This concise illustrated history of the University of Cambridge, from its thirteenth-century origins to the present day, is the only book of its kind in print and is intended as a standard introduction for anyone interested in one of the world's greatest academic institutions.

Many individuals are celebrated here who have exerted great influence upon developments within the university and beyond; but forces for change have often come from outside the university, from the crown or the church, from central government or from the aspirations and expectations of society at large. One of the prime objectives of this book is therefore to describe how the university has reacted to, or resisted, these external pressures. At the same time it conveys an impression of the day-to-day experiences of students and their teachers and administrators over the university's 800-year history.

Major university institutions, such as the University Press and the University Library, are also described briefly, while for recent years there is information not readily available elsewhere on the official sources and on the dates at which different academic disciplines have offered courses to undergraduates and graduates. In addition, the book contains many attractive and often unusual illustrations of subjects ranging from medieval manuscripts to the striking new building projects of the 1990s.

A CONCISE HISTORY OF THE UNIVERSITY OF CAMBRIDGE

A CONCISE HISTORY OF THE UNIVERSITY OF CAMBRIDGE

ELISABETH LEEDHAM-GREEN

Published by the Press Syndicate of the University of Cambridge
The Pitt Building, Trumpington Street, Cambridge CB2 1RP
40 West 20th Street, New York NY 10011-4211, USA
10 Stamford Road, Oakleigh, Melbourne 3166, Australia

First published 1996

Printed in Great Britain at the University Press, Cambridge

A catalogue record for this book is available from the British Library

Library of Congress cataloguing in publication data

Leedham-Green, E. S.
A concise history of the University of Cambridge / Elisabeth Leedham-Green.
p. cm.
Includes bibliographical references (p.) and index.
ISBN 0 521 43370 3. – ISBN 0 521 43978 7 (pbk.)
1. University of Cambridge–History. I. Title.
LF109.L44
378.42′65–dc20 96-6469 CIP

ISBN 0 521 43370 3 hardback
ISBN 0 521 43978 7 paperback

Endpapers:

Richard Lyne's bird's-eye view of Cambridge in 1574. It is noticeable that the largely robbed sites of the religious houses – Greyfriars, where Sidney Sussex College now stands; Whitefriars, or Carmelites, behind Queens'; Augustinians in Bene't Street; and Blackfriars on the site of Emmanuel – still bear their names.

WV

For Kay

CONTENTS

ILLUSTRATIONS

FIGURES

PREFACE

It is a remarkable testimony to the absence from Cambridge of one variety at least of self-regard that, to the best of my knowledge, there has been no attempt to provide a portable history of the university since James Bass Mullinger's *A history of the University of Cambridge* written as a contribution to Mandell Creighton's series, Epochs of Church History, in 1888. Recent years have, indeed, seen a striking increase in the application of serious scholarship in this area, notably in the four-volume *History of the University of Cambridge* even now issuing, volume by volume, from the press. The list of suggested further reading at the end of this volume includes a good many books of recent date devoted to particular periods or particular aspects of the university's history, and to its constituent colleges and other institutions. For a continuous and comprehensive survey, however, there has been nothing to challenge comparison with John Roach's admirable account in a hundred and fifty or so pages of the third Cambridgeshire volume of the *Victoria history of the counties of England* published in 1959, or with Christopher Brooke's contribution to the lavishly illustrated *Oxford and Cambridge* of 1988. This is a lighter book, though doubtless not without its indigestible passages, and challenges comparison with neither of these except in respect of size and weight, both of which challenges it loses easily.

In endeavouring to bring this account up to the present day I have been painfully conscious of the difficulty of discerning the wood for the trees and of having, in an attempt so to do, ignored a great many of the nearer trees, especially in the groves dedicated to advancing the frontiers of scientific knowledge and to the arts. A list of *all* the distinguished scientists and scholars who have sojourned in Cambridge in the course of this century would make an appendix almost as long as the rest of the book, and too short a list would be as invidious as it would be misleading.

In navigating so small a bark over so wide an ocean I have drawn on many aids, too many to be individually acknowledged in the notes. The list of further reading will provide chapter and verse for the great majority of the *facts*. I am, however, under a particular obligation to Mr D. P. F. McCallum, Secretary of the Board of Graduate Studies, and Mr John Easterling, the University Draftsman, who miraculously, and with the greatest goodwill, found time to furnish me with, respectively, a list of post-graduate courses and of triposes initiated, modified and discontinued in recent decades, and to Mr Geoffrey Skelsey for permission to include a large extract from his *Unofficial Guide*. For advice on the selection and interpretation of the remaining facts I have been a constant debtor to many friends of whom I cannot omit especial mention of Professor C. N. L. Brooke, Dr D. J. McKitterick, Mr Peter Searby and Mr Malcolm Underwood. If I have ignored their advice it has, I hope, been seldom, and certainly inadvertently and at my peril. Errors, nonetheless, will persist, and for them I claim full responsibility.

My debts, however, are not so easily paid: of my colleagues in the University Archives, Dr Patrick Zutshi and Mr Mark Nichols have not only provided practical assistance, but have shown almost as much tolerance as my family at the sounds of tearing hair and gnashing teeth, while the staff of the Photography Department have, against all probability, exceeded even their habitual helpfulness. My thanks are also gladly extended to all those whose permission to publish photographs is acknowledged, to Janet Keystone of the University Publications Department for giving me access to her collection of images, and to Dr Lotte Hellinga for her willing consent to my imitation of her use of plates 6 and 7. Dr Roger Morgan would be astonished to know how much he has helped. Margaret Deith has wrestled with my irregularities with unfailing patience and inexplicable good humour. Others too, who will know who they are, have assisted me in countless ways and will, I hope, accept my expressions of thanks, but most of all, perhaps, I owe to those who, for the last twenty years and more, have had recourse to the University Archives and, in the course of their researches, have posed innumerable questions to which I did not know the answer. May their shade never grow less!

1

From the Beginnings to the Late Fifteenth Century

The University of Cambridge was not founded by Athenian philosophers in the train of Cantaber, the princely Spanish son-in-law of Gurguntius Brabtruc, king of Britain, in the year 4321 after the creation of the world (in 4004 BC), nor yet by Sigebert, king of the Angles (aided and abetted by St Felix) in the seventh century AD. Greek philosophers escaping with Brutus from fallen Troy did not establish a university at Cricklade (= Greekland) in Wiltshire, presumably in the twelfth century BC, and subsequently transfer to Oxford. It is, at best, very doubtful that King Alfred founded or re-founded an academy at Oxford; and if he did, there was no continuity between that school and the later university there. These agreeable fables first appear in written records in the fourteenth century, when rivalry between the universities was already sufficient to give rise to that most venerable of contests the university lying match, and they were further elaborated by zealous antiquaries of the sixteenth century: Prince Cantaber features, along with some very favourable charters attributed to King Arthur, to Cadwallader and to Edward the Elder, in the very scholarly (and still useful) *Privileges of the University of Cambridge* presented to the university by Robert Hare in 1590, while King Sigebert held his ground, albeit somewhat precariously, in Cambridge's annual Commemoration of Benefactors until 1914. The Cambridge University Archives can show papal bulls over the names of the seventh-century popes Honorius I and Sergius I: elegant but unconvincing, they bear witness to the university's struggles for exemption from ecclesiastical authority in the early fifteenth century.

The schools of Oxford increased in stature and in numbers as a result of the migrations from Paris in 1167 and from Northampton in about 1192, but the university did not owe its origins to either of these events, although it was in the 1190s that it emerged as the premier *studium* in the country. Whether, in the earliest years of any given *studium* in medieval Europe the teaching masters were as concerned about their precise status as modern scholars have been on their account is doubtful. A master would lecture where pupils, and perhaps patrons, might be found and it was only where a group of such masters attracted an audience sufficient to give some promise of continuity that they set about establishing a guild and, as such, claiming protection and privileges as occasion demanded from pope or monarch, bishop, prince or municipality, each in turn anxious to enhance their sphere of interest.

A *studium* was simply a school with formal facilities for advanced study. It was Italian jurists of the late thirteenth and fourteenth centuries who gave legal force to the distinction between a *studium particulare* which attracted students only from its immediate vicinity and a *studium generale* which attracted an international clientele and as such could appeal for recognition from emperor or pope rather than from monarch or bishop. In practice the distinction, which was sometimes applied retrospectively, could be hard to justify. Relatively few European students came to study in Oxford in the twelfth century, yet by 1209 Oxford was one of only eight European schools generally regarded as *studia generalia*. The others – not all of them destined to survive as such – were Bologna, Paris, Montpellier, Palencia, Reggio Emilia, Vicenza and, less certainly, Salerno, where advanced studies were exclusively medical. It soon came to be expected that a *studium generale* would offer facilities for study in at least two of the senior faculties of theology, law and medicine.

If Oxford was the only British school recognised as a *studium generale* at the beginning of the thirteenth century, it should not be supposed that other advanced schools had not also been flourishing in Britain in the twelfth century. Schools throve in the cathedral cities of Lincoln and York, and also in London; both law and theology schools were to be found in Exeter in about 1200, and in Hereford in the 1190s it was claimed that all seven of the liberal arts (the *trivium* and *quadrivium*) were taught.[1] Northampton, in the late twelfth century, certainly rivalled Oxford in size and in national esteem, even after the migrations away

[1] For the *trivium* and the *quadrivium* see below, pp. 17–18.

from Northampton in 1192 and 1238. In 1261 Henry III formally approved the settlement of a university there, but when those scholars who had not removed to Oxford in the previous year ill-advisedly took the wrong side during Henry's siege of the town in 1264 the royal licence was very naturally revoked.

It is not possible to assign an exact date to the emergence at Oxford of an organised body of doctors and masters. One Theobald of Etampes taught there as early, perhaps, as 1094; Robert Pullen, who had studied in Paris, taught theology there in the 1130s. The religious houses certainly accommodated scholars, but there is no hard evidence for organised and continuous schools before the late 1180s and no single recorded event marks the beginning of a university at Oxford.

The University of Cambridge, by contrast, is alleged by Roger of Wendover,[2] an unreliable but in this instance plausible contemporary source, to trace its origins to a crime, and a bloody one. In 1209, it appears, two Oxford scholars were convicted of the murder or manslaughter of a woman and were hanged by the town authorities, apparently with the assent of King John. In normal times the ecclesiastical authorities would have exerted themselves, no doubt successfully, to claim immunity for these clerks – for the vast majority of university scholars were at least in minor orders – but the times were not normal: king and pope were in conflict, and the powers of the church were accordingly much diminished. In protest at the hanging the University of Oxford went into voluntary suspension and the great majority of scholars migrated to Paris, to Reading and to Cambridge. Migrations from one medieval university to another, both by individuals and by groups of scholars, were commonplace enough, and the Oxford scholars proceeding to Paris were but reversing the Paris migration to Oxford of 1167. Those going to Reading and to Cambridge, however, must have regarded their secession as merely temporary. The choice of Reading is comprehensible enough on geographical grounds and the sojourn of the Oxford scholars there was indeed temporary. The choice of Cambridge calls for an explanation and only hypothetical ones can be supplied.

In respect to communications Cambridge was well situated, at least in the summer when the winter floods had subsided, and had been settled

[2] Died 1236.

in turn by Romans, Saxons and Danes; it certainly had grammar schools in the twelfth century and about it lay the considerable religious establishments of Ely Cathedral, Crowland Abbey and, on its doorstep, Barnwell Priory. As much might be said for a number of other places. It is, indeed, possible that the great polymath Robert Grosseteste, later bishop of Lincoln, had lectured in Cambridge in the 1190s, but there is no evidence for continuous or organised teaching in the superior faculties of theology, law and medicine in Cambridge in the twelfth century. The band of scholars trudging into Cambridge included among their number, quite possibly as their leader, one John Grim, who had held the office of Master of the Schools (the forerunner of the chancellorship) in 1201. He was quite simply coming back to his family home, as were several others.

Five years later King John was reconciled with Pope Innocent III, whereupon the papal legate not only ruled that the Oxford townsmen must make retribution for the hanging but also tried to establish terms, favourable to the clerks, on which the town and university of Oxford could co-exist peacefully. The Reading colony returned to take its part in the newly self-confident university, and so did some of those who had migrated to Cambridge. Others, however, remained, encouraged perhaps by the graduates in the entourage of Eustace, bishop of Ely. By 1225 at the latest they had achieved sufficient status as a corporation to have a chancellor with powers delegated by the bishop of Ely. It was in about 1225, moreover, that the potential body of students was swollen by the establishment of a house of Franciscans in Cambridge, to be joined by the Dominicans by 1238.

As early as 1233 the existence of a *studium* at Cambridge had received papal recognition in an indult, or decree, of Gregory IX of 14 June awarding to the chancellor and *universitas* of scholars the *ius non trahi extra*, that is, the right not to be sued in courts outside the diocese of Ely so long as they were prepared to submit to the jurisdiction either of the chancellor or of the bishop. In 1290 a letter from Pope Nicholas IV addressed to the canons of the Order of Sempringham, some of whom were studying in Cambridge, described the school as a *studium generale* and this standing was confirmed, rather than first established, by a papal bull of 9 June 1318 granted in response to a petition from Edward II. As so often Cambridge had started after Oxford and finished first: Oxford

1. Detail from charter of Edward I, 1291/2, confirming the privileges of the university. The illuminated initial shows the king presenting the charter to two Doctors of Divinity, kneeling, a Doctor of Canon Law, standing on the left, and, beside him, a Doctor of Civil Law.

was granted the *ius non trahi extra* only in 1254 and, in spite of repeated attempts, never received papal recognition as a *studium generale*.

For practical purposes, however, it was not to the church but to the crown that the university most often looked for protection and for privileges. The crown, in turn, was increasingly in need of able administrators and of diplomats who would be internationally respected. It was in the king's interest, therefore, to foster the universities, so long at least as they proved conformable. In 1231 Henry III issued three writs, designed to promote the security and the privileges of scholars *vis-à-vis* the town. At least one of these writs clearly regarded the chancellor and masters of Cambridge as having the power to act as a legal corporation. It was on their recognition as such that the status of Oxford and Cambridge uniquely rested, and from the time of Henry III each successive king or queen was on accession routinely solicited for a charter confirming all rights granted in earlier reigns.

The speed with which the *studium* at Cambridge achieved maturity as an institution is dramatically illustrated by a compilation, dated on secure palaeographical grounds to about 1250, to be found in MS 401 (folios 54r–55v) in the Angelica Library in Rome and published by Father M. B. Hackett in 1970. The exact status of this compilation is open to question. If, as Father Hackett maintained, it represents an official code of statutes, then it is the earliest such code of any university in Europe. Other scholars have maintained that the manuscript represents rather a privately commissioned compilation comprising a mixture of formal statutes and of less official 'ordinances'. The thirteen chapters deal with such matters as university officers – the chancellor; rectors/proctors; and bedells;[3] regent masters and their assemblies;[4] judicial procedures; academical dress and discipline; hostels and rents; funerals and the commemoration of benefactors. They demonstrate conclusively that within forty years of its establishment the scholars of Cambridge had developed some institutions, notably the court of the masters, which owed nothing to Oxford origins.

So far as the ecclesiastical authorities were concerned it was the delegating of the bishop of Ely's powers to a chancellor that marked the first step in the attempts of the masters to attain autonomous status. From early in the thirteenth century chancellors were in fact chosen by the masters, but their election had to be confirmed by the bishop, who also exacted an oath of obedience. In 1374 John of Dunwich, elected chancellor for the second time, endeavoured, unsuccessfully in the end, to refuse the oath. Hitherto relations between the university and the bishop had been relatively smooth: an amicable settlement had been reached in 1264 as to the settlement of appeals from the jurisdiction of the chancellor's court, which were to be heard by the assemblies of the university before being called into the bishop's court, and there seems to have been little episcopal interference in academic affairs. Towards the end of the fourteenth century, however, matters began to come to a head. After John of Dunwich's attempted defiance the bishop, in 1392, tried to call into

[3] For the functions of these officers see pp. 11–15 below.

[4] See p. 15.

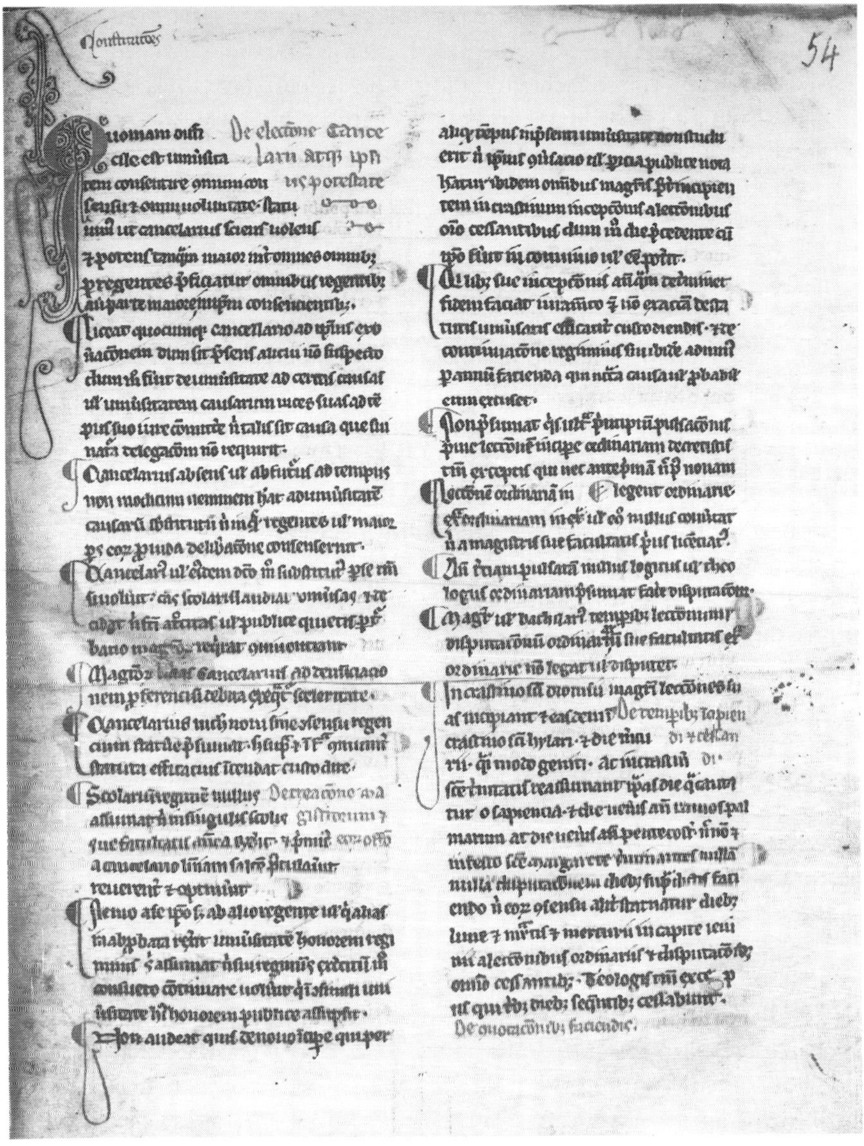

2. The earliest recorded statutes of the university, preserved in a manuscript in the Angelica Library in Rome, dating from *circa* 1250.

his court cases which the chancellor regarded as properly his. In 1401 the university was subjected to a visitation by Thomas Arundel, archbishop of Canterbury, which, indeed, passed off peaceably enough – ironically in the light of the fact that in this same year the university secured a bull from Boniface IX whereby the chancellor was no longer liable to episcopal confirmation.

The papacy, at least, seems to have held Cambridge in higher esteem than Oxford, in part, perhaps, because the smaller university was free from the taint of Wyclifism. When the Council of Constance ended the Great Schism, and the inconveniences of having two popes, in addition to an antipope, by establishing a new pope in 1417, a letter announcing the election was sent to Cambridge, but not to Oxford. Finally, in July 1430 Pope Martin V commissioned the prior of Barnwell and John Depyng, a canon of Lincoln, to investigate the claim of the Cambridge masters to be free of all ecclesiastical jurisdiction; the prior, acting alone, found in favour of the university, and his decision was ratified by a bull of Eugenius IV in September 1433. Oxford, again, had to wait, this time until 1479. These manifestations of papal favour were theoretically important in the academic arena of western Christendom: the status of *studium generale* implicitly, and soon explicitly, brought with it the *ius ubique docendi* – the right of its masters and doctors to teach in other such schools. In fact, however, it appears that at some universities at least the resident masters were capable of effectively maintaining a 'closed shop', while, conversely, more European scholars frequented the schools of Oxford, which held the title only by tradition, than those of Cambridge, which held it by papal fiat.

At a more mundane level the problems which most pressed on the university were those arising from their relations with the townsmen among whom they lived. In the first instance they required rooms and houses in which to live and to lecture, and they wished to have them at a reasonable, if not a preferential, rate. They needed also their victuals – food, drink and candles – and they wanted value for money. They wanted their streets free from ordure, and from prostitutes, and they needed the co-operation of the civic authorities in the provision of custody for those committed to prison in the chancellor's court. Their securing of these aims was proceeding satisfactorily enough, if in a piecemeal fashion, when the violent if brief eruption of the Peasants' Revolt in

1381 provided a magnificent opportunity to consolidate and increase their gains.

Brawls between scholars and townsmen were nothing new. A brawl between a northern and a southern student in 1261 had led to a general affray, joined by the townsmen, in which much damage was inflicted on persons, on property and on the records of the university. The year 1322 saw similar acts of vandalism, perhaps fomented by a clause in the university charter of 1317 which decreed that the mayor and bailiffs on taking office should swear before the chancellor to uphold the privileges of the university. This annual ceremony, known to the university as the *Magna Congregatio* and to the smarting townsmen as the 'Black Assembly', continued, predictably enough, to serve as a focus of hostility between town and gown until the last attempt to revive it in the nineteenth century.

The events of 1381, however, were of a violence hitherto unknown in Cambridge. The mayor and burgesses joined with rebels from the surrounding countryside in an assault on the property of the university, of Corpus Christi College (a substantial landowner in the town), of William Wigmore, a university bedell, as well as on the Carmelite house and on Barnwell Priory. There is a vivid account of one Margaret Sterre dancing around a bonfire of what were allegedly the muniments of the university, dragged out of the university church, crying, 'Away with the learning of the clerks, away with it!' It is, in fact, doubtful whether it was indeed muniments which burned so merrily. Some forty pre-1381 royal charters are listed in an inventory drawn up by William Rysley in 1420, of which over thirty survive to this day and not one of them is singed. It cannot be demonstrated that losses of earlier material are not due rather to the negligence of the clerks than to the fury of the town, although writs belonging to the university are also said to have been destroyed in a fracas some four years later. Some financial records may perhaps have been destroyed, but such documents were not to be regarded as worthy of systematic preservation for another hundred years or so. Some of 'the *learning* of the clerks', in the form of a number of books, may also have perished in the conflagration, but if so these were probably volumes whose owners, finding them at least temporarily inessential, had deposited them as security for loans from the university chests founded for that purpose.

3. A university chest, dating from the fifteenth century, surviving in the Old Schools. Note the multiple locks necessitating the presence of several key-holders to open it.

Nevertheless, the remaining damage was real enough, and the threat to the university's security in the town certainly provoked royal alarm. The penalties for the town were bitter. For a year the hard-won rights of the burgesses to govern their own affairs – their liberties – were taken into royal hands, and when they were restored they were shorn of the control of the assizes of bread, wine and ale, whereby the prices of these essential commodities were periodically adjusted, and of the supervision of weights and measures in the town, which powers passed instead to the chancellor of the university.

This was only the most dramatic incident in a struggle for dominance between the university and town authorities, a struggle in which for centuries the university could call on the bigger battalions. By 1381 the university had already achieved, among other privileges, an agreement whereby representatives of the town and university together were to fix rents quinquennially, some control over the supply and price of essential foodstuffs and over the arrangements for keeping the streets clean. The chancellor was allowed jurisdiction over all cases involving scholars or scholars' servants, except for cases of maiming or murder which were reserved for the king's justices, and enjoyed the right to exact fines, to impose temporary or permanent banishment, to imprison and, in certain cases, to excommunicate.

By the middle of the fifteenth century the university had established for itself a position *vis-à-vis* the church, the crown and the town which was, with some interruptions, to remain essentially unchanged until the nineteenth century. So far as its internal constitution was concerned it had, as we have seen, a chancellor, from the 1220s nominated, and from 1401 elected, by the teaching masters. His term of office was normally limited to one or two years, and it was usual for him to be a doctor of theology or of law. A vice-chancellor, empowered to exercise the office in the absence of the chancellor, appears in the records as early as 1275 or 1276 but his status as the chief administrative officer of the university did not emerge until the second half of the fifteenth century when it became the custom to elect an absentee chancellor to uphold the university's interests at court. Hitherto probably appointed *ad hoc*, the vice-chancellor now became an annually elected officer, usually holding office for two years.

Older than the office of vice-chancellor was that of taxor or rector or proctor: the terminology is confusing. The title of rector occurs in the early records and is replaced gradually in the course of the thirteenth century by that of proctor. At about the same time, probably, the office of taxor was separated from that of proctor. The duties of the taxors embraced the assessment of rents, and later the inspection of weights and measures and of all items of merchandise over which the university claimed supervision. They had no judicial powers but presented those suspected of giving short measure, or of monopolistic practices, or of exposing unwholesome food for sale, at one or other of the university courts.[5]

The powers of the proctors were far more wide-ranging. Cambridge, arguably to a greater extent than Oxford, modelled itself on Paris, but outdid its model in the extent to which it was governed by a body of

[5] It was the benevolent custom of the vice-chancellor, from time to time, to present foodstuffs which had been confiscated as unwholesome to the prisoners in the castle or the tolbooth.

self-regulating masters. As the representatives of the masters, annually elected, the proctors, in association with the chancellor, were the chief executive officers of the university.[6] In 1514 a cycle of colleges was drawn up, two by two, largely on the basis of size, which established the intervals at which each college was to present a proctor. The cycle was and is periodically revised. Trinity Hall is allotted few places in the cycle, having the obligation to fill the gap should a proctor die, resign or suffer deprivation during his term of office. This arrangement was presumably introduced on account of the customary absence of fellows of the Hall at Doctors' Commons in London where they exercised their skills in civil law in the ecclesiastical and admiralty courts. The proctors had the custody of the unique copies of the statutes which, it might be thought very imprudently, they carried about with them on all official occasions, very stoutly embossed so as to constitute formidable weapons. It fell to them also to organise the timetable of lectures and disputations and the rituals of graduation as well as of those other ceremonies, funerals and other liturgical exercises, which were common to many other guilds. In exceptional circumstances, as when the chancellor had failed to take appropriate action in the face of an offence against the masters, they were empowered to summon congregations. The observance of the statutes was their particular care, exercised as well in university assemblies as in the streets of the town, but their financial responsibilities were scarcely less important: the receipt of fees and of academic fines was theirs and from the proceeds they met a large proportion of the university's routine payments. They were also empowered after 1381 to hold a

[6] In other medieval universities it was the custom for proctors to be chosen as representatives of their respective 'nations'. In Cambridge, however, there is no evidence for this beyond the stipulation in an agreement between the university and the town in 1268 that the university's official peacekeepers (or vigilantes) should be drawn five from England and three each from Scotland, Wales and Ireland. It has, however, been observed that of the two proctors the senior was commonly a southerner. There is, indeed, nothing to suggest that 'nations' of students of distinct geographical origins were ever institutionally recognised at Cambridge, although brawls between northerners and southerners there certainly were, notably one in 1260 which led to a temporary migration to Northampton.

It may be the case also that the links which many colleges cherished with certain counties, often those in which they held land or livings, and from which they drew significant numbers of their students, lent a regional flavour to intercollegiate brawls. One may think of the Norfolk men of Gonville and Caius, and the northerners at St John's.

'court leet' at which the taxors and others might present townsmen for breaches of the regulations concerning the cleansing of streets, dressing or selling flesh in Lent, gaming on the Sabbath, and so on. Their jurisdiction in these areas was not exclusive, and in some years seems to have been exercised more as a ritual than in earnest; at other times, however, it must have served to relieve some of the pressure of business in the senior courts, as must the *pie powder*[7] court (one of summary justice) which they held at the two great fairs of Sturbridge and Barnwell.

The two figures flanking the chancellor on the (third) university Seal of 1580 are probably intended to depict the proctors carrying, as the proctors still do, the stoutly bound volumes of the university statutes (but now in the first printed edition of 1785). The precise dating of the accoutrements carried by their accompanying constables is unresolved, but their significance is clear: pike and halberd for the maintenance of law and order and the butter measure for the supervision of trading standards. It has to be admitted, however, that whatever it is that goes by the name of 'butter measure', it is unlikely at any time to have been used for measuring butter. It may perhaps be the remains of an instrument for gauging corn.

In their execution of these many and often arduous tasks the proctors called from the very earliest times upon the services of two bedells (later joined by a third) originally associated one with the faculty of arts the other with the faculty of divinity. To them fell the collection of fees and fines, the maintenance of various lists (including lists of graduates) and the haling of members of the university before the chancellor's court. Townsmen were later subject to citation and arrest by a lowlier figure, the Yeoman Bedell or Dog Bedell. The Esquire Bedells, as the senior bedells came to be called, also had important ceremonial functions, attending with their distinctive costume and their maces all congregations, funerals and exequies, as well as formal disputations, and it was their duty also to give public notice of these events and to attend the chancellor on all formal occasions. As the guardians of the details of

[7] The term 'pie powder' derives from the graphic French expression 'pieds poudreux', used of the wayfarers and itinerants who either could not or would not attend the sessions of the regular courts, and was transferred to the courts, licensed to exercise a summary jurisdiction over more or less trivial offences, before which such persons might be brought.

4. Junior Proctor's Book, complete with chains for carrying and bosses for protection in the hurly-burly of the town. The contents of the book range from the 1390s to the 1780s.

procedure and of protocol the bedells were elected for life; until the early sixteenth century they were usually non-graduates; thereafter they were nearly all MAs. At least until the seventeenth century, however, the bedells were further qualified by their status as at least moderately prosperous inhabitants of the town. They must, informally, have acted as a sort of buffer between the two corporations, although at times of friction their allegiance seems consistently to have been to the university. They also served, especially in the early centuries, as the university's men of business: not only was it they, very often, who carried letters to and from the court, it was they who, by virtue of their permanent residence and their municipal respectability, represented the university when it began to acquire real property in the town. From the thirteenth century also dates the office of University Chaplain, responsible for the conduct of the masses for the dead and the other liturgical obligations of the guild of masters. In the fifteenth century he became responsible also for the custody of the University Library.

The driving force of the early university resided, however, not in its officers but in the guild of teachers, or regent masters. Every scholar graduating as a master or doctor in his faculty was said to have 'incepted', that is to have taken his place in the senior rank of the faculty in question, and he was accordingly obliged to teach for a period of time which fluctuated over the centuries but seems originally to have been set at just under two years. Theoretically no one could proceed to the higher faculties of theology or law who had not first incepted as a master in the arts faculty. The great majority of scholars entertained no ambitions beyond the arts course, so the body of regent masters was composed overwhelmingly of Masters of Arts, typically in their early twenties. It was originally this body which was alone empowered to admit others to the guild, to elect officials, to make statutes and to grant any exemptions (graces) from the strict observation of them. Occasional instances are recorded in the thirteenth century of assemblies of both the regent and the non-regent masters (that is, those studying for higher degrees after the completion of their teaching requirement) for the purposes of legislation. Faced with the increasing dominance of the friars (who, among other things, were inclined to claim for their members the right to study in the higher faculties without first completing the arts course) the regent masters had by 1304 enhanced the voting power of the secular masters by conceding statutory powers to the non-regents also. Routine business, however, continued to lie in the province of the regent masters alone.

Some time late in the fourteenth century this model of democracy was severely modified by the introduction of a body known as the *Caput Senatus*. Apparently consisting originally of a doctor from each of the senior faculties, one doctor from among the religious houses, one regent and one non-regent master under the presidency of the chancellor or vice-chancellor, it was the business of this body to prepare the agenda for congregations. While all sections of the academic community were represented in the Caput, and any member of it had the power to defend the rights of his constituency by veto, and the membership was not constant, since the Caput was initially elected *ad hoc* whenever a congregation was called, nevertheless the creation of this body clearly bridled the hitherto dominant powers of the young regents.[8]

Such, briefly, was the organisation of the university as a corporation in the first three centuries of its existence. Nothing has been said as yet about its dual purposes: studying and teaching. The purpose of the masters in establishing a *studium* was, no doubt, principally to further their own education, but their function as teachers was essential for the provision both of succeeding generations of masters and of fees. Newly written texts in the medieval period were both scarce and costly, and there can be no doubt that in early years texts were handed down, often in the form of extracts or abstracts, from one generation to another, as indeed they continued to be even after the introduction of printing in the late fifteenth century had increased the availability of relatively cheap books. Nor would the average medieval undergraduate, or indeed the average BA, have owned copies of the actual texts he studied, but rather slim volumes of *tabulae* and of *quaestiones*: synopses of, and standard discussions of problems arising from, the text. Such a system militates effectively against frequent revisions of the syllabus.

The elementary courses in the medieval university were in grammar and in liberal arts. Relatively little is known about degrees in grammar, although the foundation by William Bingham and Henry VI of Godshouse,

[8] With the introduction of the 1570 statutes the membership of the Caput was fixed for the duration of the academic year and was increasingly dominated by the heads of houses. In this form it survived, to be translated in the 1850s into the Council of the Senate.

whose history starts as late as the mid-fifteenth century, was originally conceived as a college for grammarians only. The 1495 statutes envisage that students will first have completed at least two years in the arts faculty before turning to the study of 'Priscian, Virgil, and other poets, metrification, versification' and other such studies. This attempted revival of grammar teaching designed by William Bingham to remedy a perceived shortage of teachers for the grammar schools springing up all over the country did not, however, prove attractive and Masters of Grammar disappear from the records early in the sixteenth century. It must be recalled that, although students were often admitted with only rudimentary skills, the term 'grammar' in the medieval syllabus refers very often to the logically rigorous field of 'speculative grammar' elaborated from Aristotelian foundations. The special emphasis at Godshouse, however, was on something much closer to what we now understand by that term.

The liberal arts course is far better documented, although much of our information is derived from relatively late sources. Instruction, as in other faculties, was primarily by means of lectures and disputations. Lectures were of three categories: 'cursory' lectures, usually read by bachelors, consisting of a reading of the actual text under study with, probably, a paraphrase and a minimum of basic commentary; 'ordinary' lectures, read by regent masters on every designated lecture day (*dies legibilis*) in the calendar, in which the prescribed texts and major commentaries upon them were paraphrased and discussed; and 'extraordinary' lectures given outside the canonical hours and, from time to time, on texts other than those deemed central to the syllabus.

The liberal arts course was traditionally conceived as consisting of the *trivium* (grammar, rhetoric and logic) and the *quadrivium* (arithmetic, music, geometry and astronomy) with the three philosophies (moral, natural and metaphysical): a scheme that can be traced back to late antiquity. Although this tradition continued to constitute the formal structure of the arts course well into the early modern period, it is unlikely that it was followed precisely, even from the earliest years of the university. Cambridge students were required to attend at least three ordinary lectures a week (if so many were available) and to cover in their first year Aristotle's *Praedicamenta*, *Perihermeneias* and *Topica*, the first alongside Porphyry's *Isagoge* and the second alongside the *Sex principia* of Gilbert de la Porrée and Boethius' *Divisiones*. These constituted the

'Old Logic' and were followed in the second year by the 'New' consisting of Aristotle's *Elenchi* and his *Prior* and *Posterior analytics*. The student's powers of reasoning and disputation thus far developed, the third and fourth years were devoted to Aristotle's *Physics* with either the *Metaphysics* or one of his texts in natural philosophy: the *De generatione*, the *De anima*, the *De caelo* or the *Meteorica*, texts which bore on the nature of the universe. A further option, of Aristotle's *Ethica*, opened the door to moral philosophy, but only if some master had chosen to lecture on the text. The study of rhetoric seems to be assumed in early sources but evidence for the formal study of rhetoric texts in the medieval period is hard to find. Grammar, as we understand the term, was certainly informally taught to those who required it in later years, long after its disappearance from the official syllabus with the abolition of grammar disputations in 1527, but to the extent that it occurs in the outline above it features in the philosophical form of speculative grammar.

The MA course overlapped with that for bachelors: study of Aristotle's *Physica* and *Posterior analytics* continued along with the *Ethics* and *Metaphysics* and to these were added, in good quadrivial style, Euclid's *Elements* and other mathematical and astronomical texts, the *Algorismus*, the *Compotus* and the *Tractatus de sphera*. For the systematic academic study of music there is no evidence whatever, nor does it seem to have been even a statutory requirement before about 1500. The first surviving record of a degree in music is of the B.Mus. awarded to Henry Abynton in 1464 but it seems likely that this and subsequent degrees in music were awarded rather *honoris causa* than on the completion of a course of university instruction. If music were taught in the *quadrivium* it would have been so taught rather as a branch of mathematics or physics than as a performing art.

From late antiquity the ideal scheme had seen all study as culminating in theology, and in the earliest years of the university theology and canon law are the only two senior faculties mentioned; up to the mid-fourteenth century, while the doctorate of divinity was otherwise obtainable only from Paris, Rome or Oxford, the importance of that faculty can hardly be over-emphasised. The central text for the study of theology was, of course, the Bible, with its glosses, and with it the opinions of the early church fathers on the central concepts of Christianity and especially on the sacraments, systematically arranged in the *Sentences* of Peter Lombard and his commentators. These two texts alone are specified in the statutes. Commentaries proliferated and were variously favoured by the different religious orders, but it must be confessed that few Cambridge theologians, except for Duns Scotus (who is claimed also by Oxford, Paris and Cologne) during his residence here, compiled commentaries of an eminence to render their authors household names – even among late medieval theologians. A notable exception is the Cambridge Dominican Robert Holcot whose commentary on the Book of Wisdom, in particular, was still studied well into the sixteenth century.

As in the faculty of arts, of law and, in due course, of medicine, instruction was in the form of lectures and disputations, a number of which had to be publicly performed in order to meet the requirements for inception. In addition, senior students of theology were statutorily bound to preach both *ad clerum* in Latin to their peers, and, in the vernacular, at Paul's Cross in London. Collections of sermons therefore formed part of every theologian's reading.

If theology held the high moral ground, it was only the presence of the religious orders that gave it also numerical superiority over law. It has been estimated that by the late fourteenth century three-quarters of Cambridge theologians were regulars – members of religious orders – while among the laymen theologians were outnumbered by lawyers, four to one. By the early fifteenth century theologians all told had fallen from 40 per cent to 15 per cent of the total academic community.[9]

Among lawyers the students of ecclesiastical or canon law, mentioned in the 'statutes' of *c.* 1250, preceded the students of civil law or civilians, but probably not by very many years: the first known Cambridge doctorate in civil law was awarded (to Simon de Asceles, previously of Oxford) in 1255. For the canonists the central texts were sometimes designated the *Corpus juris canonici*, but the content of the *corpus* was continually evolving. Founded at first upon the study of the *Decretum* compiled by Gratian in the twelfth century, the syllabus had successively to take on board the later enactments contained in the *Decretals* or *Liber extra* of Gregory IX (1234), the *Sextus liber* of Boniface VIII (1298) and the *Clementines* of John XXII (1317). These texts, with their commentaries, remained central to the

[9] All such percentages should be viewed with great caution, since, in the absence of official lists of graduates, they are based largely on the biographies of graduates who attained sufficient eminence at least to occur in surviving records external to the university.

course until its official abolition in 1535 and, along with William Lyndewode's *Constitutiones provinciales*, which treated of the English canon law and may not have formed part of the official syllabus, continued to be studied in Cambridge long after that date.[10]

The *Corpus juris civilis*, comprising the codification of Roman law by Justinian in the sixth century and his subsequent legal enactments, provided the civilians with a more stable core to their studies. His *Codex* and *Digest* were the works principally studied, along with a host of commentators, notably the late medieval Italian jurists Bartolus and Baldus, for whom the faculty was to exhibit a devotion far outlasting that of their colleagues in France and Germany.

Much the smallest of the senior faculties in the middle ages, and indeed for long after, was that of medicine: only fifty-nine graduates have been recorded before 1500, far too few to provide any systematic teaching in the subject especially after the graces of 1462 and 1500 excusing them from their obligations as regents. Medical graduates were routinely excused from having attended the statutory lectures. It was expected that practical knowledge of physic and/or surgery would be found elsewhere, although the university's teaching in Aristotelian natural philosophy, in metaphysics and in astronomy were all highly relevant to the equipment of an academic physician whose claim to respectability, as well, evidently, as to his fees, rested as much on the philosophical basis of his practice as on a familiarity with the known texts of Hippocrates and Galen. Besides, a royal edict of 1421 limited the licence to practise physic to graduates of the two universities.

The statutes ordained seven years from entering the university to attain to the MA with perhaps a further ten years' study for those aspiring to a doctorate. Seventeen years is a long time to live in rented lodgings, but the earliest students had no choice in the matter. From very early days, however, they had begun to band together in hostels. The arrangement was originally, and in some cases continued to be, an informal one whereby a senior member of the university, perhaps not above the standing of bachelor, leased a house in which he rented rooms to others to whom he stood as principal. Already by *c*. 1250 the university had passed

[10] Gratian's *Decretum* remained the central textbook for canon lawyers in the Roman Catholic church until 1918.

legislation obliging principals to give a guarantee, either to the landlord or to the chancellor, for the payment of the annual rent. The principal's responsibility for his tenants implicit in this statute was made explicit by a further enactment of the late fourteenth century whereby principal and hostel were to be subject to a twice-yearly visitation by the chancellor, accompanied by the proctors and others, charged with ascertaining the fitness of the principal and his exercise of moral and academical discipline over what were now distinctly his charges. The earliest surviving decree of the university designed to ensure that all students were resident either in a college or a hostel dates from the late fourteenth century, but it is doubtful whether the aim was achieved until well into the sixteenth.

The existence of such hostels, some of them very transient, some so substantial as to have their own chapels and libraries, can be paralleled in many European universities of the time. For the colleges, as endowed, autonomous institutions, there are also parallels, if fewer. The model for the earliest colleges in Oxford and Cambridge was probably the Sorbonne, established in Paris in about 1257. Unlike the earlier Parisian colleges, whose affinity was rather with hostels, the Sorbonne was to be a community of mature scholars studying for the doctorate in theology, and it was for the support of graduate scholars that the earliest English colleges, Merton (1264), University College (*c.* 1280) and Balliol (1282) at Oxford, and Peterhouse (1284) at Cambridge, were established.[11] The scale and academic bias of early foundations varied considerably, but it is important to remember that, apart from their desire to increase the supply of graduates to church or state, founders of colleges were concerned also to secure perpetual prayers for themselves and their families

Hugh of Balsham's foundation of Peterhouse – the college of the 'scholars of the Bishop of Ely in Cambridge . . . *pro utilitate rei publice*' – was explicitly modelled on Merton's foundation. His scholars, originally housed with the brethren of the Hospital of St John, who were Austin

[11] It can be argued that the first university college in England was in fact De Vaux College at Salisbury, founded in 1262, and surviving to be dissolved in 1542; but the nascent University of Salisbury failed to materialise. The dates of foundation of many early colleges, notably Merton, University and Balliol, furnish fruitful grounds for debate, since the act of foundation comprised several distinct stages, and it was not uncommon for scholars to be in residence 'on the foundation' before any deed of foundation was finally ratified. The handsome endowment which ensured that Merton was a fully established institution by the 1280s made it the dominant model.

canons, were to be governed by the statutes of Merton College, and the earliest surviving statutes, dating from long after the removal of the scholars to a hostel adjoining Little St Mary's (then St Peter's from which they took their name) still follow the same model, albeit modified to suit the much smaller and less wealthy house. They allow for a master, who was to be appointed annually by the bishop and was to consult the fellows (of which there were intended to be fourteen, all at least BA) in all important decisions, two annually elected deans, who were to supervise the daily readings of the Bible and other theological works in the hall and to regulate disputations, two bursars, when funds allowed, to keep the accounts and, as a reminder of their association with the hospital, an almoner. Gate hours were set and were to be enforced by a porter – when one could be afforded.

The bishop's control of his foundation in appointing the master and confirming the election of fellows was not to provide a precedent for later founders, who usually allowed their fellows freedom of election. The provision for two or three needy students of grammar (bible clerks) to serve in hall and chapel and to study under the supervision of the deans was widely copied, but there was no provision for students under the degree of BA as members rather than servants of the college.

The original statutes of other early colleges are broadly similar, varying chiefly in the scale of the establishment envisaged and in the subjects of the fellows' studies, in both of which respects large discrepancies between intention and actuality persisted.

The second collegiate foundation in Cambridge, however, was cast in a quite different mould, one that was to become a pattern for many future developments, not least in the provision for undergraduates. This was the King's Hall, founded, at the prompting of John Hotham, bishop of Ely and royal Chancellor, by Edward II from about 1317 (in which year, it will be remembered, he had petitioned for papal recognition of the university). The embryo King's Hall consisted of a colony in Cambridge of the Chapel Royal: a clerk and twelve children whose expenses were met from the Exchequer.[12] Twenty years later Edward III re-

[12] The Chapel Royal consisted of a body of clergy attendant on the monarch and with the prime obligation of maintaining prayers for his soul and those of his predecessors. The boys of the Chapel Royal earned their keep and their education largely by serving as choristers.

established the college on an altogether more princely footing with a house, where Trinity Great Court now stands, and a fellowship, massive by medieval standards, of thirty-two. All the fellows on their appointment (which continued for two centuries to be by royal writ) were undergraduates, but as the fellowships could be tenable for life the college soon developed a balance of graduate and undergraduate members. Among the lay population King's Hall dominated the university, especially the faculty of civil law, up to the end of the fifteenth century.

By the time of the refoundation of the King's Hall in 1337 other colleges had appeared on the scene: Michaelhouse, founded by Hervey de Stanton in 1324 (like the King's Hall later to be absorbed into Trinity), and Clare, conceived in 1321 by Roger de Northburgh, adopted, as University Hall, by Richard de Badew, chancellor at the time, and finally established on a firm footing by Lady Elizabeth de Clare. Both foundations may be traced to the influences operating at the royal court: Hervey de Stanton was one of Hotham's successors as Chancellor of the Exchequer and the Lady Clare was a grand-daughter of Edward I; both foundations were predominantly theological. The Countess of Pembroke followed the example of her friend, Lady Clare, with her foundation of 1347, and hot on its heels came Gonville Hall (1347 to 1349), Trinity Hall (1350) and Corpus Christi (1352). Of these, the remaining fourteenth-century foundations, Gonville Hall was notable for the scope of studies allowed to its fellows, Trinity Hall, founded by Bishop Bateman of Norwich, for its emphasis on civil and canon law, and Corpus Christi for the circumstance of its having been founded by the amalgamated town guilds of Corpus Christi and the Blessed Virgin Mary under the patronage of the Duke of Lancaster: a unique example of a corporately founded institution and one which, as we have seen, provided a focus for the wrath and envy of the town in 1381.

No other colleges appeared on the Cambridge scene until William Bingham's foundation of Godshouse noticed above,[13] between 1436 and 1448. In the course of its prolonged birth pangs, there sprang to life the second royal foundation, King's (1441–5), and another, royally endowed but locally inspired, in the form of the Queen's (later Queens') College of St Margaret and St Bernard (1446–8). To these was added in 1473

[13] p. 17.

St Catharine's, a diminutive foundation, specialising, with eccentric but not absolute faithfulness to its statutes, in theology and philosophy.

King's, with its sister college at Eton, was conceived in imitation of William of Wykeham's prestigious foundations of New College and Winchester, with a lavish allowance for a provost and seventy scholars. Membership of King's was, and continued until the nineteenth century to be, confined to scholars from Eton, and the college was to be exempt from all external authority, including that of the chancellor, an idea so appalling to the other members of the university that they launched a concerted and violent assault in 1454 which led to the repeal of this particular privilege, although a measure of exemption from the examination requirements for degrees was successfully retained until the middle of the nineteenth century. The exceptionally prosperous conditions in which the college was established did not survive the king, although a limited rescue operation was launched by Edward IV for a reduced fellowship of a score or so.

Queens', by contrast, was the child of a local man. Andrew Doket, Vicar (later rector) of St Botolph's and principal of St Bernard's hostel, was a singularly accomplished fund-raiser. Having initially secured a licence for a foundation on the site of St Bernard's hostel in 1446, he obtained another in the following year to refound it where the college now stands and a year later secured the patronage of the 17-year-old Queen Margaret of Anjou (who obtained a licence for the foundation in her own name) and the building of the first court was put in hand. Momentarily disconcerted, no doubt, but unbowed by the fall of the Lancastrians in 1460, the imperturbable Doket persuaded the new queen, Elizabeth Woodville, to associate herself, as co-foundress, with her predecessor, and had even contrived to secure promises of lavish support from Richard III before his death on Bosworth Field in 1484 prevented their realisation.

Alongside these colleges, some already grandiose in appearance, others still in homely premises, stood the great buildings of the Franciscans, where Sidney Sussex College now stands, of the Dominicans, on the site of Emmanuel College, and of the Augustinian friars, at the east end of Bene't Street. To these was added in the course of the fifteenth century the Benedictine colony under the patronage of the family of the dukes of Buckingham, Buckingham College which, at the dissolution, was to be refounded as Magdalene College. Other religious houses, mostly of modest dimensions, were scattered about the town, like the Carmelite Friary destined to be absorbed into the site of Queens' College.

Even the university itself, never as wealthy as the wealthiest colleges, now had buildings of its own. The theologians launched an appeal for a purpose-built faculty building in the 1350s and their faith in starting the building, now the north side of the old (i.e. east) court of the Old Schools, in 1359 was duly rewarded by enabling benefactions of 1365 and 1372. The scheme became more ambitious and came to incorporate on the floor above a room (now the University Combination Room) which doubled as university chapel and Regent House. The west range, for canon law, was completed in the 1430s, the south, for philosophy, between 1458 and 1471 and the east, with the university consistory, or court room, between 1470 and 1473. Changing needs were reflected in different uses for many of these rooms from an early date, but initially the upper storeys of the east and south ranges were intended for library accommodation, and the handsome benefaction of Thomas Rotherham, archbishop of York, for the completion of the final range was accompanied by donations, between 1474 and 1484, of some two hundred books of which some thirty-nine remain in the University Library still.

Among the buildings of Cambridge today those which would still excite the recognition of their early occupants include the so-called School of Pythagoras (a rich man's stone house already standing when it was acquired by Walter de Merton in the 1260s as a potential refuge for his scholars from Oxford), the Old Court of Corpus, which escaped the rebuilding which transformed so many college buildings in later centuries, and the first courts of Queens', with its proud gateway, and of Magdalene.

Who peopled these streets and courts? What was their experience of Cambridge and what did they look to gain from it?

The great majority of students were probably of yeoman stock or their urban equivalent. (The nobility and the landed gentry, as Ascham was so eloquently to lament in *The scholemaster*, generally saw no need for this kind of education, although there were some notable exceptions.) They came in large numbers from East Anglia and the north-east, perhaps aged somewhere between fifteen and seventeen, supported sometimes by their families and friends, sometimes by patronage, often in the

5. Trinity Hall Library. Although constructed in the late sixteenth century, the library exhibits many characteristics of late medieval libraries.

form of ecclesiastical livings from which they had leave to be absent for part or all of the year. Some, in time, might be lucky enough to become bible clerks; others were granted licence to beg. They lived, in early days, two or three to a room in rented rooms or houses; some, later, in hostels or in colleges, where the communal hall, at least, might boast a fire at Christmas, but sleeping accommodation was shared, often between one relatively senior and one or two junior members, each with his 'study' boarded off in a corner of the room. A number, to the resentment of the lay opposition, were seduced by the relative comfort and security of the religious houses.

The academical year, then as now, was divided into three regular terms and, from at least 1456, a Long Vacation term which seems variously to have counted as a regular term or as one-third of a term for the purpose of statutory residence, reducing, for those who kept it, the BA course from four years to three. Rising at daylight the student proceeded to his ordinary lectures (perhaps 130 in the course of a year) and later perhaps to cursory or extraordinary lectures.[14] Part of his day might be spent copying his text from one lent by a fellow student or one of the stationers in the town; part of it, as the hostels and colleges evolved, in reporting progress and discussing difficulties with his principal, dean or tutor. As he advanced in seniority he might have lectures or disputations to prepare, either for the official exercises of the university or, later, for domestic consumption in his hostel or college. One has, somehow, the impression that the pressure of attending lectures and other academical exercises eased at each step towards the top of the ladder, but this may be only because we know less about the timetables of advanced scholars. Certainly as a regent master life could prove busy enough, and for a proctor downright hectic.

With the exception of Christmas, when fires were lit in halls and the embargo on card-playing was lifted, organised recreation was unknown, save to the extent that the best brawls require some initial planning. The warmth of the taverns called, as also, on the evidence of Chaucer as well as the statutes, did the ladies of the town. The life of a Cambridge student was rigorous, and few, probably, embraced it for its own sake. The intensive training in dialectic provided the basis for scholarship in any field, and a qualification in the arts faculty might be sufficient to attract a benefice (although complaints that it was not were plentiful); higher qualifications (of which those in law attracted most interest until the reaction in favour of theology in the fifteenth century) might lead to positions in the courts of bishops, or even of the king. The richest pickings made the game worth the candle – but it has to be admitted that before 1500 they went mostly to Oxford men. From 1216 to 1499 only 10 per cent of bishops were educated at Cambridge, against 57 per cent from Oxford, with almost identical figures for cathedral deanships. About one-third of recorded Cambridge alumni acquired benefices as a reward for their pains.

Of those who carved out a successful career within the university we may take as an example Andrew Doket, whose success in securing

[14] See p. 17.

patronage for Queens' College we noticed above.[15] It was as vicar of St Botolph's (from 1435) and principal of St Bernard's Hostel (by 1446) that he set about establishing the college, originally named St Bernard's College, of which he was to be the first president. He came to hold a number of benefices of which the most prestigious were the chancellorship of Lichfield, which he held from 1470 to 1476 and a canonry of St Stephen's Westminster to which he was appointed in 1479, five years before his death. Among those attaining a high position at court the fellows and especially the wardens of the King's Hall were easily the most successful. Geoffrey Blythe, for example, with the advantage of being a nephew of Archbishop Rotherham, proceeded as an Etonian to King's where he duly held a fellowship from 1486 to 1494 and served as dean from 1492 to 1493 concurrently with the wardenship of the King's Hall which he held from 1486 to 1528. From 1503 he was also bishop of Coventry and Lichfield. In 1502 he was sent as an envoy to Ladislaus II, king of Hungary and Bohemia, returning with the silver cups which he was to bequeath to Eton and to King's. He survived a treason charge in 1509 to serve as Lord President of the Council of Wales from 1512 to 1524 and was further blessed with canonries and prebends in the dioceses of York and of Salisbury and the archdeaconries of Gloucester and Sarum.

Such were the careers of the successful. Since no continuous university records of students, successful or unsuccessful, survive from before the late fifteenth century, the great majority are lost to sight entirely, and of those recorded in the earliest records no further details of their previous or subsequent lives can be ascertained. We cannot even say what proportion of them achieved ecclesiastical livings or the security of life in one of the religious orders.

[15] p. 24.

2

Cambridge under the Tudors, 1485–1603

Already in the fifteenth century a new spirit was abroad in Cambridge. With, perhaps, some seven hundred members in the 1370s, rising to thirteen hundred in the 1450s, the university was rivalling Oxford in size, if not so far in the distinction of her sons. New colleges were flourishing, several of them under royal patronage, and a new confidence can be sensed. In the universities of Europe a new learning had been spreading rapidly, and Englishmen continuing their education abroad had caught the infection. We may take as an example John Gunthorp who, after incepting as an MA in Cambridge in 1452, travelled to Italy where he learned Greek and studied under Guarino da Verona in Ferrara before returning in 1460 to the university where he became warden of the King's Hall before, like many another warden, going on to higher things, as a diplomat, secretary and chaplain to the queen and, ultimately, Keeper of the Privy Seal. Numerous other examples could be cited, especially, it must be said, from Oxford, including many who had been in attendance at the papal curia. As well as ideas, they brought back texts: new editions of Aristotle and of classical and post-classical authors, some of them only recently rediscovered. Those with the right connections had no need even to travel: the books presented to Cambridge by Thomas Rotherham, who never left England, included a number of humanist editions and texts.

We have no direct evidence that Gunthorp and other Englishmen returning to Cambridge from Italy incorporated their new learning into their formal teaching, though it seems likely. Between 1472 and 1482, however, albeit not continuously, the Italian Franciscan Lorenzo Traversagni was lecturing in Cambridge on the *Rhetorica ad Herennium* attributed to Cicero, and on Aristotle's *Ethics*; in 1478 Traversagni's *Nova rhetorica* was printed by Caxton in a rare (and doubtless unrewarding) venture into academic publishing. The new interest in literature and in literary style had sufficient support in 1488 (while Rotherham was chancellor) for a substantial alteration to be made to the requirements for the BA whereby the first two years were taken from logic and assigned rather to humane letters, leaving logic for the third year and philosophy for the fourth. At the same time the MA course was restructured, on strictly quadrivial lines, to embrace, alongside Aristotle, arithmetic and music in the first year, geometry and perspective in the second, and astronomy in the third.[1]

These changes coincided with the more or less gradual collapse of the system of regency as an effective means of instruction. Wholesale dispensations from the delivery of ordinary lectures became commonplace; the availability of relatively inexpensive printed texts started to undermine the need for cursory lectures. Those who did lecture publicly were also lecturing in their colleges or hostels and attendance at such statutory lectures as were still given must often have seemed redundant. Students voted with their feet. The university's reaction was not, however, to abandon the role of public instruction, but rather to try to improve its quality: in 1486 they hired their first paid lecturer in the shape of one 'Caius Auberinus', recently identified as the poet John Kay, who had been resident in Cambridge since at least 1483 and was to remain, as an occasional lecturer and as the university's official writer of letters to the good and the great, until 1504.

In 1495 the statute for the BA course was again redrafted substituting the single author, Terence, for the unspecified *libri humanistici* prescribed in 1488. The comedies of Terence were regarded as models of Latin style as well as furnishing, as Butler of Shrewbury (among others) was reported to have observed much later of Sophocles' *Oedipus tyrannus*, 'a veritable treasure-house of grammatical peculiarities'. As a teaching text Terence retained his popularity for centuries, and the humanities lecturer and his lecture room were long known as the Terence lecturer and the School of Terence, but it is unlikely, both on the grounds of probability and on the evidence of book-ownership, that two whole

[1] For the *quadrivium* see pp. 17–18 above.

6. Teaching before print: the master propounds the text to students sharing a single copy either of the text itself or of a summary.

¶ Formulario di lettere & di orationi uolgari con la proposta & risposta cõposto ꝑ Christofano landini

7. Teaching after print: a less depressed group of students, each of whom now has his own copy, attends a lecturer now free to devote more time to exposition of the text.

years were devoted to this author alone. The first Terence lecturer, in 1496, was again 'Caius Auberinus'.

The medieval student contrived to study the central Aristotelian works on logic, known collectively as the *Organon*, without necessarily having access, or at least constant access, to the actual texts. The substitution of literature for dialectic is one of the few landmarks we can discern in the terrain dividing a method of teaching which was largely oral from one that was based on reading. The English presses, to be sure, did not regard the university textbook as a likely starter. After Caxton's solitary venture noted above and the tentative and limited projects of the St Albans schoolmaster-printer or printers and of Thomas Hunt and Theodoric Rood at Oxford in the last two decades of the fifteenth century, it was not until the later sixteenth century that a significant proportion even of the most elementary texts was printed in England, and probably not until the eighteenth century that the English presses could supply the needs of even the most indolent MA.

The first book printed on the continent specifically for the English market (a Sarum breviary) was produced in the southern Netherlands in about 1475. In 1483 Peter Actors and John of Westphalia were offering to the Oxford stationer, Thomas Hunt, books, not from their own press alone, on a sale-or-return basis, and it is possible that similarly entrepreneurial visits were paid to Cambridge by continental printers in the fifteenth century. The Byrckmann family were actively importing academic books into England from very early in the sixteenth century (and a widow Byrckmann was a prosperous property-owner in Cambridge in 1540), and we know that in the late 1520s and early 1530s Garrett Godfrey (who had been active as a stationer in Cambridge since 1502) had a shop well stocked with the elementary textbooks printed, for instance, by Simon Colines in Paris, as well as a host of Erasmian texts, and that he could and did also procure the sophisticated Hebrew texts printed in Basle by Froben, but the degrees by which the printed textbook became commonplace cannot as yet be precisely measured.

The question is of some interest because the new technology carried with it the new learning: not only texts in Greek and in Hebrew, but also new approaches to the elementary arts course with an emphasis on the inculcation of a good (that is to say, a classical) Latin style, to be learned notably from the *Elegantiae* of the celebrated humanist pedagogue Lorenzo Valla, and a new approach to dialectic (most popularly in Lefèvre d'Etaples's *Introductiones ad logicam*) tending more and more to the ends of persuasive discourse rather than to the rigours of formal logic. Not that the new learning immediately displaced the old. Many private libraries show scholastic and humanist texts in dialectic and in grammar, as indeed also in theology and in medicine, peaceably shelved together, even if the lawyers stoutly resisted new fashions.

While the effect on Cambridge at the turn of the century of the new texts from the continent and the influence of scholars returning from studies abroad are hard to assess, there can be little doubt of the impetus given to the new approach to learning during the three years' residence of Erasmus, universally acknowledged as the chief pillar of the northern renaissance. Erasmus' first visit to England in 1499 had been prompted by three of his pupils at the Collège de Montaigu at Paris, Robert (kinsman of John) Fisher, Richard Whitford of Queens' College and William Blount, Lord Mountjoy. It was not, however, until 1506 that Erasmus paid his first visit to Cambridge, probably in the entourage of Henry VII and his mother, the Lady Margaret, who were received by John Fisher as chancellor, and it was Fisher who persuaded Erasmus to come and teach in Cambridge from 1511. He resided partly in Queens' (of which Fisher was president but never a resident himself) and partly, perhaps, with his countryman, the stationer Garrett Godfrey, with excursions to London and, to escape the plague, to Landbeach. In Cambridge he completed work on his new edition of the Gospels and Epistles, the *Novum instrumentum*, and worked on his edition of Jerome's letters and on translations from Basil, Plutarch and Lucian, as well as on those of his pedagogic texts which were to saturate the market for decades to come: the *De copia verborum*, *De conscribendis epistolis* and *De ratione studii*, along with his edition of Dionysius Cato's *Disticha*, a very elementary text but one that was bought in large quantities by Cambridge tutors.

Also, of course, he taught: both theology and Greek. His public lectures in theology, perhaps as Lady Margaret Professor, were on Jerome; those in Greek were elementary, first on Chrysoloras' grammar, which attracted a smaller audience than he had hoped for, and then on that of Theodore Gaza. It may be that the private tuition which he offered in Greek was of more lasting significance: we know that Thomas Lupset

8. Portrait of Erasmus in 1517 by Quentin Matsys now in the Galeria Corsini, Rome.

and others were paid in Greek lessons for their research assistance. Of the generation who came to prominence in the university between about 1515 and 1525 many had embraced humanism and many are known to have experienced Erasmus' teaching.

The mantle of public instruction in Greek, however, was inherited by Richard Croke, who had been away from Cambridge for the whole period of Erasmus' residence. After graduating BA from King's in 1509 he had pursued his studies in Paris, Louvain and Cologne before, at the age of twenty-six, becoming the professor of Greek at Leipzig, where he published an elementary Greek accidence and an edition of book four of Gaza's grammar. He returned to Cambridge to take his MA in 1517 and was appointed lecturer in Greek in 1518. Attempts to attract an endowment for this post having failed, the university ingeniously established on a regular basis the office of Orator and appointed Croke to that either in the same year or the next. Typical of many of his generation Croke made it clear in his inaugural lecture that he regarded the study of the classical languages, especially Greek, essentially as a handmaid to theology and was at pains to express his esteem also for Scotus and other scholastic theologians.

Greek flourished, attracting the attention, among many others, of Nicholas Ridley (BA 1522), who taught it in turn to Nicholas Carr, later Regius Professor of Greek, and of John Cheke (Croke's successor as Orator and son of Peter Cheke, Esquire Bedell), who passed on his learning to Roger Ascham, to William Cecil, later Lord Burghley, and to William Bill, later to be Regius Professor of Greek and Master of St John's and of Trinity in succession. Meanwhile, the public lectures in philosophy, logic and rhetoric had by 1524 been put on a firmer footing by the endowment of Sir Robert Rede and the university had responded by assuring an income from fees for the mathematical lecturer.

When Henry VIII's 'reforming' injunctions of 1535 addressed the arts syllabus, prescribing as authors Aristotle, Rudolph Agricola, Melanchthon and George of Trebizond and proscribing Scotus, Burley, Trombetta, Bricot and Bruliferius, as exemplars of the 'frivolous questions and obscure glosses' of the scholastic dialecticians, they were addressing themselves to a non-existent problem.[2] Scotus, indeed, remained a useful

[2] For the religious and political context of these injunctions see p. 47 following.

source for theologians, and a few editions of Burley and of Bricot were still to be found in private collections, but if Trombetta and Bruliferius were still studied anywhere it was in Oxford, not in Cambridge. More positively the injunctions laid on all colleges the obligation to provide two daily public lectures, in Greek and in Latin, an obligation that seems to have been widely accepted by those colleges that had not already made such arrangements. Later in the year the injunctions of Thomas Leigh, the great suppressor of the monasteries, now deputed by Cromwell to conduct a visitation of the university, required the establishment of public lectures in Greek and in Hebrew. College contributions duly financed the continuation of lectures in Greek, and a lectureship in Hebrew was financed from 1535 to 1539 by the suppression of that in mathematics. From 1535 to 1540, moreover, additional public lectures in Greek and Hebrew seem to have been funded by King's Hall alone.

The studies of the higher faculties were also addressed in the 1535 injunctions, notoriously with the suppression of the faculty of canon law. Public disputations and degrees in canon law accordingly ceased, but there is ample evidence that it continued to be studied by many of those who graduated in civil law since canon law continued to inform proceedings in the church courts, which still opened an avenue to advancement, even if the Act of Supremacy, establishing the king as supreme head of the church in England, meant that no new canon law was to be enacted in England. In theology the injunctions directed that lectures, both public and domestic, should be on the Bible 'according to the true sense thereof and not after the manner of Scotus, etc.' and the study of the *Sentences* and of commentaries on them was formally banned. This, if totally effective, would have marked a dramatic break with tradition, but many theologians were already directing their attention more to the fathers of the church than to the scholastic doctors while, on the other hand, editions of Scotus and other schoolmen continued to be used and cited.

The Edwardian visitors of 1549, continuing the work of reformation, proposed further adjustments to the arts course, laying down directions on the one hand for the lecturers and on the other for the students. The philosophy lecturer was to supplement readings in Aristotle with some from Pliny or Plato. Pliny again, with Pomponius Mela, Strabo and Ptolemy for cosmography, Tonstall and Cardan for arithmetic, Euclid for geometry and Ptolemy for astronomy were recommended to the mathematics lecturer. Mathematics was to supplement literature as the first study of the undergraduate. Those studying for the BD were to study the apostolical epistles, doctors were to be admitted to study the whole of scripture, Old Testament and New. In an attempt to increase the learned ministry a route to the BD was devised comprising three years' study in arts and four in divinity, bypassing the MA, while an English sermon in the university church was added to the necessary exercises.

Two years later the Marian visitors again addressed the arts syllabus, directing the philosophy lecturers to teach, as very likely they were already teaching, Aristotle's *Problemata*, *Moralia* and *Politica*. Lectures on Aristotle were to be in Greek – a requirement that called in 1560 for the more realistic rider: 'as far as possible'. The return of catholicism was marked, therefore, by no significant changes in the basic curriculum, and, by the same token, no alterations to the syllabus marked its retreat on the accession of Elizabeth.

As for the university statutes of 1570, they propose no significant alterations to the arts course, merely deigning to recommend as suitable texts in rhetoric Quintilian, Hermogenes and the speeches of Cicero. That Bartholomew Dodington as Regius Professor of Greek did indeed lecture on Hermogenes is clear from his annotated copy in the University Library, but the text seems not to have become a widely used one. Quintilian and Cicero, on the other hand, had been routinely used at least since the beginning of the century. Here, as with the earlier statutory regulations for the curriculum, we may see with what caution such regulations should be interpreted. Where, as so often, they merely codified existing practice, they serve as mileposts rather than signposts; when they attempted a radical reform they were commonly ignored. Many of the authors whose works in reality formed the backbone of the arts course – authors like Valla and Erasmus and, later, Seton and Ramus – are never mentioned. The 1570 statutes remained in force, but for a few hiccoughs, until the middle of the nineteenth century. It would be absurd to suppose that no curricular developments took place in the interim.

In broad outline, the changes in the curriculum between the second half of the fifteenth century and the end of the sixteenth were marked in arts by a move away from formal logic and modal grammar to literature, rhetoric and some arithmetic for undergraduates, from further logic and

Aristotelian natural and moral philosophy to a more widely based natural and moral philosophy for BAs. Real control over the reading of undergraduates and to some extent of BAs, was exercised by college tutors, who made it their business to acquire, for loan or sale to their pupils, the texts which they were to study and who may have been more or less influenced by, for example, the Ramist approach to learning with its assault on traditional Aristotelianism which so stirred the University of Paris in the middle of the century.

Theology, meanwhile, underpinned by an increasing familiarity with Greek and to some extent Hebrew, became concerned less and less with the schoolmen and more and more with the text of the Bible itself, and with the commentaries of the western, and increasingly, the eastern fathers, constantly to be cited in the controversies that racked the middle years of the century. In medicine, new and better texts of Galen and Hippocrates came to be supplemented by a wide variety of continental texts, not excluding those of Paracelsus and his school, while the lawyers continued predominantly to follow the Italian schools, both in civil and in canon law.

While these developments were not conspicuously influenced by state interference their acceleration early in the sixteenth century was not without encouragement at a different level. Among those who had been exposed to the ideals of reform and who had, moreover, turned their academic labours to good account was John Alcock, Doctor of Civil Law of Cambridge in 1459, and subsequently bishop of Rochester, Worcester and Ely successively, as well as serving, in the absence of his friend Thomas Rotherham, as royal Chancellor in 1474 and as Comptroller of the Royal Works under Henry VII. He it was who, after attempting, perhaps with more earnestness than he has been given credit for, to reform the lives of the remaining nuns of the convent of St Radegund at Barnwell, resolved instead to dissolve the house, and replace it with the College of the Blessed Virgin Mary, St John the Evangelist, and the Glorious Virgin St Radegund near Cambridge – to be known at his request as Jesus College. The premises to hand, although in need of repair, were certainly spacious in respect of the modest establishment proposed of a master, six fellows and six boys studying grammar. The inspiration for the six grammar students, as for the common name of the college, may well have been Thomas Rotherham's Jesus College at

Rotherham in Yorkshire, although the precedent of Merton could also be adduced.[3]

The greatest architect of the university's fortunes in these years, however, was John Fisher (BA 1488) who, after active service as senior proctor (1494–5), lecturer (1496–7), vice-chancellor (1501), first Lady Margaret Professor of Divinity (1502) and chancellor annually from 1504, was seldom to be seen in Cambridge, although he was elected President of Queens' in 1505 and chancellor for life in 1514. In his constant endeavours to promote active religion and a learned church he never let go of the university as an instrument for realising his aims. We do not know on what university business he dined, as his accounts as proctor show, with the Lady Margaret in 1494, nor whether this was their first encounter. Shortly after, however, he withdrew temporarily from Cambridge to join her household as her confessor. From then until the end of her life and beyond it, he directed her favours to Cambridge.

The first manifestation of this favour was the foundation of the Lady Margaret Professorship of Divinity in 1502 (of which we have seen that Fisher himself was the first holder), and this was closely followed by a preachership in 1504 (a clear reflection of Fisher's ambitions for a preaching ministry) and this in turn by the refoundation, as Christ's College, of Godshouse, with its strong tradition of internal lectures in the arts, now designed as a school of arts and theology whose fellows were obliged to enter the priesthood within a year of their admission and were to have preference in elections to Lady Margaret's preachership. The founder's statutes show that the Lady Margaret envisaged the college primarily as a chantry for herself and her family, then as a house of devotion, and only then as a place of study. On her death in 1509 the task of realising her final benefaction, the foundation of St John's College, fell to her executors, John Fisher and Henry Hornby.

The idea of suppressing the Hospital of St John (where Cambridge's first college had awkwardly originated)[4] had been discussed by her council as early as 1505, but without visible results, and one must admire the pertinacity with which her executors fought to secure both the licence for the foundation and what funds they could from the Lady Margaret's

[3] See p. 21.
[4] See pp. 21–2.

9. Portrait of John Fisher, by Hans Holbein.

estate and elsewhere. Fisher himself contributed a huge sum, in excess of £1,000. St John's was in many ways to be a less conservative foundation than Christ's with provisions, probably modelled on those of Richard Fox for Corpus Christi College, Oxford, for teaching in Greek and Hebrew (albeit the Hebrew lecture, if it seemed at any time not to be 'useful', could be replaced by a Latin lecture on Scotus) and for internal examinations as well as lectures. Parallels may also be adduced with Wolsey's foundation of Cardinal College, not least in the refusal of both Fisher and Wolsey to deny all merit either to the tradition of scholastic theology or to the disputation as an educational instrument. Unlike Wolsey and Fox, however, Fisher refrained from throwing open the lectures of the fellows of his college to outsiders.

The position which Fisher occupies as the friend of Erasmus, as an admirer of the schoolmen, as the effective founder of colleges well abreast of the latest educational developments and as a bitter opponent of Luther and others is very properly no longer seen as anomalous. Many others of his generation entertained the same respect for the content of medieval theology, while deploring its Latinity, even if few were to be called, as he was, to demonstrate their faith on the scaffold.

Erasmus attributed to Fisher's support the successful launch of Greek studies in Cambridge, and it was in this direction that his foundation at St John's was to distinguish itself. Fisher would surely have smiled, as we must smile (even if, like us, he might also have raised an eyebrow) at Ascham's rosy account of the university and particularly of St John's in 1542 as compared with its state twenty years earlier when his correspondent, John Brandesby, had graduated:

> Aristotle and Plato are now read in their own language by the boys – as indeed we have done for five years in our own college. Sophocles and Euripides are more familiar that Plautus was when you were here. Herodotus, Thucydides, Xenophon are more on the lips and in the hands than Titus Livius was then. Now you would hear of Demosthenes what once you did of Cicero. More copies of Isocrates are in the boys' hands than there were formerly of Terence.[5]

We may question this as an accurate description of the university at large, but as an account of the academic élite, and of the group around

[5] *The whole works of Roger Ascham*, ed. J. A. Giles (4 vols., 1865) i p. 26.

Cheke, which came to be known as the 'Cambridge Athenians', at that precise moment it is hard to fault.

For those on whose shoulders fell the defence of the ivory tower, however, the years since Fisher's vice-chancellorship had been anything but tranquil. In that year (1501–2) the disputes between the town and the university had once again come to a head and arbitration was sought at the hands of the Lady Margaret, who appointed to hear the submissions of each party three lawyers, one of them, confusingly, being another John Fisher, Justice of the Common Pleas. The arbitration concentrated on problems concerning scholars' servants (college cooks, launderers, etc., and others, such as stationers, employed by the university who were entitled to claim the privileges of scholars in being largely free of the jurisdiction of the town courts); disputed areas of jurisdiction; tolls on victuals coming into the town and the filthy state of the streets. The town evidently felt that the number of people claiming scholarly privileges was getting out of hand with the increased employment opportunities offered by the colleges, and the arbitrators devised rules to prevent such privileges being claimed by those whose employment was only sporadic, or had in fact ceased. The town in turn had to reduce the tolls levied on fresh food coming in to the market and on wood and coal intended exclusively for college consumption. Both of these issues were prophetic of countless disputes between town and gown in the course of the century, often focusing on their respective rights in Sturbridge Fair, a very significant source of all manner of commodities, including books from the continent, and a mart which was on its way to becoming the largest annual fair in the country, vividly depicted as Bunyan's Vanity Fair. The concern with 'nuisances', with the butchers' habit of using the street as a slaughterhouse and with the uncontrolled spread of middens, was not new, but these were problems which became increasingly urgent as the town became more and more overcrowded: fires broke out constantly and throughout this century and the next 'plague' of one sort or another became endemic in the town, frequently forcing the evacuation of the university, the postponement of terms and dispensations from residence and from the performance of academic exercises.

Troubles brewing further afield had even more impact on the university. In 1517 Luther nailed up his theses in Wittenberg, and Cambridge's fat was soon to be in the fire. When Geoffrey Knight (DD 1500/1), a pillar of the university establishment, died in 1520 he left, among other things, funds to support two priests studying at Gonville Hall, and, to the Prior of Walsingham books, including one by Luther. A month later Luther was excommunicated and his books banned, and in 1521 Henry Bullock, Robert Ridley, Humphrey Walkden and John Watson, all friends of Erasmus, rode up to London at Wolsey's command to assist in the formal examination of Luther's works. The cardinal pronounced the condemnation at Paul's Cross on 12 May and the preacher after the bonfire of books was Fisher. There was a bonfire at Cambridge too, and the papal condemnation was posted on the schools doors. It was defaced, but the young man responsible recanted when he was caught.

At about this time, probably, there started those famous meetings at 'Little Germany': the White Horse tavern on the site of the present insalubrious passage between King's and St Catharine's, where Thomas Bilney, Robert Barnes, Hugh Latimer, Miles Coverdale, Thomas Cranmer, Matthew Parker, William Tyndale, Nicholas Shaxton, John Bale, even Stephen Gardiner, gathered with others to discuss the latest theological developments in Germany. They can scarcely have foreseen the extent to which these interests would dictate their fates on the whirling wheel of ecclesiastical favour, but Luther's excommunication must have sent a shiver down some of their spines, and they knew, also, that Wolsey had an eye on Cambridge. He had been in Cambridge in 1520 (when Henry Bullock's speech welcoming him became the first product of John Siberch's short-lived Cambridge press) and as long ago as 1514 Fisher, conscious that the deaths of the Lady Margaret and of Henry VII must diminish his own influence at court, had twice offered to resign the chancellorship in his favour. Wolsey had then declined the offered honour, but it was now becoming clear to the university that he was a power to be reckoned with nonetheless.

In 1523 Wolsey had set about the establishment at Oxford of Cardinal College on a scale of spectacular munificence which, if realised, would, as the Oxford authorities wrote to him, have equalled all the rest of the university put together. Moreover, if Wolsey as an East Anglian was unusual in having found his education at Oxford rather than Cambridge, it was overwhelmingly to Cambridge that he looked to staff his new college in Oxford. Prominent among his recruits was Richard Cox, first dean of the college and chancellor of the university from 1547, who as a result of his firm action in purging the University Library during the Edwardian visitation of Oxford in 1549 was to become known, unfairly enough, to his less rigidly protestant detractors as 'not so much the chancellor as the cancellor of the university'. Meanwhile both universities were swept off their feet by the apparition of so princely a patron as Wolsey. Cambridge, like Oxford, in a gesture of extraordinary abasement, voluntarily surrendered into his hands the entire corpus of statutes, ordinances and customary regulations, inviting him to revise them. Wolsey was no supporter of Lutheranism, but his new foundation at Oxford clearly demonstrated his enthusiasm for the new learning. He did not, however, find time to modernise the Cambridge statutes.

Late in 1525 the persecutions began when the vice-chancellor instituted proceedings against Robert Barnes, Prior of the Augustinian friars, for heresy on the basis of a Christmas Eve sermon directed chiefly against ecclesiastical abuses; Barnes was sent to London and on this occasion recanted, was confined to the Augustinian houses in London and then escaped to Germany. He was not to burn until 1540. In 1527 Thomas Arthur, Thomas Bilney and George Joye were also charged with heresy, but conformed for the time being. With Hugh Latimer's 'Card Sermons' of December 1529, in which he employed similes from games of cards (allowed in the colleges only at Christmas) in an attack on superstitious practices, and the 'Dice Sermon' of Dr Robert Buckenham, prior of the Dominicans, in reply, war was openly declared, although the university again managed to construct a temporary truce. Bilney, who had been such an inspiration to Latimer and to others, both in doctrine and in charitable works, was burned in the Lollards' Pit at Norwich in 1531. Wolsey, meanwhile, barred a proposed episcopal visitation of Cambridge to root out heresy.

In 1529 or 1530 the bookseller Sygar Nicholson was convicted of holding not only protestant opinions but also a stock of heretical books, which were duly burned. The university had recently, on the pretext of the suppression of error, petitioned Wolsey for the right to license three booksellers who should be subject to their supervision. The booksellers were to be foreigners, so as to be capable of the art of printing, and would have the right to buy foreign books. Almost certainly they had in mind three of the existing booksellers, Garrett Godfrey, whom we have already encountered,[6] his 'cousin' Nicholas Spierinck, and, possibly, Nicholson. The university's request was to be met, but not until 1534, and then by the crown.

In 1530 Wolsey fell, to be replaced by Thomas Cromwell, but not before Thomas Cranmer (previously a fellow of Jesus, and a lecturer at Buckingham College when his short-lived marriage forced the resignation of his fellowship) had suggested to Henry VIII that the university of Cambridge might be found willing to interpret in favour of the king the legal questions bearing on the pressing matter of the divorce. Cranmer was in a position to know that there were men in Cambridge who would not shrink from a confrontation with Rome, but he cannot have supposed that such inclinations were universal there. Nonetheless, the 'request' for a ruling was sent to Cambridge before Oxford. In the event the university dragged its feet until a letter of February 1530 from Edward Fox, Provost of King's, royal almoner, and, with Richard Croke (now estranged from his doomed patron, Fisher) one of Henry's agents in Italy, forced the university into giving an opinion on 'whether it is prohibited by divine and natural law to marry the childless widow of one's brother'. It was a close-run thing. Congregation was summoned, discussed the matter at length, and came to no conclusion. The next day the vice-chancellor, William Buckmaster, proposed a grace in the king's favour. It was defeated on the first vote; the second vote was inconclusive. Finally the opposition abstained, the vote was carried, and a heavily weighted panel was deputed to formulate the final decision. The university's actions were greeted, according to Buckmaster, with shock and dismay, but Oxford, if with less docility, finally followed suit.

From this time the university's fortunes were to be as intricately involved with state and church as ever they had been, but now church and state were one and, moreover, very able and no less willing to intervene at every turn. Not that the cause of protestantism was triumphant, either in Cambridge or in the court. In 1530 the king ordered each university to send twelve delegates to sit in judgement on 'certain books' – including part of Tyndale's translation of the Bible and a selection of Lutheran texts. Latimer and Shaxton were in the Cambridge team. Early in the next year Shaxton was summoned before the vice-chancellor for

[6] pp. 33–4.

preaching against purgatory. He came to heel and agreed to swear an oath never to maintain the opinions of Wyclif, Hus or Luther, or any opinion contrary to the doctrine of the catholic church. The same oath was imposed on all those graduating in theology that year, but seems to have lapsed on the change of vice-chancellors. As yet the quarrel was officially with the pope, not with the catholic church. Dr Heynes of Queens', the vice-chancellor, and Dr Skyppe were sent to London to preach against the authority of the pope and in favour of the royal supremacy, but in a public disputation held in Cambridge on their return the contrary was stoutly maintained by others, including the prior of the Dominicans.

The year 1535 saw the deaths of two of Erasmus' Cambridge friends: of William Blount, Lord Mountjoy, High Steward of the university, and, on the scaffold for his denial of royal supremacy, of John Fisher, the chancellor. Both were replaced by one man: Thomas Cromwell. Backed by royal authority he prepared for a visitation of both universities. The visitation of Cambridge was preceded by royal injunctions demanding a universal oath of allegiance to the royal succession and supremacy, and imposing the reforms to the syllabus discussed above including, since papal legislation would henceforth have no force in England, the banning of public lectures and degrees in canon law.[7] The actual visitation was carried out, not by Cromwell himself but by Thomas Leigh, Doctor of Civil Law, a graduate of King's and notorious as a suppressor of monasteries. It resulted in further injunctions forbidding the sale of college fellowships which were to be awarded purely on merit and not on geographical grounds, ordering a commemorative mass for college and university founders and benefactors and for the king and his lawful queen Anne, and, potentially much more seriously, commanding the officers of the university, the colleges and the hostels, to deliver up their 'papistical muniments' with a list of all their rentals and moveable property. They did as they were told, and in due course received confirmation from the crown of privileges previously held of the pope.

Great grounds for anxiety remained: many of the religious houses had already been dissolved, and the scramble for their lands and revenues proceeded apace. The colleges of the university were also seen as religious

[7] pp. 36–7.

houses, and the vultures looked at them with interest. For the time being all was well. In 1536 Oxford and Cambridge, Winchester and Eton were granted a perpetual exemption from the tax of 'first fruits and tenths' levied by the king on other religious houses, in recognition of which favour they were to celebrate two masses yearly for the king, Queen Anne and the Princess Elizabeth, and to institute the lectureships called for in the injunctions and discussed above.[8] Cromwell meanwhile enjoined on all clergy with benefices worth £100 or more the obligation to support, either at one of the universities or at grammar school, one scholar for every £100.

The axe fell first on the houses of the friars. They had long seen it coming, and the numbers who remained to sign the deeds of surrender in Cambridge in 1538 were small: twenty-four Franciscans and sixteen Dominicans. Several found accommodation in the secular colleges; others had made arrangements elsewhere. The Carmelites had tried to establish a friendly transfer of their premises to Queens', who had in the end to go to law for them, and pay for them. Buckingham, the college of the Benedictines, seems, as recent research has shown, to have survived the dissolution as an anomaly until, under the ostensible patronage of the time-serving Thomas, Lord Audley, whose mother had been a benefactor, it was refounded by Henry VIII in 1542. The university, ever hopeful, petitioned the king that the houses should all be re-established as colleges: then they started to carry away the stone for use in their own more modest establishments.

In 1540 Cromwell followed Fisher to the scaffold to be replaced as chancellor by Stephen Gardiner, a Cambridge graduate. Cromwell had been a graduate of no university but was nonetheless an enthusiast for the new learning. The adaptation of the scheme for lectureships propounded in 1536 whereby, in 1540, they were transmogrified into the five Regius Professorships (Greek, Hebrew, Theology, Civil Law and Physic) may have been a legacy of his influence or a new initiative of Gardiner's. They were initially funded out of the revenues of the newly established bishopric of Westminster and were all filled, by crown nominees, by 1542. Gardiner was certainly interested in education: in 1542 and 1543 he deeply upset the proponents of the new learning in

[8] p. 37.

Cambridge by banning the new pronunciation of Greek as advocated, with some pains, by that great polymath Thomas Smith, Regius Professor of Civil Law (later to be secretary to Edward VI and to Queen Elizabeth, and ambassador to France), and by John Cheke, now Regius Professor of Greek (also destined to be a royal tutor, and a royal secretary as well as, briefly, brother-in-law to his young fellow Johnian, William Cecil).

Meanwhile the king's coffers rattled hollowly and the vultures grew more insistent. In 1545 an Act was passed for the dissolution of all major chantries and all colleges, placing all the foundations in the university at the king's disposal. This was the threat to end all threats. By now the colleges *were* the university to all those extents and purposes to which they were to remain so for centuries.

The precise means by which the universities snatched themselves from ruin remain obscure, but their defence was conducted on three fronts. First the king was persuaded to save the expense of sending expert surveyors down from London by appointing rather men already in place (in the case of Cambridge John Redman, warden of the King's Hall, William Mey, president of Queens', and Matthew Parker, master of Corpus); next they appealed successfully to Queen Katherine Parr, a staunch protestant to be sure, and an unlikely supporter of chantries, but then the vultures were predominantly catholic. The credit for securing her support has been attributed to Thomas Smith and John Cheke, both royal tutors, and indeed both of them constant friends to their university. Both had had the same teacher there, John Redman, and it is mainly to him, most probably, that the university owes its survival of this crisis.

Surveys of the colleges' lands and income were duly presented, evidently by bursars already forming the mould in which their successors were to be cast, since the king, who was not perhaps unfamiliar with their breed, and was not without wit, on studying their returns observed that 'he thought he had not in his realm so many persons so honestly maintained in living by so little land and rent'. Questions were indeed asked as to how the colleges managed to survive in a permanent state of deficit, to which the reply was made, truthfully if economically, that it was done by the levying of fines on the renewal of leases in those years in which they fell due and by sales of wood.

The third line of defence is obscure in its mechanism but visually pre-eminent in its results. Wolsey's college in Oxford had largely fallen with him. It was Richard Cox,[9] very probably, the sole commissioner for Oxford, who persuaded Henry to re-establish it as his own royal foundation, Henry VIII College (later Christ Church) to stand as a monument to his princely liberality and a source not only of learned clerks for state and church but also of continual prayers for the king and his successors. John Redman, meanwhile, pointed out that the same effect might be achieved in Cambridge, by absorbing into his own royal foundation, the King's Hall, both Physwick Hostel (the thriving property of Gonville Hall) and Michaelhouse, making of the three establishments one Trinity. The king proved susceptible to this line of argument and, moreover, found the means to complete at long last Henry VI's lavish chapel at King's.

The situation had been saved, and the university as an institution was perhaps never again to face so grave a threat; for many individuals, however, life was about to become even more interesting. The accession of Edward VI in 1548 was hailed by the protestant party as heralding a new dawn. The universities were expressly omitted from the Act for dissolving chantries, and there was time for rows with the town again. The chancellor, Gardiner, was in prison because of his resistance to the reformation. He was replaced by Protector Somerset due in four years' time to follow Cromwell along what was becoming a well-trodden path to execution, thus yielding place to Protector Northumberland, hot on his footsteps. The university cross (which had been carried by Nicholas Ridley, as university chaplain in the 1530s) was sold. The university's charters were duly confirmed. The obligation on the more prosperous clergy to support scholars was once again promulgated, but the fact remained that students were in short supply. Theologians had disappeared in large numbers in the previous reign, and now the young gentlemen who, as Latimer lamented to the king,[10] had filled their place were inclined to bide their time. Ascham wrote to Archbishop Cranmer that 'the university was then in so depressed and drooping a condition, that very few had hope of coming thither at all, and fewer had any comfort to make long tarrying when they were there; and that abroad it retained not so much as the shadow of its former dignity', a remark that at first

[9] For whom see also pp. 44–5.

[10] 'There be none now but great men's sons in colleges, and their fathers look not to have them preachers.'

strikes us as strange in the light of the number of Cambridge graduates personally known to him who were already occupying, or who were shortly to fill, so many eminent positions in church and state.

Meanwhile, the new reign brought a new visitation at the friendly hands of Thomas Goodrich, bishop of Ely, Sir Thomas Smith, Dr Thomas Wendy, Nicholas Ridley, bishop of Rochester, Sir John Cheke, Sir William Paget and Dr William Mey. They brought with them a new code of statutes whose bearing on the syllabus we have noticed above.[11] In constitutional matters they looked back in spirit to earlier days: the chancellor was to be elected by the regents and non-regents in open scrutiny, the vice-chancellor, proctors and taxors by the regents alone. Students were to live more soberly: fencing schools and dicing taverns were singled out for disapprobation; the Christmas *Dominus ludorum*, close cousin to the Lord of Misrule, was to rule no more, although cards were to be allowed at that time, if no other. The responsibility of tutors for the moral conduct of their charges was clearly recognised.

In 1506, perhaps under pressure of having so often to produce ammunition for their battles with the town, the university had created the post of registrary and appointed to it Robert Hobys, a bedel. He had been succeeded by another bedel, John Meres, who not only fulfilled assiduously the duties of scribe to the university, but also kept a record of the course of the visitation, nervously enough, no doubt, since his sympathies were perhaps with the old religious practices. College statutes were called in and amended where necessary. Disputations were encouraged, and several were held in honour of the visitors, focusing often on the eucharist, which had replaced predestination as the central topic for theological debate. Nothing too terrible had happened: the Master of Clare (Roland Swynborne) was expelled, altars were pulled down at Jesus. There had been a proposal that Trinity Hall and Clare should be merged to form a single college for the study of civil law, but that had been deftly warded off on the part of Clare. Ascham, who was abroad at the time, wrote to Cecil lamenting the opportunity lost in confining the studies of non-regent masters to the existing faculties when some might have been more profitably engaged with the study of languages or the sciences, but he was ahead of his time.

[11] pp. 37–8.

Protestant scholars on the continent had high hopes of Edward's England and willingly accepted invitations to come and assist in the advancement of godly learning. Peter Martyr went to Oxford, and to Cambridge came in 1549 the irenical Martin Bucer to take up the regius chair in theology, and Paul Fagius (Büchlein) that in Hebrew. Both were internationally distinguished as scholars and as protestants. Fagius barely survived his arrival, dying in Bucer's arms within the year. Bucer's tenure lasted only until his death early in 1551, but in that time he won such esteem, not only for his skill in disputation and for his teaching, but also for his way of life, that for a generation at least his pronouncements and his example were cited with intense reverence, even by some of those who had opposed him in his lifetime. As we shall see, the posthumous fate of his body was to be bizarre. Within in a year or so the astonishing prospect was entertained of Bucer's being succeeded by none other than the great European teacher Philipp Melanchthon. There is no evidence that he himself regarded the proposal with enthusiasm, but even if he had the scheme would certainly have foundered with Edward's untimely death.

The university chancellor, the duke of Northumberland, proclaimed Lady Jane Grey queen in London on 10 July, and Mary queen in Cambridge ten days later. He was arrested nonetheless, in King's College, and set off very shortly afterwards for the scaffold, to be replaced by Gardiner once more. On Mary's accession the mass was reintroduced, exequies were revived, the Henrician statutes, on the queen's command, were restored and a new cross bought. The vice-chancellor, Dr Sandys, who had preached for Northumberland in Cambridge during the reign of the ten-days queen, was immediately imprisoned. Committed protestants left for the continent, for Strasbourg, for Frankfurt-am-Main and for Zurich. Dr Sandys in due course contrived to join them.

Of the colleges only Gonville Hall, Jesus and Magdalene retained their heads: Bill, at Trinity, was ousted in favour of John Christopherson, Andrew Perne replaced Ralph Ainsworth (who was married) at Peterhouse, Swynborne was restored at Clare, Ridley at Pembroke was replaced by the vice-chancellor, John Young, William Mowse by Gardiner himself at Trinity Hall, Sir John Cheke (who had been Secretary of State to Lady Jane Grey) by Richard Atkinson at King's and so on. Of the deprived Heads five, if we include Matthew Parker who seems to have prudently resigned, were to be appointed bishops in the next reign.

In April 1554 a deputation of eight Cambridge men, led by the vice-chancellor, proceeded with the blessing of Convocation to Oxford to dispute with Cranmer, Ridley and Latimer in prison there, and in October Gardiner sent articles for subscription by all members of the university: the king and queen were to be properly styled in all sermons (it was a mouthful),[12] scholars were to wear the gowns proper to their degrees – and the old pronunciation of Greek was to be enforced. At Gardiner's direction the university appointed the vice-chancellor and two other doctors of divinity to draw up further articles for subscription. These were concerned entirely with the dogmas of the catholic church. They appear to have been subscribed by twelve doctors, nineteen BDs, two bachelors of canon law and two of civil law, eleven non-regent masters, seventy-six regent masters and five BAs, a total of a hundred and twenty-seven; although an alternative account maintains that only fifty-one subscribed. Either way, the rate of the exodus increased.

In October 1555 Ridley wrote his moving farewell to the university and to his college:

> Farewel therefore Cambridge, my loving mother and tender Nurse. . .. What benefits hadst thou ever, that thou usest to give and bestow upon thy best beloved children, that thou thoughtest too good for me. Thou didst bestow on me all thy school degrees, the common offices, the chaplainship of the University, the office of the Proctorship and of a common Reader, and of thy private commodities and emoluments in Colledges what was it thou madest me not partner of? . . . Farewell Pembroke Hall . . . In thy orchard (the walls buts and trees, if they could speak would bear me witness) I learned without book almost all Pauls Epistles, yea, and I ween all the Canonical epistles . . . The Lord grant that this zeal and love towards that part of God's word, which is a key and a true commentary to all the holy scriptures, may ever abide in that colledge so long as the world shall endure.

He went with Latimer to the stake in Oxford, before the eyes of Cranmer, shortly, and after much wrestling with his conscience, to follow them. In the following year John Hullier, previously conduct (or chaplain) of

[12] 'Philip and Mary, by the grace of God, king and queen of England, France, Naples, Jerusalem, and Ireland, defenders of the faith, princes of Spain and Sicily, archdukes of Austria, dukes of Milan, Burgundy, and Brabant, counts of Hapsburg, Flanders, and Tyrol.'

King's, after elaborate procedures in Great St Mary's, was handed over by the university to the town authorities to be burned on Jesus Green. Sir John Cheke recanted, but died shortly afterwards.

In 1556 a commission was set up to seek out heresy. John Meres again recorded it. The commissioners included, as usual, university trusties, but also representatives of the town authorities. A search was made of the stationers' premises, of college rooms and of private houses for heretical books. Meanwhile, those who remained in Cambridge awaited the inevitable visitation which was duly ordered by Cardinal Pole, the replacement for Gardiner, who had died, a troubled soul not long lamented in Cambridge. The visitors were led by Cuthbert Scott, bishop of Chester, and included the Master of Trinity and other graduates now eminent in the church. Their task was to establish conformity. Great St Mary's and St Michael's were laid under an interdict as containing the remains of Bucer and Fagius, college and university statutes were inspected and information solicited by various means; all this interspersed with masses and with sermons. The climax, certainly for the townsmen, who found it hugely amusing, took the form of the ceremonial burning of the chained coffins of Bucer and Fagius, exhumed for the purpose. The sermon on this occasion was preached by Andrew Perne, Master of Peterhouse.

There followed a new code of statutes notable for limiting the nomination of the vice-chancellor to the heads of houses, the doctors of all faculties and the bachelors of divinity, and the nomination of lecturers to the vice-chancellor and Heads. The membership of the Caput was to be fixed from one year's end to another, and, except under exceptional circumstances, graces were to be voted upon at only four congregations in the year. As we have seen, the statutory syllabus remained virtually untouched.

Before the end of the reign there were positive developments also. Under licence from the king and queen Gonville Hall, crippled as it had been by the confiscation of Physwick Hostel, was refounded as Gonville and Caius by the sole efforts of the learned and autocratic John Caius, MD, a conservative in religion and a pioneer in the establishment of accurate Greek texts of Galen. The fellows were, if aged at least twenty at their appointment, to pursue those studies specified by the founders

10. The burning of Bucer's and Fagius' remains in 1556; John Foxe, *Actes and monuments* . . . [Foxe's Book of Martyrs], 1st edn, 1563.

of the fellowships, if under twenty to make their own choice. Of the three fellowships endowed by Caius himself one was in theology, the other two in medicine, and the college was to become a notable centre (by Cambridge standards) for the study of medicine. John Meres, dying in 1558, left to the university his house in St Bene't's parish (to be assigned for many years to the Lady Margaret Professor of Divinity), and eleven volumes and two bundles of documents which he had compiled or purchased over the years as registrary. The sermon founded by the university in his memory is still preached annually. Finally, in her will

Queen Mary herself left £500 to each university for the relief of poor scholars.[13] She was also a notable benefactor to Trinity College.

Mary's death in November 1558 was closely followed by that of Cardinal Pole and the exiles were soon packing their bags. Many of them, however, hesitated before setting out, and they judged well: they were not to have everything their own way (any more, indeed, than they had had in Frankfurt). The devices and desires of Elizabeth in matters of religion were anything but transparent. The Act of Supremacy was, however, swiftly reinstated, and many of the catholic heads required no further warning. Some fled to the continent; others, once they had resigned their headships, continued to reside in Cambridge.

Meanwhile, of course, there had to be a commission and a visitation. The commissioners were William Cecil, already chancellor of the university, Sir Anthony Cook, Matthew Parker, William Bill, Robert Horne, James Pilkington, Walter Haddon and, once again, William Mey and Thomas Wendy. Several of them were coming back into their own. Statutes, substantially the same as the Edwardian ones, were imposed on the university, and the statutes of several colleges revised, not without opposition, especially, it seems, at King's. In 1560 Bucer and Fagius were solemnly reinstated with a sermon by the vice-chancellor, that same Andrew Perne who had presided over the burning of their remains.

There were several signs of royal favour: without actually putting her hand in her pocket the queen saw to it that work on the chapel and library of Trinity, started in the previous reign, was completed; she asked for lists of those worthy of advancement in the church; in 1564 she visited the university herself in considerable state, attending sermons, disputations and plays. Gradually the university became accustomed to a level of stability; the young gentlemen came back. New colleges were to be founded: Emmanuel in 1584, Sidney Sussex in 1596, both with the aim of increasing the godly ministry, both built on the sites and with the stones of earlier religious houses and both with their chapels defiantly facing to the north rather than the east.

The second half of the century was not, however, to prove peaceful. As the 'wolves' returned from Zurich and from Strasbourg they enacted

[13] There is no evidence that the bequest was in fact received, although the records of the university chests are such that there can be no certainty in the matter.

dramatically in Cambridge the struggle for a more radical protestantism than the queen or her Cambridge advisers, Cecil, Parker and Whitgift, in particular, were minded to tolerate. Notable among them was Thomas Cartwright, a hugely successful preacher in the late 1560s, who was expelled from the Lady Margaret Professorship and from his fellowship at Trinity in 1570, but not before he had rallied the previously flagging spirits of the 'puritan' party. The university and the colleges were torn apart by disputes over vestments and over more serious disagreements as to the relative authority of scripture and of the church. Those who had been in exile kept up a steady flow of correspondence with their continental mentors and colleagues. Presentments in the vice-chancellor's court were frequent, as were appeals to Cecil at court and to Archbishop Whitgift at Lambeth, who, jointly and severally, were hard pressed to contain the situation.

The statutes which they, principally, constructed for the university in 1570 may well reflect their exasperation with the hot-headedness of the radicals. Their anti-democratic tendency certainly met with protest from the proctors, the traditional upholders of the rights of the masters, and the proctors were of Cartwright's Calvinist camp. The statutes indeed increased the number (and average age) of the regent masters by extending the period of regency, which by now had little to do with lecturing, to five years, but the power of the vice-chancellor and the Heads, which had long been increasing in practice, was now statutorily recognised, granting them the sole right to interpret the statutes and giving them a voice in most university appointments; nomination for membership of the Caput was indeed vested in the vice-chancellor and the proctors each of whom made five nominations but the electoral body was now to consist not of the regent masters but of the Heads, all doctors, the proctors and the two scrutators of the Non-Regent House. The vice-chancellor had hitherto been freely elected by the regents; from 1570 the non-regents were also given votes and the field was limited to two candidates nominated by the Heads. John Copcot, in 1586, was the last vice-chancellor not to be a head of house on his election. He became one during his term of office and the ladder was pulled up smartly under him. Finally, it is worthy of remark that these statutes, promulgated twelve years after the lapse of the catholic obligation of celibacy on the clergy, endorsing a royal proclamation of 1561, enforced celibacy on the

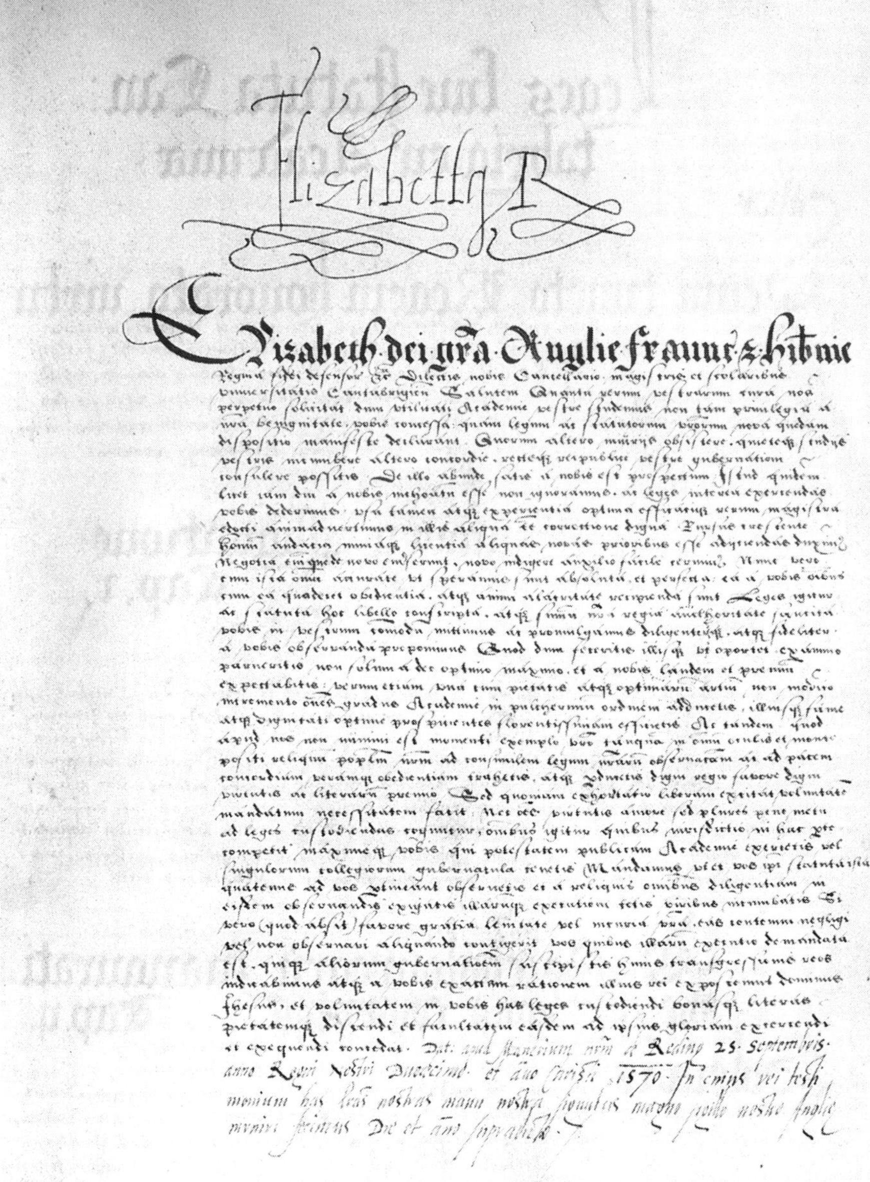

Elizabeth R

Elizabeth dei gra Anglie fraunc z hibnie

11. University statutes of 1570: the preamble, signed by Queen Elizabeth, and with the date and place of signing – 25 September at Reading – inserted in the hand of William Cecil, Lord Burghley.

fellows of colleges. The ban on matrimony was also embodied in college statutes and was to be enforced with regard to fellows until 1861, and in many colleges until later. The Heads, on whom also celibacy was nearly always imposed by college statutes, for the most part ignored them.

Such Heads as chose also attended the not infrequent heresy trials, sitting as assessors to the vice-chancellor and so sharing in his judicial role. It was to the vice-chancellor and Heads that letters from the court or from Lambeth were commonly addressed, and it was very probably in this reign that it became their custom to gather weekly in the porch, after the service at Great St Mary's. Was the sermon acceptable? If so, what other business have we to discuss?

Recusants there were, notably in Peterhouse and in Caius, but they gave little real trouble, melting away to the continent as need arose. The charge of 'papistry' was more often levelled at the ecclesiastical establishment by the radicals than by the establishment at an identifiable cadre at the university, at least until the end of the century when Peter Baro, Lady Margaret Professor from 1574 to 1596, and his adherents were denounced for what we would now call 'High Church' sympathies. After the foundation of the college at Douai in 1559 many English catholics sought their education there just as, conversely, the fifteenth-century universities of St Andrews, Glasgow and Aberdeen, reviving from 1560 under the influence of John Knox, provided potential havens for committed presbyterians. Trinity College Dublin, founded largely on the Cambridge model in 1591, was in its turn to accommodate Cambridge men tending towards radicalism in religion, including its first five provosts.

With Cecil and his son at Elizabeth's right hand throughout her reign, and with Parker, Grindal and Whitgift, all Cambridge Heads, succeeding each other at Canterbury and with her graduates promoted constantly to the high offices of church and of state, Cambridge had never been closer to the centres of power and was, perhaps, never to be so close again. It was an association which was to prove essential to, among others, Thomas Thomas, MA of King's, and, in 1583, the first university stationer since John Siberch in the 1520s to exercise the university's right to a printing press. Thomas intended a learned press, and was regarded, not without reason, as running a puritan one. His immediate successors had less exalted aims. All were obliged either to do battle, or to

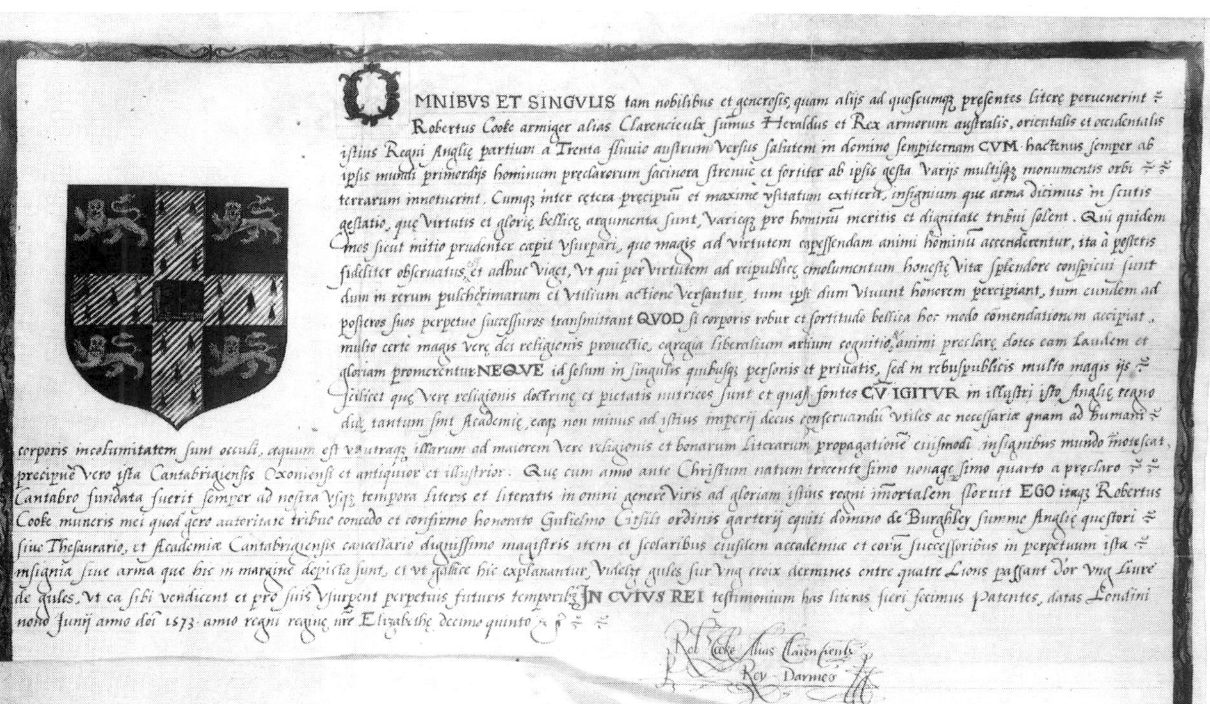

OMNIBUS ET SINGULIS tam nobilibus et generosis, quam alijs ad quoscumque presentes literę peruenerint Robertus Cooke armiger alias Clarencieulx Sumus Heraldus et Rex armorum australis, orientalis et occidentalis istius Regni Anglię partium a Trenta fluuio austrum versus salutem in domino sempiternam CUM hactenus semper ab ipsis mundi primordijs hominum preclarorum facinora strenuę et fortiter ab ipsis gesta varijs multisque monumentis orbi terrarum innotuerint. Cumque inter cętera precipuū et maxime vsitatum extiterit, insignium que arma dicimus in scutis gestatio, quę virtutis et glorię bellicę argumenta sunt, varieque pro hominū meritis et dignitate tribui solent. Qui quidem mos sicut initio prudenter cępit vsurpari, quo magis ad virtutem capessendam animi hominū accenderentur, ita à posteris fideliter obseruatus est et adhuc viget, Vt qui per virtutem ad reipublicę emolumentum honestę vitæ splendore conspicui sunt dum in rerum pulcherimarum et vtilium actione versantur, tum ipsi dum viuunt honorem percipiant, tum eundem ad posteros suos perpetuo successuros transmittant QUOD si corporis robur et fortitudo bellica hoc modo cōmendationem accipiat, multo certe magis verę dei religionis prouectio, egregia liberalium artium cognitio, animi preclarę dotes eam laudem et gloriam promerentur NEQUE id solum in singulis quibusque personis et priuatis, sed in rebuspublicis multo magis ijs scilicet quę verę religionis doctrinę et pietatis nutrices sunt et quasi fontes CU IGITUR in illustri isto Anglię regno duę tantum sint Academię, eæque non minus ad istius imperij decus conseruandū vtiles ac necessariæ quam ad humani corporis incolumitatem sunt oculi, equum est vt vtraque illarum ad maiorem verę religionis et bonarum literarum propagationē eiusmodi insignibus mundo innotescat, precipuē vero ista Cantabrigiensis Oxoniensi et antiquior et illustrior. Quę cum anno ante Christum natum trecentesimo nonagesimo quarto a preclaro Cantabro fundata fuerit semper ad nostra vsque tempora literis et literatis in omni genere viris ad gloriam istius regni im̄ortalem floruit EGO itaque Robertus Cooke muneris mei quod gero autoritate tribuo concedo et confirmo honorato Gulielmo Cecill ordinis garterij equiti domino de Burghley summo Anglię questori siue Thesaurario, et Academiæ Cantabrigiensis cancellario dignissimo magistris item et scolaribus eiusdem accademiae et eorū successoribus in perpetuum ista insignia siue arma que hic in margine depicta sunt, et vt gallice hic explanantur, videlicet gules sur vng croix dermines entre quatre Lions passant d'or vng liure de gules, vt ea sibi vendicent et pro suis vsurpent perpetuis futuris temporibus IN CUIUS REI testimonium has literas fieri fecimus Patentes, datas Londini nono Junij anno dñi 1573 anno regni reginę nrē Elizabethę decimo quinto

Rob Cooke alias Clarencieulx Roy Darmes

12. Grant of arms to the university, 9 June 1573, signed by Robert Cooke, Clarencieux King of Arms.

compound, more or less honourably, with the Stationers' Company in London. Without support at court, they could never have succeeded.

Of those whose careers prospered outside Cambridge, all of them devoted, if sometimes irritated, sons, we have had frequent occasion to mention such luminaries as Thomas Cranmer, Sir John Cheke, Roger Ascham and Matthew Parker. Many others could be singled out, not least some of the earliest figures in the noble procession of Cambridge poets: Sir Thomas Wyatt, George Gascoigne, Edmund Spenser, Fulke Greville, Sir John Harington the elder, Christopher Marlowe, Thomas Nashe, Robert Greene. It would be long yet before an academic career would be an end in itself rather than a stepping stone to distinction in the 'real world' but of those who dominated the university during these years two perhaps reflect in their lives the flavour of the university, William Whitaker and Andrew Perne.

Whitaker was from his youth a very accomplished scholar, as witness his Greek verses written at the age of sixteen on the occasion of the queen's visit in 1564. He was revered as such internationally, even by his adversaries, and had established himself by his death at the early age of forty-seven as the intellectual leader of the moderate Calvinists prominent in Cambridge and in the nation at large in the 1570s and 1580s. He was suspected of sympathies with the more extreme Calvinists and his mastership of St John's was not without its tribulations but his stature as a man of learning and of principle is beyond dispute.

Perne, long a laughing stock for his tergiversations among the tornadoes of religious change, also deserves our respect as a true servant of the university, perceiving as he did that her prosperity depended on visible conformity to the powers that be; powers that he slightly, but understandably, misjudged in a disastrous disputation before the queen in 1564 when he allowed himself to be forced by his opponent into too papist a position. Perne was not the stuff of which Elizabethan bishops were made, although he may have come close to it. He did achieve the deanery of Ely. Whatever his own religious convictions (and we need not doubt that he had some), his sympathy with other men's consciences led him at different times to protect from certain trouble men as different in their beliefs as Cartwright and Whitgift. As vice-chancellor he was assiduous as a record keeper and as Master of Peterhouse a munificent benefactor, leaving to the college all the more substantial volumes in his colossal library as well as substantial gifts in land and in money. It was Perne, in his lifetime, who was chiefly responsible for the re-establishment of the University Library, energetically soliciting his powerful friends for donations to make good its depleted stock and himself transferring or bequeathing to it his collection of manuscripts including those which he had 'rescued' from Norwich Cathedral priory. It was almost certainly he, moreover, who proposed to its ostensible architect, Sir Thomas Smith, the scheme realised in the Act for the Maintenance of the Colleges (1571) whereby one-third of the rents of college lands were to be paid in kind or (as seems usually to have been the case) in the cash equivalent, thus giving to college incomes both a measure of stability and a rational relationship to the cost of provisions.

What of the average consumer? Between 1500 and 1600 both the numbers and the social backgrounds and expectations of undergraduates changed. Numbers fluctuated, partly at least in response to the winds of religious change, partly as a result of plagues, including the sweating sickness. From 1544, thanks to Registrary John Meres, we have matriculation registers – except from 1590 to 1602 when, thanks to the indolence of Registrary Thomas Smith (not to be confused with Sir Thomas Smith), we have none. The registers record variations from 59 matriculands in 1557, when both deterrents operated, to 527 in 1578, a sharp rise on the 239 of the previous year, to be followed by a more or less gradual decline to 300 in 1589.

For the purposes of extracting fees for matriculation and graduation the university divided students into three categories: noblemen, pensioners and sizars. Noblemen paid high fees, but were entitled to proceed to their degrees without, or with only an empty formality of, examination. Pensioners and sizars, save for fees, were of equal footing in the eyes of the university. In colleges, noblemen and other wealthy individuals soon came, as a rule, to occupy the status of fellow commoners, men who took their meals, or commons, at the fellows' table. They were later to be distinguished by their elaborate gowns and caps. Pensioners were students who paid the college fees for their board and lodging, and sizars those who, for lack of money, earned their keep by performing more or less menial tasks, such as waiting at table, cleaning the courts or, later, assisting in the library. The date of a man's admission to his college dictated his seniority if and when it came to the award of fellowships and it soon became the custom to seek formal admission some time before actually coming into residence. Many men following this course were admitted, at a cheap rate, as sizars and 'upgraded' to pensioners either when they started their university career in earnest or shortly thereafter. Younger brothers of pensioners, or even of fellow-commoners, already in residence, very often sought admission as sizars and were no doubt regarded as retainers to their elders. Both pensioners and sizars, moreover, might be elected to college scholarships, so becoming 'members of the foundation' and entitled to allowances in respect of their keep. Thus, neither the matriculation registers nor the college admission books give an accurate picture of the social standing of the student body. The fact remains, however, that at least until the late nineteenth century many sizars were genuinely poor. For these men success at the university was essential and many of those who were to be leaders, both within the university and in their subsequent careers, rose from the ranks of the sizars.

Colleges varied greatly in size from, say, twenty-one fellows and students at St Catharine's in 1564 to 306 at Trinity, and these differences must have been reflected in the daily lives of their students. College plays, in Latin usually, came to be one of the forms of recreation approved, when seen as educational rather than subversive, by the authorities, but only in those colleges with a sufficient student body to support them. Most, perhaps all, colleges witnessed over the century an increase of students from the propertied classes, fewer of them, though still a substantial number, destined for the church. Many came with no intention of completing even the BA course, finding their way rather, after a year or two, to the Inns of Court or to travels abroad to finish their education.

Such students sought more cosmopolitan diversions than their predecessors and reckoned to cut more of a dash, as witness the ever-increasing flow of injunctions from the vice-chancellor and Heads, and from the court itself, against 'great galligaskins' and other outrageously flamboyant attire; against football; attendance at bear-baiting and at plays in the town. Entertainments of this kind in the town and nearby countryside, indeed, were seen as such a real threat to the proper deportment of the young as to be subject to the licensing authority of the vice-chancellor, who customarily forbade them, at least in term time. Even the least serious student, however, was subject to his tutor, whose task it was not only to dictate the course of his students' reading, but also the opening of his purse-strings, parents generally committing to tutors the requisite monies for extras as well as for fees and commons. Come the summer the tutors sometimes rode home with their charges, especially those whose sponsors were either in debit or, conversely, in a position to extend patronage. Most colleges had strong affinities with geographical regions, typically where fellowships had been endowed by lands and livings. The colleges supplied the incumbents, who knew the landowners, who, with them, might recommend local boys to tied scholarships in a continual give and take. The mechanism was in place from medieval times, but improved communications and, for many, the necessary funds to travel home at least once a year, drew the net closer.

At the same time, many students, whatever their background, were certainly caught up and inspired by the religious currents in the university. William Perkins (1558–1602), allegedly a profligate student, then a fellow of Christ's and, briefly, a protestant radical, was to spend his entire career in Cambridge. His success in inspiring others with his brand of Christian ethics and spirituality, both as the author of theological works, notably his *Armilla aurea*, or *Golden chain*, and as a preacher, spread far beyond Cambridge, beyond England even. There must have been hundreds of those, still a sizeable proportion, if no longer the majority, who went from Cambridge to country livings, for whom the inspiration of Perkins, or of other notable preachers such as William Whitaker, or Laurence Chaderton, or, a little later, John Preston, was the chief legacy of their days at the university.

Their visual recollections will have varied enormously according to their generations. It was the generation of the 1540s which saw the great screen go up in King's College chapel; that of the 1570s which saw realised Parker's initiative in opening up University Street (between two brick walls) joining the university schools to the university church; the eclectic, symbolic and entirely charming gates adorning the court built by John Caius for his refounded college and (probably) the magnificent timbered (but alas no longer turreted) gallery which now serves as the lodge of the President of Queens'. For those leaving in about 1600 was reserved the astonishing vision of Trinity Great Court.

13. Drawing of Clare Hall (now Clare College). The drawing, by Edmund Prideaux, fellow-commoner of the college, is dated 1714 but must be copied from an earlier drawing recording, as it does, the college as it was before the rebuilding of 1638–42.

3

FROM THE ACCESSION OF JAMES I TO THE ELECTION OF THE DUKE OF NEWCASTLE AS CHANCELLOR, 1603–1748

Queen Elizabeth's visit of 1564 was regarded by the university as having been a great success; even Cecil had had only minor criticisms to make. As to the queen herself, who can say? Certainly she had completed a rigorous programme with considerable aplomb and had entirely charmed her scholars by what appears to have been a genuinely impromptu Latin speech vouchsafed under protest, but she never again came closer than Saffron Walden, where she was ceremonially visited by the university. There are times, on the contrary, when one gets the impression that her successor, King James, regarded the ceremonial antics of his scholars in Cambridge as providing a sort of raree show. It was a very convenient raree show, within easy reach of Newmarket, amply provided with board and lodging, and able to produce on demand Latin plays at which the wisest fool in Christendom could laugh knowingly, and disputations in which he could, ineptly enough, take part. Better still, perhaps, it would provide these entertainments, with degrees thrown in, for visiting ambassadors and other grandees, and for the royal progeny, leaving the royal personage free to enjoy Newmarket.

In James's reign, moreover, the interference by the crown and by courtiers in elections to college fellowships, of which the university had already had occasion to complain in the previous reign, steadily increased. Cecil, while promising that a tighter control would be exercised in future, had then pointed out that royal mandates for fellowships and for degrees were now part of the royal prerogative, and although the university's objections were from time to time sustained, care had to be exercised in deciding when a complaint might prove acceptable. All mandates were signed by the king, but it was not always immediately obvious at whose request he had done so.

It would be misleading, however, to suggest that James's interest in the university was entirely frivolous, especially in matters of religion: one of his earliest acts was to be the setting up of the team of translators, from Oxford, from Cambridge and from Cambridge-dominated Westminster, whose labours were to see the light of day as the Authorised Version of the Bible in 1611. Moreover, as he rode down from Scotland James had been presented, by a Cambridge graduate, with the Millenary Petition, a radical attack on the established church and on the alleged misappropriation of its endowments, especially of tithes which had been acquired (impropriated) by laymen and by institutions and diverted to their own purposes when they should have been making provision for a preaching clergy. The university moved swiftly to dissociate itself from the Petition, passing a grace forbidding any member of the university to speak or write against the established church. James, however, was clearly impressed by the Petition and, very shortly afterwards, expressed the intention of returning to their proper use such tithes as had fallen, or would in future fall, into royal hands. He wrote, moreover, to the universities urging that the colleges should follow his admirable example. Financially this would have been disastrous for the colleges (and indeed for the king had he attempted it) and both universities were prompt in dilating upon the impracticability of such a course of action, however worthy.

No colleges, no learned clergy: the universities were by now the chief, though they were never to be the sole, breeding grounds of the clergy, and the moderate Calvinism which characterised the ecclesiastical establishment and the consensus of the authorities in Cambridge was more attractive to James than it had been to his predecessor. That consensus, however, was now being threatened not only by the more extreme Calvinists but also by the so-called Arminians, with their emphasis on salvation by works and their affection for ritual, as the episode of Peter Baro, recounted in the last chapter, had already demonstrated.

The bishops who assembled to discuss these matters between themselves and with the king at Hampton Court in January 1604, however much they differed on individual points, were predominantly Cambridge Calvinists. The outcome is well known, and in the interests of uniformity James in 1613 obliged the university to impose religious tests on all those proceeding to doctorates in any faculty and to the BD in the form of subscription to the Act of Supremacy, to the use of the Book of Common

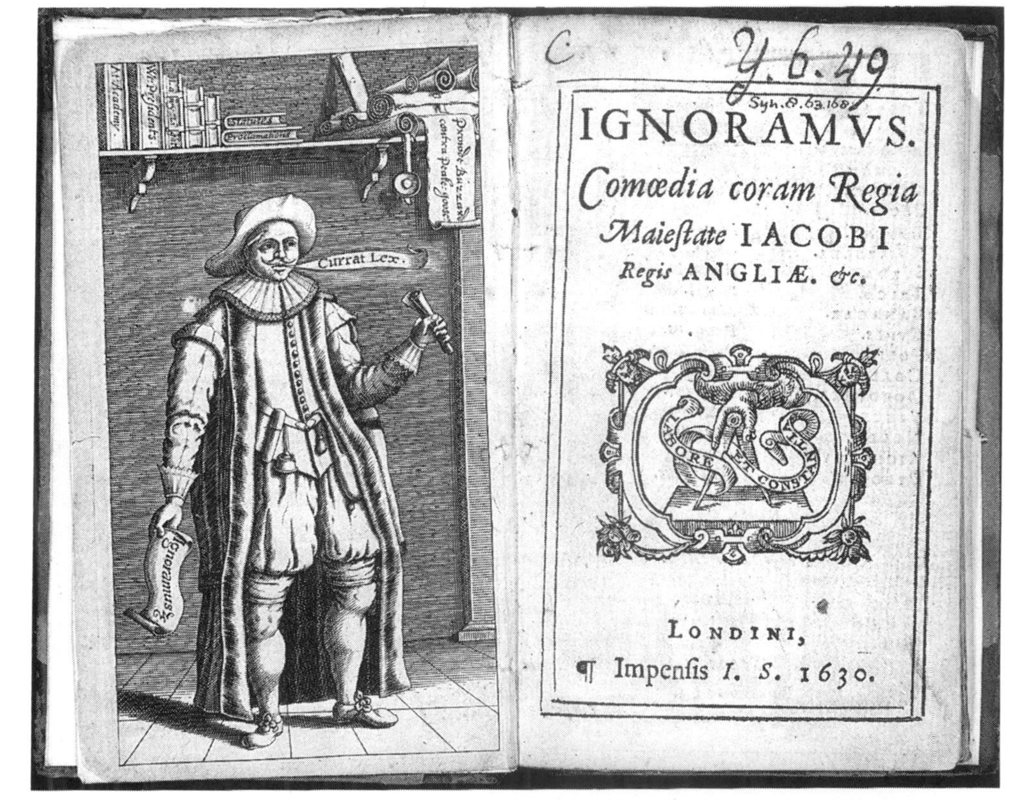

IGNORAMVS.
Comœdia coram Regia
Maieſtate IACOBI
Regis ANGLIÆ. &c.

LABORE ET CONSTANTIA

LONDINI,
¶ Impenſis I. S. 1630.

14. Student theatricals: frontispiece and title-page of George Ruggle's *Ignoramus* (London, 1630), first performed before James I in 1615.

Prayer and to belief in the Thirty-Nine Articles of Religion first promulgated in 1563. In 1617 the same triple oath was made obligatory for those proceeding to any degree in the university.[1]

The number of matriculations recorded in 1619 amounted to 509. Except in 1631 and 1667, when those who had been prevented by plague from matriculating in the previous year were also entered, this figure was not to be equalled until 1864. It would be unreasonable to attribute the decline in numbers from this point entirely, or perhaps at all, to the introduction of subscription, but the very attempt to enforce conformity and so to ensure stability presages, however distantly, its own failure, and, as we saw in the mid-sixteenth century, times of uncertainty were usually not good for recruitment. In the civil war years, however, the numbers of students attending Cambridge were doubtless enhanced by the fact that Oxford was a military camp. By the late seventeenth century it was the lay element, which had swollen in numbers from the late sixteenth century, which departed, leaving the university to revert to something more like a clerical seminary. Meanwhile, however, the royal endorsement of the stand against Arminianism taken in 1618 at the Synod of Dort (where two of the four English representatives were from Cambridge) lent support to the still predominantly moderate Calvinist establishment in the university.

On James's death in 1625 this official support from church and crown began to crumble while those of a more Arminian tendency could and did look more and more for encouragement from William Laud. In 1625 he was ex-President (Master) of St John's College, Oxford, and bishop of St David's, and we might wonder why two Cambridge Heads (Beale of Pembroke, and Wren of Peterhouse) should have seen fit to write to him reporting on 'the defects in the University of Cambridge', but Laud was a friend of the duke of Buckingham who, on royal instructions, was, even on the very brink of his downfall, to be elected chancellor of Cambridge in the following year. The election was anything but

[1] There was, however, no requirement of conformity for admission to the university, so the option remained for those so inclined to complete the course of studies for the BA and to 'supplicate' for the degree without actually graduating. This expedient was occasionally employed, and was open to those whose doubts had arisen in the course of studying for higher degrees. The failure to graduate BA or MA would, however, be a bar to proceeding further at the university.

unopposed and was only achieved by forceful action by those Heads who favoured it. Several Heads were mysteriously called away from Cambridge and so were unable to vote; nor is it possible to categorise the supporters of the election at this dramatic moment as uniformly Arminian and its opponents as solidly Calvinist. Nonetheless, Buckingham *was* elected, if only by four votes, and with this backing Laud, now bishop of Bath and Wells, was able to write to Cambridge in 1627 asking for copies of all royal injunctions and directions sent to the university since Elizabeth's accession. He and Buckingham were also able to suppress the history lectureship founded in Cambridge by Fulke Greville, Lord Brooke, with the intention, as they with some justice suspected, that analogies unfavourable to the political status quo might be drawn from the study of classical history.

Buckingham's assassination in 1628 removed Cambridge for the time being from Laud's sphere of influence, but by 1635 he was archbishop of Canterbury and as such determined to exercise his metropolitical power in carrying out a visitation of both universities. Here was a dilemma, even for those who were most inclined to favour both his principles and his person. Laud might easily enough have obtained a royal commission to visit the universities, but he insisted rather on his right to do so as metropolitan. Cambridge was asked to search its muniments for any privilege exempting them from metropolitical jurisdiction. The question had not arisen in this form before; exemption from papal and from episcopal authority they had achieved long since, but they had not since then been threatened by an archbishop.

William Beale, the vice-chancellor, wrote in July to the chancellor, now the Earl of Holland and a staunch protestant, to say that they were much too busy preparing for commencement to worry about the archives. Officially he was obliged, whatever his private convictions, to defend the university's rights as a self-regulating body. In August he wrote to Laud himself claiming that the dispute over the mastership of St Catharine's had unavoidably delayed the preparation of the university's defence. In October he wrote again, describing the university's resistance to the proposed visitation 'under color of our privileges' while emphasising the need for a visitation to reform the university and suggesting the use of royal powers; but this letter was sent from outside Cambridge and Laud was asked to keep it secret lest its author be misunderstood: 'as though

I labored to betray the University, or upon any Occasion were redy to passe by our Chancellor'. Finally, in response to an angry letter from Laud, the new vice-chancellor, Henry Smith, submitted the university's defence, blaming the delays on Beale. In May Laud formally rejected the defence and called on the university to submit or to go to arbitration by the king. Smith was all compliance – but was unable to take immediate action as many of the Heads were once again mysteriously away from Cambridge. The time for wriggling, however, was drawing to a close. In June the King in Council at Hampton Court ruled in favour of his archbishop. In the face of the imminent threat Trinity, Christ's and Caius raised and enclosed their altars and carried out those other 'seemly' alterations to their chapels which others had made earlier, but miraculously the threat never materialised 'for', as Laud was to recall, 'my Troubles began then to be foreseen by me, and I visited them not'.

To Oxford Laud had proved a busy chancellor, constantly interfering in such minutiae as the wearing of the proper academical dress, and attempting to enforce the adequate use of colloquial Latin as a qualification for the BA and its fluent use as a qualification for the MA (thus, allegedly, precipitating a flight from Oxford to Cambridge); but he had rendered them great service also in organising their statutes into a manageable corpus, in his munificent donation to the Bodleian Library of Greek and oriental manuscripts and in his foundation of a chair in Arabic. His benefactions to St John's College, where he had been president, were spectacular. His effect on Cambridge was to strengthen the hands of those who shared his theological sympathies. It would be an over-simplification, however, to say that he was responsible for a split in the university as, in many ways, the university was not split. Battles indeed there were in matters theological, and acts forbidding the stirring up of *odium theologicum* could be and were used by either side against the other. Some colleges, to be sure, favoured one side of the theological divide and some the other; yet in other colleges both parties contrived to co-exist without too much friction. Both sides saw eye to eye on the standing of the university and of the colleges within it just as both, no doubt, had been delighted with the right that had been conferred by King James in 1604 to elect two burgesses to Parliament, and it is impossible to draw clear battle lines on the basis of votes on political and theological issues.

The correspondence of Joseph Mede, fellow and tutor of Christ's, vividly illustrates both the interest taken in Cambridge in national affairs and in their local repercussions, and also, what is too seldom recorded, the serious attention which he gave to his pupils.[2] Seriousness was certainly not lacking: it was during these years of the 1620s and 1630s that so many Cambridge men, notably from Emmanuel, set sail for the New World, there to establish their own religious empires.

For the young early seventeenth-century Cambridge was an exhilarating place. Some, like Milton, evidently took seriously the political and theological debates which so engrossed their seniors; others found them a source of amusement. This was a second great age of university wits, of Cleveland, Randolph and many others including, indeed, Milton himself; the breeding ground of Marvell and George Herbert and many other poets. One has the impression that everyone was versifying. Countless manuscript collections bear witness to the exchange of verses and of ingenious in-jokes. Scurrilous speeches by the Praevaricator at Commencement were regularly censured: he may have been a licensed jester, but there was a limit to licence. Plays flourished (to the distress of the puritans); saltings (theatrical *jeux d'esprit* serving to introduce and to initiate freshmen to their colleges) were revived. Cambridge was closer to London in sophistication than it had ever been or was to be again for many years. There is a theatricality everywhere, even in the records of the vice-chancellor's court. Rapiers, as well as tongues, flashed in the street.

The backdrop was the plague. Never far from Cambridge, in 1610, in the 1620s and in 1630 its visitations were savage. Mortality within the university was low, since from medieval times it had been customary for it to disband when infection threatened, but fear of the plague must have impressed itself forcibly on many imaginations, as it was to do later in the century on the young Newton's. Not everyone could leave Cambridge in times of plague, and in accordance with epidemiological theories evolved in the course of the seventeenth century those that remained remained as it were in prison. We recall that when Thomas Hobson the carrier, and great benefactor to the town, died in 1630 at the age of eighty-six, Milton wittily assumed that the primary cause was inertia,

[2] See below, pp. 98–9.

since his travels to and from London were forbidden on account of plague.

The embargo on entering the town, like an earlier embargo on bringing in goods, which had forced Hobson to leave his cargo, much of it perishable, outside the town for days on end, was the work of Dr Henry Butts, Master of Corpus and vice-chancellor. Butts's heroic struggles to combat the plague are eloquently recorded both in the records of the court, where he sat almost daily with the mayor attempting to enforce compliance with such regulations as they could devise for isolating the infected, and for preventing movement in and out of the town, and in his increasingly chaotic accounts. These record the receipt of such monies as he managed to raise from all over the country on a warrant certifying Cambridge to be the equivalent of a national disaster area, and his expenditure of these monies on building a pesthouse on Coldham's Common, on payments to a German plague-specialist, Dr Milde, whom he had brought to the town (the town physicians having probably fled, as was usual) and on individual cases of extreme hardship. The plague had not come out of the blue. Before its onset had reached its final level of ferocity, Dr Butts had taken other steps including, to the fury of many, especially the young wits, the closing of taverns.[3] At the height of the infection Butts had to report on its progress, which he did with harrowing effect, ending up 'myself am alone, a destitute and forsaken man, not a scholler with me in college, not a scholler seen by me without'. The plague abated in due course, as it always did, and the university reassembled. On 20 March 1632 a congregation was to be held for the conferring of a number of honorary (mandate) degrees. Recipients of such degrees were usually liable, as were those graduating without benefit of mandate, to fees, and substantial fees at that: it was one way in which the university sought to protect itself from incessant pressure to confer them. On this occasion, however, it became known that Edward Martin, chaplain to Laud and a thoroughgoing Arminian, and several others were to receive their degrees gratis. When Butts, still vice-chancellor, arrived at the Regent House he found it in an uproar, and it was only with difficulty, and a measure of brute force, that he was able to bring the ceremony to completion. As

[3] There is a legend that the whole of Green Street, where plague was particularly rife, was sealed off, and that the grass growing in the street when it was reopened gave it its name.

¶ There Died in *Cambridge* of the Plague and of other Diſeaſes from *July* 2d 1665 to *March* 29th 1666————————366

Whereof of the Plague————————171

A GENERAL BILL

Of all thoſe that have died in *Cambridge* of the Plague, or of other Diſeaſes, from *June* the 5th to *January* the 1. 1666

All the Colledges (God be praiſed) are and have continued without any Infection of the Plague.

	Bur.	*Pla.*	*Infected & Recovered*		*Bur.*	*Pla.*	*Infected & Recovered*
St Andrews *Cambridge,*	162	139	100	St Giles	027	015	010
St Andrews *Barnwell*	063	053	083	St Maries *Great,*	048	032	020
All-Saints	097	090	030	St Maries *Leſs,*	024	012	008
St Bennetts	062	051	023	St Michael	019	013	008
St Botolph	030	013	009	St Peters	012	003	003
St Clements	021	012	006	St Sepulchres	024	017	012
St Edwards	016	006	003	Trinity	153	138	069

The total of Burials in the fourteen Pariſhes————————758

Whereof of the Plague————————594

And at the Peſthouſe————————155

In all of the Plague.————————749

Perſons infected that are recovered————————384

The total of Burials in both Viſitations————————1124

Whereof of the Plague————————0920

Francis Wilford *Vice-chancellour.* John Herring *Major.*

15. Plague Bill, recording total mortality in Cambridge from 2 July 1665 to 29 March 1666 (366, 171 of them from the plague) with a more detailed breakdown, by parish, of the next visitation of plague from 5 June 1666 to 1 January 1667 (758 deaths, 749 from the plague).

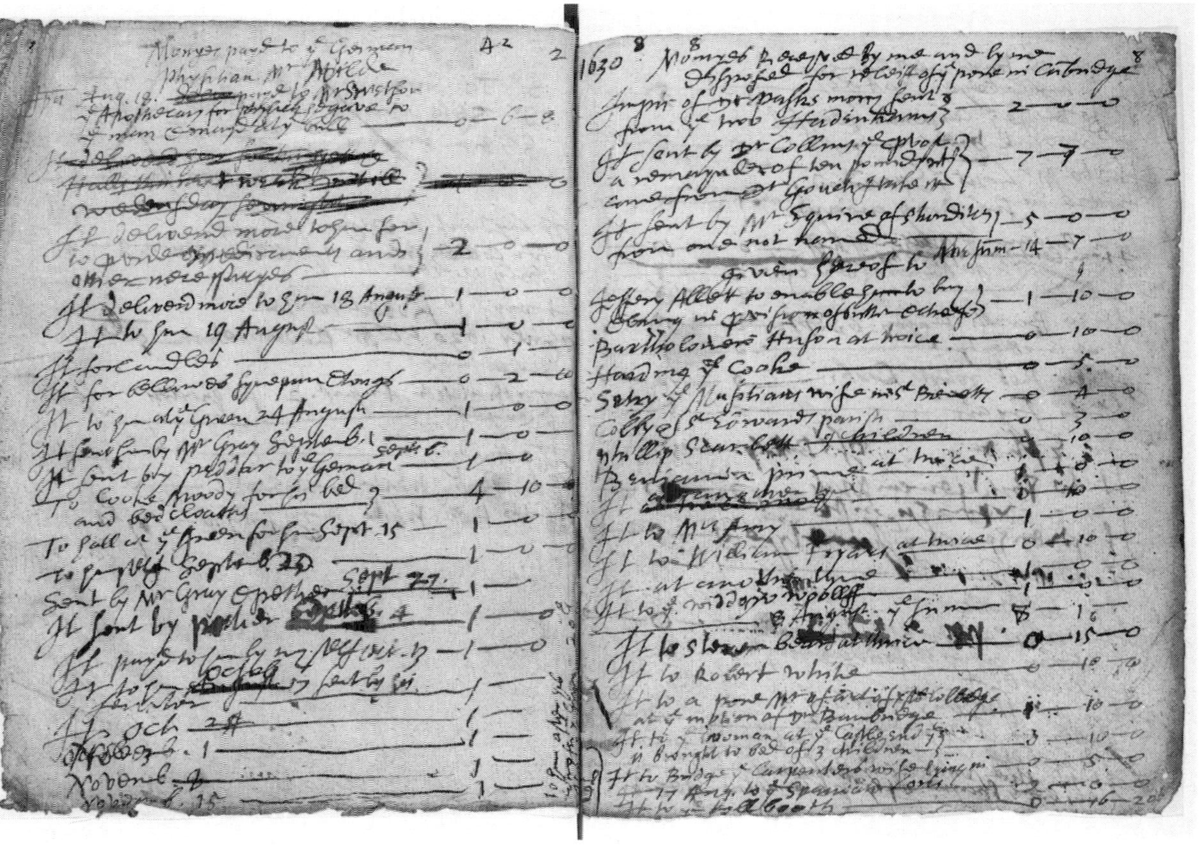

16. Dr Butts' account book, showing payments made in 1630 to 'the German physitian Mr Milde', apparently an itinerant plague-specialist, and, on the right hand pages, income and expenditure on poor-relief.

17. Grave digging at Great St Mary's: detail from David Loggan's *Cantabrigia illustrata* [1690], Plate IX.

he left, precipitately, a voice from the crowd called, 'Let him go hang himself.' On Easter Sunday, 1 April, Dr Butts was due to preach before the university. He was found that morning, hanging from his garters in his own room at Corpus. For all his great concern for the destitute he appears to have been an unclubbable man in a clubbable age, and had apparently been much vexed over a dispute with Dr Comber, Master of Trinity, about the precedency of the comedies at Trinity and at Queens'; he was certainly much mocked by the young blades, but it is hard not to attribute his suicide largely to mere exhaustion and despair arising from the great battle he had waged, unseen by so many of his peers.

In spring 1640, for the first time in eleven years, Parliament was summoned. The university elected as its representatives Thomas Eden, Master of Trinity Hall, who had also served them in Parliament in the 1620s, and Henry Lucas, secretary to the chancellor, the earl of Holland. To its fury the Parliament was dismissed in May, but not before it had stated among its objectives the protection of parliamentary liberties, the defence of religion from innovations and the fight against popery. Indignation was aroused when, in spite of the prorogation of Parliament, Convocation continued to sit, and in June issued canons including the so-called Etcetera Oath, which was to be imposed at the universities, binding its takers not 'to seek to alter the government of the church by archbishops, bishops, deans and archdeacons, etc.'. When Parliament was recalled in November tempers had worsened. The university returned the same two members, but the election was fought with more bitterness, and, it was alleged, with sharp practice. One of the two defeated candidates was Sir Henry Spelman, who had recently founded a lectureship in Arabic in the university for Abraham Whelock, the university librarian and a noted linguist. Among the first acts of the Parliament was to set up a Grand Committee for religion which, in its turn spawned a sub-committee to examine 'the state of Magdalen College Chappell [at Oxford]; and other abuses in the Universities, especially in matters religious'. In December the sub-committee was made a full committee with the remit to 'consider the Abuses in matters of Religion and Civil Government either done or suffered by the Universities'. Early in the following year the universities were ordered to put an end to subscription on graduation, not because of any objection to the oaths, but because their imposition had not been sanctioned by Parliament. The universities paid little attention, and had to be sent reminders in February 1642 and January 1643.

Parliament, of course, was out after the 'Arminians' or those who, whether or not they accepted that particular label, favoured religious practices which Parliament associated with papistry. They should have known what they were about, as more than half their members had attended either Oxford or Cambridge, although only just over a quarter of them had actually graduated. On the basis of information solicited from the universities on 'Arminian' sermons and the harassment of anti-Laudians since 1634, a report was drawn up on 'Innovations in religion and abuses in government in Oxford and Cambridge', but a Bill for regulating the universities, which was given its first reading in August 1641 was not proceeded with. Orders for the moving of communion tables from the east end of churches and chapels, and for the removal of altar rails and images, however, expressly included the universities.

Rather than proceeding directly against the university and colleges as institutions at this time, Parliament, which had more pressing business, chose rather to direct its attack against individuals, notably John Cosin, Master of Peterhouse and one of Laud's staunchest Cambridge supporters, who was arrested in November 1640 and impeached in March of the following year. The Lords dragged their heels, and Cosin was still at liberty, on bail, in Cambridge in July 1642. Shortly afterwards he fled to the continent. William Beale was reported on, for a sermon against Parliament, but he and others were left unmolested until the summer of 1642. In July 1641 the universities petitioned against the proposed abolition of cathedral chapters, an obvious target for the increasingly presbyterian aims of Parliament but a useful area of employment for graduates. Throughout the year these patterns were repeated: Parliament passed measures tending to presbyterianism to which the colleges, in the variety of their religious tone, paid more or less attention; the universities registered occasional, rather half-hearted protests, which met with a lukewarm reception.

Generally speaking the sympathies of the university were royalist: it celebrated the king's return from Scotland in November 1641 with bonfires and with verses, and entertained the king and Prince Charles in the usual splendid style in March 1642. The town was predominantly for Parliament: it had returned Oliver Cromwell, a graduate of Sidney

Sussex College, and a like-minded alderman to the second, or Long, Parliament. Increasingly, both in the council chamber of the mayor and in the streets, the town threatened the university.

When civil war finally broke out, many left the university, some to join the king's forces, fewer to join those of Parliament, often as chaplains. East Anglia was militarily important. It was potentially a base of major parliamentary power, but it was not yet a secure base. The Eastern Association was sct up to tighten Parliament's control, but met with little success until the second earl of Manchester took command in August 1643. Meanwhile the king wrote to the vice-chancellor in June 1642 requesting a loan of money. It was to be reported later that he received from the university £5,118, but the university as such sent nothing and only five colleges record contributions: Queens', Peterhouse, St John's, Sidney and Emmanuel. At Queens' and Peterhouse sums contributed by individuals easily exceeded those from the college coffers, and Emmanuel's contribution was entirely from the pocket of the master, Dr Holdsworth. There may have been other, unrecorded, private donations. In July 1642 fifteen chests full of arms on their way from London to the Cambridge royalists were ordered to be stopped: the mayor endeavoured to comply, but five chests were successfully seized by royalists from Trinity.

A few days earlier the king had written again to the vice-chancellor, this time calling for college plate. His argument was that it would be safer with him than in Cambridge, where it was likely to be plundered by the parliament men. Probably nobody expected any plate sent ever to be returned, but the possibility of parliamentary confiscation may have been a real fear. It seems that some colleges at least preferred to be plundered by the king. The whole exercise was carried out with a lack of secrecy which was to characterise the Cambridge royalists for the next eighteen months. Townsmen gathered cheerfully to witness the transfer of the plate to King's College and Captain Docwra of Fulbourn with his trained band marched in 'with his colours flieing and drums beating' to take delivery of it. Barnabas Oley, of Clare, managed to get away with some of the plate during the night, but the rest, probably most of it, was stopped at King's by Cromwell and a scratch force. St John's, Queens' and Jesus succeeded in sending their plate; perhaps also Peterhouse. Magdalene tried, but their contribution was confiscated by the Commons, allegedly on the road to York, and later handed to the earl of Manchester to be disposed of for the common good. Such, at least, is the tenor of the royalist accounts, but their accuracy is doubtful.

On 17 August martial law was imposed on the town when Cromwell was 'put in charge of the defence of Cambridge'. William Beale of St John's, Edward Martin of Queens' and Richard Sterne of Jesus, the Heads who had sent their college plate to the king, were arrested, along with Matthew Wren, lately Master of Peterhouse and now bishop of Ely, who was taken at Ely, and sent to the Tower. They were all to survive. Meanwhile the vice-chancellor, Richard Holdsworth, blithely licensed the university printer, Roger Daniel, to put to press Henry Ferne's decidedly royalist *Resolving of conscience*. Ferne and Daniel were both arrested. When the Commons realised that Daniel was only acting on the vice-chancellor's instructions they released him and arrested Holdsworth instead. In January following they were to seize from Daniel's press a royalist tract by Lionel Gatford (who contrived, impudently enough, during his subsequent imprisonment to write and publish his royalist *Exhortation to peace*).

Meanwhile the presence of the garrison in Cambridge made itself felt: troops surrounded a meeting of the Heads in the hope of persuading them to vote for the loan of £6,000 requested by Parliament and, more successfully, ensured the election of Richard Minshull as Master of Sidney Sussex by kidnapping one of the opponent's supporters. Royalists were afterwards to claim that during these months they went in perpetual fear of their lives, but this did not abate their foolhardiness. Richard Holdsworth had long been the object of parliamentary suspicion and had been in and out of prison several times already when he was elected Lady Margaret Professor of Divinity. It was too much. In January 1644 Parliament approved the ordinance 'for regulating the University of Cambridge and for the removing of scandalous ministers in the seven Associated Counties'.

At that very time Cambridge was already experiencing a vivid representation of the shape of things to come in the visit of William Dowsing, Parliament's agent in the eastern counties for 'the utter demolishing, removing and taking away of all Monuments of Superstition or Idolatry'. Cambridge occupied him from 21 December to 3 January. King's and Christ's had obediently dismantled their altars in 1641, and Peterhouse,

St John's, Jesus and Trinity had taken some action in advance of the visitation but much remained. Superstitious pictures and statues were destroyed (including sixty-eight cherubim at Caius and forty pictures at Magdalene); chancels were levelled and all Laudian trappings destroyed. Emmanuel, Sidney and Corpus alone provided no work for the iconoclast.

Manchester descended on Cambridge in February with authority to establish a committee to summon all Heads, fellows and members of the university considered scandalous or ill-affected, to have them expelled and their estates confiscated (reserving at his will one-fifth for wives and children of Heads). He was, moreover, to administer the Solemn League and Covenant, denouncing prelacy and approving the presbyterian model of ecclesiastical government, an oath which Parliament aimed to impose nation-wide. Replacements for those expelled were to be first approved by the Westminster Assembly of Divines. Heads were obliged to submit lists of all their members, noting those who were absent and recalling them. Non-appearance was to be grounds for ejection, as was also refusal to take the Solemn League and Covenant. On 13 March 1644 Benjamin Laney, Master of Pembroke, along with Beale, Martin and Sterne, already in prison, and Dr Cosin of Peterhouse, who had fled the country, were ejected from their headships 'for opposing the proceedings of Parliament, and other scandalous acts of the University of Cambridge' – an ambiguity which caused much merriment among the royalists. On 8 April Manchester, sitting in person, ejected sixty-two (or sixty-three) fellows; by the time his committee had completed its work the total had risen to over two hundred, half the total fellowship of the colleges. Of these about a quarter were to return on the restoration.

The colleges were allowed to nominate replacements, subject to the approval of the Westminster Assembly, and the new fellows inherited the seniority of those they replaced, leading sometimes to predictable squabbles within colleges. But squabbles in colleges are of the order of nature, and by and large the new fellows and the old managed comfortably to accommodate one another. Ten new Heads were intruded in 1644–5 and the election of a further three approved in 1646–7. Nine of them were members of the Westminster Assembly (and so inclined to be often absent from Cambridge), seven of them were members of

Emmanuel.[4] All except Ralph Cudworth at Clare and Benjamin Whichcote at King's (both to become celebrated as leaders of the Cambridge Platonist movement)[5] were presbyterians. Whichcote's position at King's, as not having been previously a member of Henry VI's foundations as the statutes required, must have been particularly delicate. He showed his awareness and his humanity by making over half his stipend to his ejected predecessor, Samuel Collins, for life.

After the excitement of August 1645 when the royalists took Huntingdon, occasioning the temporary flight or attempted flight of many students, and the quartering of the army in and around Cambridge when the captured king was accommodated at Childerley, some six miles from Cambridge, and cheerfully received a number of rain-sodden students, the military presence evaporated; later in that year Cambridge's fortifications were dismantled, although soldiers continued to be quartered on the colleges until Cromwell, as Lord Protector, forbade the practice in 1652.

The execution of the king in 1649 and the enforcement of the 'Engagement' – an oath to uphold the current regime in church and state, entailing the use of the Presbyterian Directory in place of the Book of Common Prayer, and the abolition of the House of Lords as well as of the monarchy – prompted the exile of five Heads, including some of the intruded ones, and the replacement in 1651 of Manchester, now chancellor of the university, who refused the oath. He was to be restored in 1660.

Records of Cambridge during the protectorate are scarce: their destruction was ordered on the restoration. Cromwell's commission 'for the carrying on and perfecting of the regulation and reformation of the University of Cambridge', established in 1654, did not report until 1657. The commissioners included the Heads, and their brief, which was chiefly to put an end to dissension and to impose a basis for religious toleration,

[4] Recalling the much-quoted diplomatic reply of the founder, Sir Walter Mildmay, when accused by Queen Elizabeth of having established a puritan house in Cambridge: 'No, Madam, far be it from me to countenance anything contrary to your established laws, but I have set an acorn, which when it becomes an oak, God alone knows what will be the fruit thereof.'

[5] See below, p. 92.

extended to the scrutiny and revision of college statutes. They seem to have encountered in Cambridge little of the fractiousness which enlivened the work of their Oxford colleagues.

After the death of Cromwell in 1658 Parliament was to prove unable to sustain the republic, and the restoration of Charles II in 1660 was greeted in the university with extravagant enthusiasm manifested in the usual bonfires, verses and sermons (and also in a deplorable assault on the local Quakers). The king confirmed the charters granted by his royal predecessors, and also validated degrees conferred, college leases granted and free elections made during the protectorate. It remained to restore to their places those who had been ejected in 1644–5 and 1650–1, first among them the earl of Manchester as chancellor. As some of the intruded fellows had been replaced on their deaths by others, freely elected, there were now too few places for too many fellows, and some confusion ensued. Some of the intruded fellows were popular with their peers, at least one ejected fellow was paid to stay away; instant ejections were few among the fellows, but by 1662 the total had risen to some fifty. As for the Heads: twelve of the intruded sixteen resigned or were ejected by 1662, seven of them to be replaced by their ejected predecessors. John Lightfoot, intruded at St Catharine's, offered to resign in favour of his predecessor, but the fellows wisely preferred to keep him. Richard Love at Corpus and Richard Minshull at Sidney alone held office from before the parliamentary purges into the restoration. Cudworth retained the mastership of Christ's, for which he had left Clare in 1654, but Whichcote's best endeavours were not sufficient to overcome the insistence of the fellows of King's that their statutes be observed. He was, however, shortly afterwards presented to the nearby college living of Milton. Meanwhile the Book of Common Prayer was once more printed in Cambridge (as the Directory had never been) and chapels were restored to their former state.[6]

In 1662 the use of the Book of Common Prayer was once more enforced and denial of the Solemn League and Covenant imposed by the Act of Uniformity. Whatever the king's intentions for liberty of conscience, the

[6] At Emmanuel the Book of Common Prayer and the Directory were used alternately until the election, on the crown's recommendation, of William Sancroft as master in 1662. He soon set about fund-raising for a less unconventional chapel, designed by Christopher Wren and consecrated by his uncle, Bishop Matthew Wren, in 1677.

18. Domestic arrangements: detail from Loggan's engraving of Christ's College showing, in the background, the Master's garden with its washing-line, beehives and dovecote. Outside the Master's Lodge (labelled 'D') a large dog pants in the shade of a tree (*Cantabrigia illustrata* [1690], Plate XXV).

19. Examples of academical dress from Plate VII of Loggan's *Cantabrigia illustrata* [1690]: '1', an undergraduate; '4', a fellow-commoner; '21', a nobleman; '8', an MA wearing his hood as a regent master; '9', a non-regent

master wearing his hood 'squared'; '12', a proctor, carrying the statutes; '18', DD in scarlet, festal robes and '20' in 'Congregation habit'; and (over) an Esquire Bedell.

19. (continued)

national impetus for the restoration of the old Anglican order could not be stemmed. Crown intervention in appointments to headships and to chairs, especially those in divinity, was frequent until about 1670, and met with but little effective opposition. The university docilely accepted a succession of court favourites as chancellor: the duke of Buckingham from 1671 to 1674; the duke of Monmouth, from 1674 until his deposition by the king in 1682; and the duke of Albemarle from 1682 to 1688; and it celebrated with the customary verses both the king's escape from assassination in 1683 and the accession of James II in 1685.

Although James II, an avowed catholic, had promised to uphold the Church of England he saw no reason why such a promise should be incompatible with the removal of the bars to office operating against his co-religionists. The country at large was inclined to think otherwise, and when James turned for support to the dissenters as allies in the struggle for religious tolerance, the upholders of the established church were naturally alarmed. When Monmouth's rebellion failed in the summer of 1685, orders were given that his picture, which had been removed from the Regent House on his disgrace in 1682, was to be burned. It is pleasing to report that the bonfire was delayed for twenty-four hours by the school-keeper, Titus Tillet, who insisted on sight of the warrant before surrendering the portrait.

In March 1686 an order forbade the preaching of sermons on controversial topics. The order must have had a familiar ring to it, as must also the news of the setting up of an ecclesiastical commission, under Lord Chancellor Jeffreys (of the 'Bloody Assizes'), with jurisdiction in all ecclesiastical and spiritual causes and with authority once more to revise college statutes – presumably with a view to removing bars against catholics. In November a mandate arrived for the appointment to the mastership of Sidney Sussex of Joshua Basset who promptly, and to nobody's surprise, officially declared himself a catholic. More resistance was shown than had been at Christ Church earlier in the year when the catholic John Massey was installed as dean. Nevertheless, contemporary opinion was that the fellows of Sidney had lost the opportunity of pre-empting the intrusion by a rapid election of some other candidate. With Basset's connivance Sidney's statutes were called in by the ecclesiastical commission and revised to allow the admission of catholics.

In February 1687 the university itself had an opportunity to show fight, and did not miss it, refusing to honour a mandate for the conferring of an MA on Alban Francis, a Benedictine monk and an active proselytiser. The vice-chancellor, John Peachell of Magdalene, and other Heads were summoned before the commission, and although Peachell proved to be no match for Judge Jeffreys, and suffered deprivation of both the vice-chancellorship and his headship, the university's stand was greeted nationally with acclamation.

In November 1688 William of Orange landed to the usual Cambridge bonfires, but they were reported to burn less brightly than was usual. When the oath of loyalty came to be imposed some four hundred clergy refused it, including Archbishop Sancroft, formerly Master of Emmanuel (who was one of those who had approved the invitation to William but

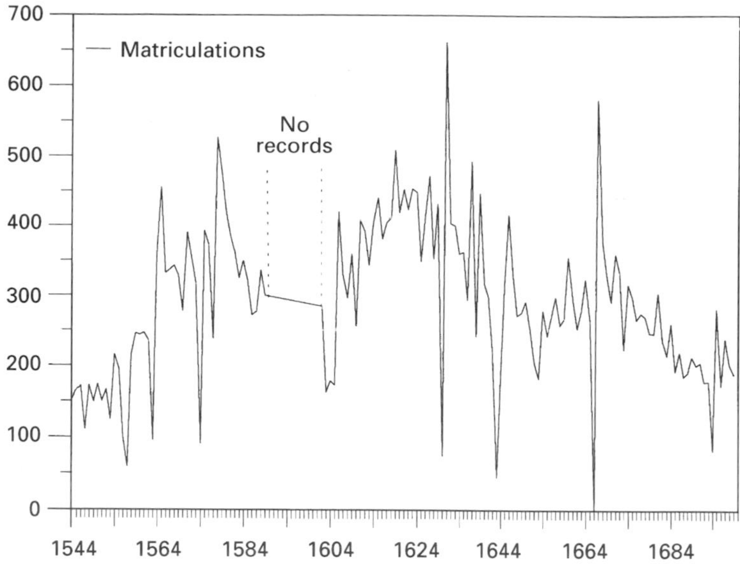

Figure 1. Matriculations 1544–1699

in the capacity of regent only), five other bishops and some forty resident members of the university. Of these forty fellows now technically ejected, a good many, especially at St John's where they were mostly to be found, in fact retained their places. The same phenomenon was to be observed in 1717 when, belatedly, a similar oath was administered after the Hanoverian succession, an oath refused most memorably by Thomas Baker, who continued to reside at St John's and to sign himself *socius ejectus* for the rest of his days. With the partial exemptions won by the universities from the full force of the Mortmain Act of 1736, which would have prevented the acquisition of lands by the colleges, the last direct threat to the well-being of the universities was past.

As noted above,[7] the university had reached its numerical apogee in 1619 (see Figure 1). The decline in numbers in the years leading up to the civil war was due to the disappearance not so much among the young gentlemen, whose attendance indeed increased in the late 1650s and early 1660s, as among those destined for the church – a situation which was

[7] p. 69.

to be reversed later in the century. The insistence of the radicals on an extreme presbyterianism, in which preaching was no longer to be confined to the ordained, may have deterred many, but even the most radical of the new Heads, such as William Dell, who had argued publicly against the traditional studies and, indeed, against the very notion of degrees, did not seem to deduce from these premises any necessary diminution in the status of the universities. Many, however, both within the university and without were arguing for an expansion of the field of higher education. Claims were advanced at about this time for universities at Manchester, at York and at London; but they came to nothing.

More persistent were demands that the existing universities expand their syllabus. Among their proponents John Hall, disappointed of advancement at St John's, published in 1649 his *Humble motion to Parliament concerning the advancement of learning and reformation of the universities*, comparing them unfavourably with their continental counterparts and deploring, among other things, the absence of provision for the teaching of chemistry, anatomy, botany, mathematics and history. Hobbes in his *Leviathan* attacked the deference paid to Aristotle and the barbarous Latin of his commentators; and Milton himself, released in 1659 from the duties of the Latin secretaryship by the fall of Richard Cromwell, denounced, in his *Considerations touching the likeliest measures to remove hirelings out of the church*, the emphasis on dialectic and on disputations in theology in the training of the clergy. Already in 1620 Francis Bacon had presented the University Library with his *Instauratio magna* or Great Instauration (renewal), to be followed, three years later, by the Latin edition of his *Advancement of learning*, both of them urging the claims of a more broadly based education with particular emphasis on an experimental approach to natural philosophy.

As with the edicts of the previous century, many of these critics, knowingly or unknowingly, were to some extent calling for a statutory recognition of changes already in effect. The 'Directions for students' composed for the use of his own students almost certainly by Richard Holdsworth in the 1640s, and current in later versions, laid far greater stress on rhetoric than on logic; the commentators on Aristotle were to be used chiefly as signposts to problems and were not to be studied in detail; ancient history and geography are early introduced, as essential to the study of classical literature as well as to an understanding of world events. Bacon and Descartes were routinely studied in the second half of the century. An anatomy lecturer was receiving payment in 1647, two years before Harvey's publication of his *Exercitatio anatomica de circulatione sanguinis*, embodying his theory of the circulation of the blood first propounded in 1615, and three years before the appearance of Francis Glisson's celebrated treatise on rickets, *De rachitide*. Harvey and Glisson, to be sure, spent almost all of their careers outside Cambridge, but there is ample evidence that their work gained rapid recognition there among the intellectually curious, who were not necessarily confined to the faculty of medicine. John Wallis was a notable teacher of mathematics in Cambridge before his departure to the Savilian chair in Oxford in 1649. In 1660 Henry Lucas established the chair of mathematics which was to be occupied with distinction by Isaac Barrow, and with glory by Isaac Newton, to whom Barrow yielded succession in 1669.

The latter part of the seventeenth century was indeed to witness lively and substantial developments in Cambridge many of which exhibit a cast of mind which can be traced back to Ralph Cudworth, Benjamin Whichcote, Henry More and others who came to be known as the Cambridge Platonists, and whose influence was to spread well beyond Cambridge. The group was never well defined and was, indeed, inclined to deny that it was a group at all. As we have seen, they rose to prominence at a time of extreme Calvinism and they survived, although they were occasionally threatened by, the Anglican backlash. Among the attitudes which they shared was a mystical and metaphysical approach to religion which had as little respect for the Calvinist belief in predestination as it did for the rituals of the High Anglicans, and which they endeavoured to reconcile with a philosophy broadly Cartesian. Such aloofness from the dominant dogmas was equally unpleasing to both sides of the religious divide and they, and especially their successors with their increasing tendency towards rationalism in religion, were dismissively christened the 'Latitude Men'. As a result of their teaching and their example Latitudinarianism and the intellectual curiosity to which it gave rein gained increasing currency until by the end of the century it characterised not only Cambridge but most of the bench of bishops.

Without endeavouring to trace specific influences, it is not difficult to see how liberating such an outlook proved in many fields of enquiry; nor should we be surprised to find from this time on much intellectual endeavour in the university that bore little relationship to the immediate demands of the official syllabus. Not that the new influences thus admitted remained altogether aloof from the university's teaching: Cartesianism in particular made rapid strides in the years following the restoration, in spite of the opposition of those who saw doors opening on atheism.

More conventional scholarship had been spectacularly exhibited by the publication from 1655 to 1657 of the fruits of the labours of Brian Walton (of Magdalene and Peterhouse) and a team of scholars overwhelmingly from Cambridge in the great Polyglot Bible.[8] Oriental languages, though never, with the partial exception of Hebrew, widely studied, had had an impressive pedigree in Edward Lively, Abraham Whelock (also noted as an Anglo-Saxonist), Thomas Comber (described as 'dextrous in Hebrew, Arabicke, Coptick, Samaritane, Syriack, Chaldee, Persian, Greek, Latine, French, Spanish and Italian') and others. Late in the century serious editions of classical authors began to issue from the press with some regularity and in the works of Richard Bentley a whole new dimension to textual criticism became domiciled in Cambridge.

Nor were Bentley's efforts confined to the editing and dating of classical texts and to those theological controversies for which his skills were most notably apt.[9] As Master of Trinity he may have been, and indeed undoubtedly was, a greedy tyrant and a bully; so was he also as vice-chancellor; but he was also a notable patron of scholars in other disciplines, notably of Roger Cotes the mathematician and astronomer and of Henry Sike the Regius Professor of Hebrew, and he could be as energetic in pursuit of the university's interests as he was in pursuit of his own. To Bentley we owe the establishment of the University Press on a new footing in 1698 as not only a printing house but also a publishing house. He it was whose vision inspired the chancellor, the duke of Somerset, to part with a substantial sum to that end and to encourage others to do likewise, and he it was who brought the printer Cornelius Crownfield (or Cornelis van Groenveld) from the Low Countries and ensured

[8] *Biblia Sacra Polyglotta, complectentia textus originales, Hebræum cum Pentateucho Samaritano, Chaldaicum, Græcum, versionemque antiquarum Samaritanæ, Græcæ, LXX. Interp. Chaldaicæ, Syriacæ, Arabicæ, Æthiopicæ, Persicæ, Vulg. Lat. quicquid comparari poterat* ... (London, 1655–7).

[9] Witness his masterly defence of Christianity in his Boyle Lectures of 1692.

that he was equipped with type suitable for the production of impressive scholarly volumes. Bentley was also, very probably, active in the abortive attempt to establish a physic garden, for the cultivation and study of medicinal plants; this too in the 1690s, a decade, incidentally, in which he was resident in London as, first of all, chaplain to Bishop Stillingfleet, and then Royal Librarian and Chaplain in Ordinary to the king.

As for the allegedly neglected natural sciences, botany at least was almost certainly privately taught in the university in the 1650s by John Ray who, when the Act of Uniformity obliged him to set off on his travels, left behind him for the like-minded his *Catalogus plantarum circa Cantabrigiam nascentium*: a handbook to the flora of the region. The first professor of botany, Richard Bradley, was appointed in 1726, and endeavoured strenuously, as he was bound, to raise funds for a physic garden. His reputation was mishandled by John and Thomas Martyn who succeeded him,[10] but his published course of lectures and his other works have since been found worthy of respect. John Woodward, MD, who was in 1728 to found the chair in geology and endow it with his collections, demonstrated in his *Essay towards a natural history of the earth* that he had recognised the existence of different strata in the earth's crust, although he failed to make any sense out of them. From 1683 lectures in pharmaceutical chemistry were given by Giovanni Francesco Vigani of Verona, whose labours were rewarded by Bentley's provision for him of a laboratory in Trinity and, in 1700, by the university's investing him with the title of Professor. His cabinet of curiosities was still being used for teaching in 1729, and it remains to this day in Queens' College.

It was to be in the study of mathematics, however, and the associated fields of physics and astronomy that Cambridge men, with Isaac Newton at their head, were to be chiefly distinguished. Newton's predecessor in the Lucasian chair, Isaac Barrow, an accomplished classical scholar and a notable preacher, has claims on our attention as a profound mathematical practitioner, well versed in recent work on the continent, and as the author of published lectures, mathematical, geometrical and optical, which, however briefly, stood high in contemporary esteem.

Newton's claims to be self-taught should be taken with some caution.

[10] For Thomas Martyn see p. 116 below.

Although Barrow, who resigned the chair in Newton's favour in 1669, is no longer seen as having directly influenced the precise direction of his successor's studies, he had familiarised the university, and Trinity in particular, with new mathematical concepts and procedures. From 1661 to 1696 Newton resided, with only occasional absences, as an object of awe in Trinity. Essentially solitary and deeply intent on his studies, he was, however, content to display his learning on request and took comfort in the enclosed garden which the college allowed him where, no doubt, he scratched diagrams in the gravel, as he did in the fellows' garden, where his peers reverently walked around them. Nor should the argument that the remainder of Newton's career was spent away from Cambridge be allowed to detract from his local significance: his great mathematical works were products of his Cambridge years and his *Optics*, *Arithmetica universalis* and *Principia* were soon incorporated into the teaching of the university. The glory of his reputation, and the substantial attainments of his successors in the Lucasian chair, William Whiston (1702–10), whose textbooks remained in use long after his alleged Arianism had driven him from the university, and Nicholas Sanderson (1711–39), who, though blind, lectured very successfully on, among other things, optics, ensured that henceforth distinction in mathematics was a goal for many of Cambridge's most ambitious students. Nor can we, in this context, pass over the illustrious name of Roger Cotes, first Plumian Professor of Astronomy and Experimental Philosophy (1707–16), on whose early death, aged thirty-four, Newton, who had employed his talents in the reissue of the *Principia*, memorably exclaimed: 'Had Cotes lived we might have known something.'

Opportunities for the pursuit of natural philosophy in Cambridge were also seized by Stephen Hales, whom we know to have gone 'herborising' with William Stukeley, the antiquary, and with Ray's *Catalogus* in hand.[11] It is true that, like Newton, Hales spent only a relatively short time in Cambridge, holding his fellowship at Corpus, where he had a private laboratory, only from 1702/3 to 1719, and spending the rest of his life as a country clergyman. In this capacity, however, he produced notable works on the physiology of both animals and plants (*Statical essays*, comprising the *Haemastaticks* and the *Vegetable staticks*,

[11] See p. 94.

20. Sir Isaac Newton's laboratory and garden: detail from Plate XXIX of Loggan's *Cantabrigia illustrata* [1690]. Newton's rooms were in the upper storey, above his laboratory, in the arcaded building jutting into the garden.

DOMVS MEA DOMVS
A

separately issued in 1727), as well as on chemistry, health, and agriculture. Many of his practical inventions, for artificial ventilators and for desalinating salt water, had a philanthropic bent, aimed as they were at improving the lot of prisoners and of seamen.

The endowment by George I at Cambridge and at Oxford of professorships of modern history, whose holders were to maintain out of their stipends (£400) at least two lecturers in modern languages, was specifically intended to address 'the prejudice that has accrued to the said universities' through 'persons of foreign nations being often employed in the education and tuition of youth both at home and in their travels' and, less chauvinistically, 'the opportunities frequently lost to the Crown of conferring on' members of the universities 'such employment both at home and abroad as necessarily requires a competent skill in writing and speaking the modern languages' – very much the motives which inspired royal patronage of humanist studies in the universities in earlier centuries. The extent to which such teachers of modern languages were indeed employed is uncertain, as their employment was a private matter for the professor. We do know, however, that Thomas Gray, the poet, who held the chair from 1768 to 1771, maintained out of his stipend teachers of French and Italian, and it may well be that other teachers of modern languages, who occur sporadically in unofficial records, were in fact maintained at least in part by the professors. As historians, it has to be admitted, the early holders of the chair were notably lacking in distinction.

It would appear then that the university had a good deal to offer to the industrious and to the intellectually curious, but it is almost impossible to give any general picture of the usual course of undergraduate studies at this time: the evidence is scattered, often among private papers, and often contradictory, suggesting that there was considerable variation in the instruction offered by individual colleges and that students in fact enjoyed a good deal of scope for choice. So much, indeed, is implied in John Worthington's account, in the preface to his edition of the works of Joseph Mede (d. 1638), biblical scholar, letter-writer, and tutor of Christ's, of his subject's style of teaching:

> After he had by daily Lectures well grounded his Pupills in Humanity, Logick and Philosophy, and by frequent converse understood to what particular Studies their Parts might be most profitably applied, he gave them his Advice accordingly. And when they were able to go alone, he chose rather to set every one his

daily Task, than constantly to confine himself and them to precise hours for Lectures.[12]

It seems likely that conscientious tutors, at least, followed a similar procedure for at least the next hundred years. John Byrom of Trinity, for instance, in the first decade of the eighteenth century included in his undergraduate studies Plutarch, Locke's *Essay on the human understanding*, Nehemiah Grew's *Cosmologia sacra* (on his father's recommendation), Ray's *Wisdom of God in the creation*, Whear's *Method of reading histories*, a manuscript chronology drawn up by his tutor, and texts in French, Italian, Spanish and Hebrew. He attended lectures in geometry and composed themes and declamations. He also made serious preparation for his academical exercises in the schools, but was disappointed in his opponents. Pembroke College in 1746 drew up a scheme for their tutors, in what appears to be an attempt to impose some uniformity, specifying the number of lectures in mathematics and natural philosophy to be given weekly and the classical texts to be studied in each year and requiring the regular performance of dissertations and orations.

Possibilities for serious study not only in the fields traditionally grazed in the university but also in newer pastures improved dramatically, albeit in fits and starts, in this period with the fortunes of the University Library. The example of Sir Thomas Bodley's refoundation of the library at Oxford at the end of the sixteenth century, even before the splendid apparition of the Sheldonian Theatre there in 1669, naturally aroused the desire for emulation, and various schemes for new public buildings, to include accommodation for the library, were buzzing around Cambridge from early in the seventeenth century. Great hopes for a substantial endowment for such a building centred on the duke of Buckingham, elected chancellor in 1626. He it was who donated the handsome silver maces still carried by the Esquire Bedells, but his assassination in 1628 put an end to more extravagant expectations, although the university, with some difficulty, finally extracted from his widow the valuable oriental manuscripts of the Dutch scholar, Erpenius, acquired by the duke on its behalf.

During the protectorate the library profited greatly from the services,

12 John Worthington, ed., *The works of the pious and profoundly learned Joseph Mede* (London, 1677) iv.

more memorably associated with Oxford, of John Selden, who in 1647 persuaded Parliament to buy for Cambridge £500 worth of Hebrew books offered for sale by the London bookseller, George Thomason; and who little more than a year later successfully advocated the deposit in Cambridge of the Lambeth Library. This move was in accordance with the wishes of the founder, Archbishop Bancroft, who left his substantial collection of books first of all to his successor, on condition that he in turn left them to his successors, failing which they were to go to Chelsea College of Divinity if it were by then fully established, and otherwise to Cambridge. The library had been confiscated by Parliament on the impeachment of Laud in 1640; Chelsea College of Divinity still had but a shadowy existence, so Cambridge's claim was a reasonable one, even if it took some eight years to bear fruit. The arrival of the ten thousand volumes of the Lambeth Library increased the holdings of the University Library ninefold, but they had scarcely been catalogued and shelved when, on the restoration, they were reclaimed by Archbishop Juxon. Recognising the blow that this represented to Cambridge, Juxon urged that the library of Richard Holdsworth should instead be given to Cambridge. This was decidedly unfair on Emmanuel. Holdsworth had indeed left his books (10,281, including 186 manuscripts) to Cambridge, but his bequest was dependent on the manifestly unfulfilled condition of the church's having been resettled by 1654; otherwise the books were to go to his college. Notwithstanding Emmanuel's protests, the books were adjudged to the university in December 1664.

Holdsworth's library was, predictably, largely scholarly and theological. It was complemented in the same year by the arrival of some four thousand volumes bequeathed by Henry Lucas, MP for the university up to the outbreak of the civil war and founder of the Lucasian Professorship of Mathematics. His collection embraced contemporary history, geography, modern languages and a certain amount of science and thus neatly reflected the increased range of subjects studied, if not examined, at the university. Several lesser bequests followed including that of Tobias Rustat, who in 1667 left the university £1,000 to provide a fund, such as was previously unknown, for the purchase of books. Meanwhile, the passing of the Licensing Acts of 1662 to 1679 and 1685 to 1695 brought in many hundreds of books. All this was more than the librarian could cope with, as witness that connoisseur of chaos the learned

Zacharias Conrad von Uffenbach, who visited Cambridge in July and August 1710 and found the library in 'two mean rooms', the first containing 'the printed books . . . very ill-arranged, in utter confusion' and the second, 'half-empty', with more printed books and manuscripts, which, in the absence of the librarian, he would not have been able to see at all but for the fortuitous presence of Thomas Baker of St John's. Such indeed was the chaos that von Uffenbach could not believe the statement, slightly underestimating the actual total, in Chamberlayne's *Present state of England* that the library contained fourteen thousand volumes.[13]

Accessions continued to arrive. In 1709 Cambridge was named as one of the nine privileged libraries under the first Copyright Act, a faulty Act in that only those books had to be deposited which for fear of piracy had been entered in the Stationers' Register. The scholarly books which the library needed were often not so entered, and much of what was deposited was as soon disposed of as so much dross. Better use, however, might have been made of the Act by a less lackadaisical beneficiary. It has been calculated that the university probably received (and kept) only about a sixth of the 17,000 odd titles entered between 1758 and 1814. This is perhaps the less remarkable when we consider the enormous practical difficulties attendant on the arrival in 1715 of George I's munificent gift of John Moore's library comprising some thirty thousand books. The only room available for expansion in the Old Schools was the upper floor of the west range. This was totally inadequate. There remained the first floor of the north range, previously the university chapel and by now the Regent House,[14] but this could not be colonised until alternative accommodation could be provided for the conduct of the university's formal business. Grand schemes for an academic piazza were once more floated and 1734 saw the opening of the Senate House. Objections were, however, raised, notably by Gonville and Caius College which would have lost its outlook to the south past the Gate of Honour, to the construction of a matching building to face it and a new range to join the two. The final solution, entailing the demolition and rebuilding of the east range, was not completed until 1758. Meanwhile proper

[13] It is true that von Uffenbach's account of Cambridge, and in particular of Cambridge libraries, is uniformly disparaging, but there is some plausibility in his account of the University Library.

[14] Now the University Combination Room.

provision could only be made for the rarest of the rare books and manuscripts, including as they did the Book of Cerne and the Book of Deer; a manuscript of Bede's *Ecclesiastical history* written *c.* 737, and numerous other treasures including a number of books printed by Caxton and Wynkyn de Worde. The remainder lay about in untidy heaps, gradually diminishing at the hands of predators. Nevertheless, when at length the Royal Library (so called from its donor) was shelved and catalogued, Cambridge could at last boast a library which, if it could not compete with the Bodleian, could at least be mentioned in the same breath. Recognition of the increased burdens laid on the Librarian by the acquisition of the Royal Library came in 1721 with the creation of the post of Protobibliothecarius (First Librarian) to which the university elected, as a deliberate rebuff to Bentley, his arch-enemy Conyers Middleton, DD, fellow of Trinity and, from 1731, also Woodwardian Professor of Geology.

Mention has already been made of Richard Bentley's part in the establishment of a press that would be directly controlled by the university in respect both of texts chosen for printing and of such day-to-day business as the purchasing of suitable types, with the aim of producing accurate scholarly texts of a handsome appearance which would enhance the reputation of the university both at home and abroad. Previously the university, under its charter of 1534, had licensed stationers, some of whom had indeed printed in Cambridge and nearly all of whom had been obliged to enter into agreements, more or less advantageous to themselves and disadvantageous to the university, with the London stationers. The university had had no financial stake in the affairs of its stationers beyond, from time to time, contributing to the costs of litigation. Nor was it envisaged under the new arrangement that the university should undertake the usual risks of publishing. The intention was rather to acquire and equip a press capable of high-quality work and to ensure that the work for which it was employed was scholarly in itself and competently proof-read. To this end the chancellor, the duke of Somerset, whose letter to the university of 29 June 1696 marked the culmination of earlier negotiations of some obscurity, offered £400, half of it as a loan; other contributions followed and in October the university itself set about raising £1000, half of which was earmarked for the press. A site was secured, in what is now Queens' Lane, involving a complicated arrangement with the sitting tenant, the printer John Hayes.

21. Provisions: detail from one of Loggan's engravings of St John's College, apparently showing provisions and fuel being carried into the college (*Cantabrigia illustrata* [1690], Plate XXVI).

22. 'A View of the Public Library, the Senate House, and St Mary's Church. . .', by P. S. Lamborn [1769]. Notice the rubble still in place from the clearing of the buildings on the south side of Senate House Yard, and the arcading running from the new library façade to what is now Senate House Passage. (CUL: Views x.2 (26))

It was not until 1699, however, that the fruits of this endeavour saw the light of day; but they were fruits of great promise, including as they did the fine quarto editions of the Latin poets printed for Jacob Tonson, a duodecimo Greek New Testament (1700), and Stillingfleet's *Origines sacrae* in folio (1702). The university's boldness in undertaking to print the magnificent edition of Suidas prepared by Ludolph Kuster of Berlin and issued in 1705 proved, however, something of an embarrassment. It represents the finest product of the Press until the end of the eighteenth century, but on the insolvency of the original publisher, John Owen, the university was obliged to assume the mantle of publisher. It was a discouraging experience. The final copies were remaindered in 1752. A happier experience was the issuing, after some bullying of the author by Bentley, of the improved second edition of Newton's *Principia.*[15]

Of the appearance of the exteriors of the colleges and the public buildings of the university between 1675 and 1690 we have the superbly accurate record of David Loggan, 'Engraver to both the universities'. In his pages, at first glance, each floats tidily on its own island, a few decorous academics pacing thoughtfully by. Closer inspection is rewarded by a more intimate view of the Cambridge of his time: the horses grazing outside King's College chapel, the burial party and the barrow outside Great St Mary's, the waggon creaking reluctantly past Pembroke, the coach passing Sidney Sussex, pack horses outside Queens', a chimney-sweep and, as ever, an impending traffic jam outside Christ's, provisions being carried into St John's and the boats, here and in the view of Magdalene where, also, we see the exercise of the university's ancient right to expel prostitutes; and everywhere there are dogs, even fighting in King's College chapel. Street-sellers call their wares, a young man seeks a purchaser for a hare. The gardens and orchards are accurate too: formal flower beds alternating with orchards and meadows. His distant prospects, with their hunters, harvesters and grazing beasts emphasise the rustic setting, yet this was, in many ways, a far grander Cambridge than it had been a hundred years earlier. Clunch walls, once almost universal and nowadays to be seen only in such rare spots as the Old Court of Corpus, had been faced with stone and brick; pleasure gardens

[15] See p. 95 above.

were beginning to replace the vegetable plots and orchards of earlier times.

Among the newer buildings depicted by Loggan are the chapels of Peterhouse, the work of an unknown architect, and of Emmanuel and Pembroke, both the work, like the spectacular new library at Trinity, of Christopher Wren. Of the developments in the next half century certainly the most striking was the clearing away of the untidy clutter of houses between Great St Mary's and the Old Schools to create the space, known by a locution essentially Cantabrigian as Senate House Hill, visually bounded by the university church, King's College chapel, the east face of the Old Schools and the Senate House itself. Here the university puts itself on display with a new sense, however ill-founded in academic terms, of confidence.

4

FROM THE ELECTION OF THE DUKE OF NEWCASTLE TO THE BEGINNINGS OF REFORM, 1748–1840

In the eighteenth century Cambridge, like the rest of the country, came to be divided not between Calvinists, Latitudinarians and Arminians but between political parties: Whigs and Tories. Originally the Whigs had been those who, in 1679 and thereafter, had opposed the succession of James II and upheld the rights of Parliament while the Tories believed in the right of succession. The terms 'Whig' and 'Tory' came to change their meaning over the years and continued to denote broad divisions in Cambridge long after they had been abandoned, as politically meaningless, at Westminster. Nevertheless, it is more or less safe to say that in Cambridge the Tories were usually to be closely identified with the High Church party and the Whigs with the Latitudinarians, the remaining Calvinists dispersing among the increasingly successful dissenting churches and so, until the later nineteenth century, forbidden full access to the university.

The battle lines between Whigs and Tories came to be drawn in the university, not so much in the sense that each party had a distinct vision of the university's place in society or the direction in which it should bend its endeavours, but in the sense that every election to a university office, however minor, was strenuously fought along party-political lines. The same was true of many college headships and fellowships, at least in those colleges which were not entirely dominated by one party or the other. Elections of major officers, such as the chancellor or the university's representatives in Parliament, absorbed a vast amount of time and energy, and often displayed organisational skills otherwise rarely exhibited within the university.

The spur to all this endeavour, however, was not necessarily political zeal so much as the pursuit of patronage. Just as the university Whigs and Tories contended to elect a Whig or a Tory Public Orator, so the Whig and Tory lords and bishops contended to present their protégés to more or less lucrative positions. It was essential therefore for any member of the university with the least spark of ambition to make it clear at the first possible opportunity, and at every opportunity thereafter, where his allegiance lay. Those in the university who were conspicuous in their exertions for the election to the chancellorship of the Whig duke of Newcastle in 1748, for example, looked for and largely received their reward in the form of high ecclesiastical office.

National politics were, of course, highly relevant in so far as patrons in office had more to offer; but even out of office they still maintained impressive power bases. A delightful story was current that, when William Pitt, prime minister since December 1783 and elected member of parliament for the university in April 1784, paid his first visit to Cambridge in that capacity and attended the university church, the preacher, none other than William Paley, later the author of *The principles of moral and political philosophy* and *Evidences of Christianity*, took as his text John vi. 9: 'There is a lad here, which hath five barley loaves and two small fishes: but what are they among so many?'[1] George I and George II were notable benefactors to the university, but otherwise the Hanoverian kings impinged on the university chiefly as sources of an exasperating stream of mandates for degrees, against which, with ultimate success, the university protested. In other respects the crown became more and more remote from the universities as the power of Parliament increased.

The successful politician in Cambridge depended, of course, on good communications: he needed up-to-date information about developments in London and he needed, as polling-day approached, to be able to summon his supporters from the country. Joseph Mede's correspondence with Sir Martin Stukeley in the first half of the seventeenth century demonstrates vividly the frequency with which newsletters came from London – and also their occasional unreliability. A hundred years later carriers travelled daily between Cambridge and London, such that on every weekday one carrier left and another returned. It was thus just possible for a letter to London to receive a reply by the following evening.

[1] Sadly the story is not true: Paley was away from Cambridge at the time, but in discussing with a friend the likely effect on the university of Pitt's visit said that, had he been chosen to preach, he would have taken this as his text.

Stage coaches, moreover, made it possible for the electorate outside Cambridge to be summoned with haste, as was often necessary since university and college statutes, based on the assumption that voters would be resident, normally set a limited number of days for a vacancy to be filled before the intervention of the chancellor or the college Visitor. By the mid-nineteenth century elections of university representatives in Parliament ran for four or five days.

The improved availability of news, once limited to individuals, soon extended to the many. Newspapers, certainly, were expensive, but they could be read in combination rooms, no doubt, and certainly in clubs and coffee-houses in the town. Coffee-houses, indeed, became such popular places of resort that an order against attendance at them in the morning was one of a set of disciplinary regulations drawn up in 1750 partly by the vice-chancellor and Heads, but at the instigation of the chancellor, the duke of Newcastle, who, with the assistance of the archbishop of Canterbury and the bishop of London, both old Cambridge hands, also took a part in their drafting.

The duke was anxious that Cambridge should be seen to be putting its house in order and so avoid the commission of inquiry with which Oxford was threatened on account of the alleged prevalence of Jacobite sympathies there. The regulations themselves were not unreasonable, but their imposition by the vice-chancellor and Heads rather than by the Senate was a cause of offence eagerly fomented by entrenched Tories. Their passage through the Regent and Non-Regent Houses was stormy and they were immediately and dramatically challenged, when certain senior members of the university, including Thomas Franklin, Regius Professor of Greek, and Thomas Ansell, fellow of Trinity Hall, were found, after the witching hour of 11 p.m. when, under the new regulations, all undergraduates and BAs should have been in their colleges, presiding at the Three Tuns tavern over a gathering of the Westminster Club.[2] The repercussions continued for eighteen months and called into question the procedure for appeals from the vice-chancellor's court, a question not, apparently, resolved in the event.

[2] The club consisted of old members of Westminster School, many of whom went up to Trinity on closed scholarships.

Local newspapers made their appearance, of which the most successful in the long run was *The Cambridge Chronicle* (later *The Cambridge Chronicle and Journal*) founded in 1762. Official and unofficial university news was regularly reported, and university issues were disputed in the correspondence columns, alongside reports of the proceedings of the corporation and of the town and county courts, and essential agricultural information. Like its predecessor, *The Cambridge Journal and Weekly Flying Post*, founded in 1744, the *Chronicle* was first of a mildly, later of a more rabidly, Tory complexion. *The Cambridge Intelligencer* (1793–1803) and the *Cambridge Independent Press* (1839–1934), with its short-lived forerunners, were of a radical hue. Town and gown surveyed each other, usually dispassionately enough, but sometimes to good effect. The university and colleges had, since the seventeenth century at least, made more or less regular contributions to the relief of the poor in the town, and had also, through the leet jurisdiction, long been concerned with the state of the streets. Several times in the second half of the eighteenth century town and gown together petitioned for a Paving Act. In 1769 the university chancellor, the duke of Grafton, and Trinity Hall both offered £500 towards the project, but the proposal crumbled under opposition in the House of Commons. In 1788 an Act was at last obtained, again as a result of a joint petition, and a commission of over seventy persons was established, just under thirty of them from the university, to supervise its operation. Two-fifths of the cost of lighting and paving the town was to be defrayed by the university and in the event the nine years' work could only be completed with the assistance of an interest-free loan from the university in 1792 of £1,500. Before the end of 1788, however, the first lamps were lit and the first street (Petty Cury) paved. Gas lighting followed in 1823: the poet Wordsworth came down from the Lake District to admire the effect – also, no doubt, to visit his brother Christopher, now Master of Trinity. Meanwhile, university and college contributions to poor relief were regularly increased. Addenbrooke's Hospital opened in 1766. The original trustees and governors who had struggled to bring Addenbrooke's bequest to fruition were all senior members of the university, acting as individuals, and the vice-chancellor and Heads were among the trustees of the established hospital. Just over half of those who subscribed annually towards its maintenance were to be fellows of colleges.

23. 'Gown! Gown! Town! Town! or The Battle of Peas Hill', from *Gradus ad Cantabrigiam*, 1824.

These involvements of the university with the town reflect not only the generally increased interest in philanthropic matters throughout the university at this time but also the increased indigence in the town, suffering as it was simultaneously from an increase in population without any extension of housing and from the general depression of agriculture and the fall in student numbers, the two main sources of its income. By the early nineteenth century the rick-burning activities of the desperate agricultural labourers were a cause of alarm to the university as well as the town. The streets may have been paved and lit, but they could also be violent, and not only as a result of juvenile high spirits. Under the Act for the Better Preservation of Peace and Good Order in the Universities of England (1825), the vice-chancellor was empowered to appoint university constables with the duty of keeping a general watch in the town.

Academically the eighteenth century has long been represented as the nadir of the university, but this has in part been due to a simple failure to distinguish between the minimum requirement for graduation and the scope, and increasingly the necessity, for intensive study for those who joined the race for fellowships – a race in which success, indeed, might win a lifetime's subsequent torpor. There is also a sharp distinction from now until the second half of the nineteenth century between subjects which might be studied for their own sake and those which the tutors determined to be necessary for those seeking academic distinction.

We know, for instance, that French and Italian teachers were active in Cambridge from the 1740s, although no such persons appear in the official lists of university teachers.[3] Instruction in Hebrew was also available, if not from the professor of Hebrew. Between 1700 and 1808 new chairs were endowed in chemistry (by the university in 1702), in astronomy and experimental philosophy (by Thomas Plume in 1704), in anatomy (by the university in 1707), in modern history (by George I between 1724 and 1728), in Arabic (by the Lord Almoner in 1724), in botany (by the university in 1724), in geology (by John Woodward in 1728), in astronomy and geometry (by Thomas Lowndes in 1749), in divinity (by John Norris in 1777), in natural experimental philosophy, with special reference, seldom if ever applied, 'to that *opprobrium medicorum* called the gout' (by Richard Jackson in 1783), in the laws of England and in medicine (by Sir George Downing in 1800), and in mineralogy (by the university in 1808). The university foundations were usually set up initially in recognition of teaching already being supplied on a free-lance basis. Plume, Woodward, Norris and Jackson had been members of the university and presumably envisaged an audience for their professors. Several of the professors did in fact lecture, though they have often been censured for their failure so to do. In some cases, indeed, they seem to have given only a single course, presumably abandoning the attempt in many cases from lack of support. Tutors were unlikely to send students to hear lectures that had no bearing on their essential studies. It was a problem with which the university would grapple in the nineteenth century. Meanwhile, there is a certain amount of evidence that many, though not all, of the non-lecturing professors were not only pursuing their own researches but also teaching informally among such of their peers and of the student body as were interested, and that some provision

[3] See above, p. 98, for the obligations of the Regius Professor of History in this respect.

was being made for teaching in the required subjects in the form of inter-collegiate lectures in the 1740s.

Provision was made for the practical study of certain subjects both curricular and extra-curricular. Astronomy, which had formally been an element in the curriculum since medieval times, was now in the ascendant. The need for an observatory had been recognised by Thomas Plume in his endowment of the chair in astronomy and experimental philosophy in 1704. The sum which he provided, however, was not adequate both to maintain a professor and to build and stock an observatory for him. Accordingly, on the appointment of Roger Cotes, fellow of Trinity, as the first professor, his college provided for him, with the aid of funds raised by subscription, a dwelling and an observatory on top of Trinity Great Gate. This was dismantled in 1797, not having been used for at least fifty years. Meanwhile, in 1790, a syndicate had been set up to examine ways and means for its replacement. Nothing came of this initiative. More success attended the syndicate established on similar terms in 1818. Its deliberations must have been complicated, but when it finally reported in April 1820 that the need could and should be met with a grant of £5,000 from the University Chest and a like sum to be raised by subscription, the Senate cheerfully approved the report and between May and December of that year a sum in excess of £5,000 had been raised. Meanwhile a site had been identified on St John's College land off Madingley Road and the college's consent to the sale obtained. By the end of 1823 the building, by John Clement Mead, was completed – but at a cost of no less than £19,241. A disgruntled university contrived to make good the deficit, adjusted after some haggling, of £7,115. George Biddell Airy, now the Plumian Professor, reported in 1828 that in the opinion of all the astronomers who had seen it, both English and foreign, it was 'better adapted to its purpose than any similar building in Europe'. Further accommodation was, however, soon found to be necessary. Happily the cost of the adjoining building, erected in 1835, was met by the duke of Northumberland, High Steward and later chancellor of the university, who also provided for it a very splendid telescope.

Physic, similarly, had formed part of the medical curriculum from the earliest times, although there is little evidence that it formed a significant element in the studies of Cambridge's still modest medical school. In 1762 Richard Walker, Vice-Master of Trinity, presented to the university

24. John ('Maps') Nicholson, by Philip Reinagle, RA, 1788. Celebrated in his day as a bookseller, proprietor of a circulating library, and purveyor of manuscript 'themes' to demand, it is appropriate that this fine portrait of 'Maps' (1730–96) now hangs in the entrance hall of the University Library.

in trust 'for the purpose of a public Botanic Garden' some five acres of land adjoining Free School Lane, now part of the New Museums Site, which he had bought two years previously. As its founder Walker took the old-fashioned view that the garden should be a physic garden giving first priority to trials and experiments with medicinal plants, 'in comparison whereof Flowers and Fruits must be looked upon as amusements only': pure botany and agricultural and horticultural research, such as had been advocated by Richard Bradley, the first professor of botany (1724 to 1732), were not envisaged. The subsequent history of the old Botanic Garden was not as prosperous as it might have been: Walker's death in 1764 and the departure of the first curator, Charles Miller, to the East Indies in 1770 removed two essential stimuli. Nevertheless, Thomas Martyn, who succeeded his father in the chair of botany in the year of the garden's foundation, lectured there in the old Mansion House (previously the Augustinian Friary, on the site now occupied by Barclay's Bank) in the early years of his tenure and in 1771 published his splendid *Catalogus horti botanici Cantabrigiensis*. Further catalogues followed under the hands, probably, of the Curator, Philip Salton, in 1794, and of his able successor James Donn, in seven editions between 1796 and 1812. The distinguished Austrian botanist Joseph August von Schultes, visiting in 1826, was impressed by the arrangement of the garden and the number of species ('from five to six thousand') successfully cultivated in 'very bad ground'. There were, however, drawbacks besides the poor soil, not least the perception of the local jackdaws that the wooden labels of the plants and seeds represented excellent building materials. The site was too small for many scientific purposes, and, thanks to the endeavours of John Stevens Henslow, elected to the professorship in 1825, an Act of Parliament was procured in 1831 enabling the sale by Trinity Hall to the university of the present site where the new Botanic Garden was officially opened in 1844.

Meanwhile, that part of the Augustinian Friary in which Martyn had lectured had, in 1786, been leased to the banker, John Mortlock, for 999 years, and it fell to the university to provide an alternative lecture room not only for the professor of botany but also for the Jacksonian Professor of Natural Philosophy. A building as unloved as it was unlovely, comprising a lecture room with private rooms for the two professors at either end, was duly erected towards the southern end of what is now Corn

Exchange Street near the corner of the old Botanic Garden. Disagreeable though the building seems to have been, it was an object of envy at least to the professor of chemistry who, since 1716, had been sharing with the professor of anatomy a house adjoining the old Press in Queens' Lane. He moved in on the Jacksonian Professor, leaving the professor of anatomy and his collections still in the old building and, such was the shortage of lecture rooms, still sharing his with the professors of physic and of modern history. Proper provision for anatomy was made in 1832 (consequent on the sale of the old Press site) on the corner of Pembroke Street and Corn Exchange Street, next to the building of 1786, once again at a cost wildly exceeding the estimate.

Until the election of John Hailstone in 1788, the lack of accommodation for geology, other than a small, dark room under the University Library for the Woodwardian collection and for the professor, was probably of little concern as, with the exception of Charles Mason (1732–62), who industriously confounded the order imposed on the collection by Woodward, the occupants of the chair had regarded it as an easy one. On Adam Sedgwick's election in 1818 the matter became more urgent. It was not, however, to be remedied until the opening of the Cockerell Building, alongside the old University Library, in 1842. The plight of the professors, especially those in scientific subjects, with nowhere suitable to house their specimens and nowhere to lecture, is depicted in a magnificently incantatory statement to the Senate, now known to be by Whewell, in 1828. Through it rings the increasingly awful refrain: 'He has no lecture room.' Whewell even offered practical suggestions, for a building complex on the site of the old Press warehouses, but they fell on deaf ears. The university having recently acquired the Old Court of King's as an extension to the Library complex[4] blithely hoped that their accommodation problems were at an end. Funds, moreover, were unquestionably short.

Developments at the University Library in this period were such as to exercise all the fortitude of the staff, with the frequent exception of the university librarians themselves, many of whom were torn between conflicting avocations. The successful prosecution of a publisher in 1812 for failure to deposit a book under the terms of the Copyright Act forced the

[4] The west court of the Old Schools site, opposite Clare.

Library into a position in which it felt obliged henceforth to retain those Stationers' books which had previously been disposed of as unsuitable and so to enter in earnest upon its responsibilities as a national repository. Additional staff were appointed, rising to the dizzy height of five in 1823, but sinking to four again in 1828 when the offices of University Librarian and Protobibliothecarius were merged. Among those usefully employed was John Bowtell, who compiled, between 1819 and 1826, a manuscript catalogue of the Library in forty-two volumes.[5] Funds for acquisitions grew. In 1825 a 'library tax' of 1*s* 6*d* a quarter was imposed on all members of the university except sizars; and in 1829, on the death of the first beneficiary, the library inherited from John Manistre, fellow of King's, the sum of £5,000 specifically earmarked for purchases, the first bequest calculated to provide a regular income since that of William Worts in 1709.

Probably the most notable, if also the most inconvenient, episode in the Library's history at this time arose from Viscount Fitzwilliam's munificent bequest to the university in 1816 of 144 pictures, substantial collections of books and illuminated manuscripts and the income arising from £100,000 South Sea Annuities to build a museum to house them. In the event, the building of the Fitzwilliam Museum could not begin until 1837, by which time a site had been secured and the dividends had accumulated to a sum of something over £40,000, and it was not until 1847 that it was possible to move the collections into the still unfinished building.[6] Meanwhile the collections were housed in the old Perse Grammar School in Free School Lane until, in 1842, eight years after the Perse Trustees had expressed the wish to reoccupy the site, space had to be found for them elsewhere. The Library, which had long served as a repository for such curiosities as the mummy presented by Captain Townshend in 1743, and which in this year looked to enjoy the increase

[5] This John Bowtell was nephew of the celebrated bookbinder of the same name who acquired in the course of his trade a notable collection of documents bearing on the history of the town and donated it to Downing College.

[6] The original building was not completed until 1875. Some of the delays were due to the untimely death of the original architect, George Basevi, who fell through an opening in the floor of the West Tower of Ely Cathedral in October 1845, leaving his business papers in considerable disarray. He was succeeded by C. R. Cockerell, but the entrance hall, the final portion to be completed, was from the designs of E. M. Barry. The total cost of the building was about £115,000.

in space provided by the opening of the Cockerell Building, magnanimously vacated the East Room with much attendant and subsequent inconvenience. Some time after the collections had finally moved into the museum the Librarian had the consolation of sending many of his curiosities, mummies, coins, and all, to join them, along with a number of paintings which, uncared-for as they had been, were nonetheless perhaps more to be missed.

The fortunes of the Press, by contrast, prospered increasingly in this hundred years both physically and financially. In 1716 the building erected in 1696 had been converted into lecture rooms for the professors of anatomy and chemistry, as we have seen, while the printing house transferred itself to the premises next door which had been the private property of the University Printer John Hayes. The arrangement was unsatisfactory and from 1762 the university set about acquiring properties on the other side of Silver Street, culminating in 1821 in the purchase of the site of an old inn spacious enough to allow the erection in 1826–7 of a printing house. At this opportune moment the question arose as to the best use of the surplus funds raised for Pitt's Hanover Square statue,[7] a question answered by the erection of the Pitt Press, started in 1831 and opened with due pomp in 1833. Four years later estimates were obtained for a steam engine and four printing machines. Other technical developments had occurred much earlier, in an abortive attempt to introduce stereotyping in the 1730s and a successful one, with Andrew Wilson, in the first decade of the nineteenth century. From the middle of the eighteenth century the university had begun to appreciate what profits it was forgoing in abandoning to the London stationers its right to print bibles and prayer books. After the failure of the 1730s experiment, when the right to print bibles had been leased to William Fenner, and then to his widow Mary, the university entered in 1740 into a similar arrangement with Joseph Bentham and, by this move, into protracted litigation with the Stationers' Company. A short-lived contract with John Baskerville in 1758 to print bibles and prayer books resulted in some of the most typographically interesting books to issue from the Press in the course of the century, albeit financially the experiment was a disaster. Meanwhile,

[7] See p. 141. The statue was recently, and very appropriately, acquired by Pitt's college, Pembroke.

however, the proliferation of societies for the dissemination of the scriptures early in the nineteenth century created a demand for cheap bibles and prayer books in large numbers; with the introduction of stereotyping and with the litigation behind it, it was a challenge the Press was well equipped to meet and one which was soon to provide a financial cushion which could support the publication of more specialised, academic books.

Notwithstanding some lack of institutional support for the professoriate, it was possible for a young gentleman destined for the church who knew how to use his tutor, his college library and such university lectures as were on offer, to take away from the university a useful grounding in classical literature, moral philosophy and political philosophy, natural history, perhaps a smattering of medicine, and even some theology – all that a well-equipped clergyman needed; but of these only moral philosophy formed part of the official curriculum and that curriculum included also a heavy dose of mathematics. If his living were tolerably secure he would be wasting time taking the Mathematical Tripos, the only route, until the 1820s, to an 'honours' degree. It must be added that it was equally possible for a young scallywag to come away from the university with a BA and precious little else except advanced skills in drinking and driving a coach and pair. We have no way of knowing what the proportion of these last were, since it is only those who hit the headlines, in the form of the records of the university courts, for drunken driving, duelling, consorting with prostitutes and brawling, whether in Cambridge or in Newmarket, who can be singled out.

College tutors who, with the continuing fall in student numbers, were in a good position to assess their pupils, divided them into 'hard-reading men', 'reading men' and 'non-reading men', the last category sometimes referred to as 'rowing men' but with no reference to aquatic pursuits – the rhyme was with 'ploughing'. Colleges varied, according to the dispositions of their tutors, in the teaching they provided for each of these groups. Several introduced or revived compulsory exercises, written or oral, in Greek and, more commonly, in Latin. This, after all, remained the official language of the university such that it was still used not only ceremonially and in the recording of university transactions but also for the abstruse mathematical disputations which distinguished the graduations of those who aimed at fellowships. Even the least talented had to muster a few words of Latin to acquire a BA. Teaching was certainly

25. Academic dissipation and its imminent come-uppance as depicted by Hogarth for the frontispiece of James Miller's *Humours of Oxford: a comedy* (1730). Such scenes were, of course, quite unknown at Cambridge, and any resemblance to the Old Combination Room of Trinity College, Cambridge, is purely fortuitous.

provided in mathematics and in moral philosophy, notably Locke and, later, Paley, Bishop Butler and Hume and others. At St John's twice-yearly examinations were held from 1765 with a dramatic effect on the academic standing of the college such that it is hard to explain why Trinity did not follow suit until 1790 and other colleges until later still.

The excellence of the St John's scheme was not, however, lost on John Jebb, a former fellow of Peterhouse, and a man ardently devoted to reform but handicapped as a man of influence in the university by his (rightly) suspected unitarianism, his overbearing manner and, in the eyes of some, the very active part he had taken in the moves to abolish religious tests.[8] To him it was clear that the examinations introduced at St John's were so evidently beneficial that they ought to be embraced by the university as a whole, and, reacting to a speech on the low state of Cambridge education by Dr Cooke the provost of King's, on his election to the vice-chancellorship in 1772, Jebb presented him with a proposal for annual university examinations for all undergraduates, including noblemen and fellow-commoners, in international law, chronology, history, classics, mathematics, metaphysics, and natural and moral philosophy. It was, of course, an insanely over-ambitious proposal and doomed to failure. How were the colleges to provide the necessary teaching? In the course of the next two years, before openly avowing his unitarianism, resigning his livings and generally burning his university boats, Jebb proposed a succession of schemes each more reasonable than the last, either for examinations, or for the establishment of a syndicate to consider the matter; and a syndicate he at last obtained, though he was not to be a member of it. Its proposals for the examination of second-year students (with different schemes for noblemen and fellow-commoners and for the rest) were voted out in April 1774, but not overwhelmingly. Attempts to rescue something from the wreckage also failed: the objections were not simply practical, they were rooted in a passionate belief in the tutorial system, a belief expressed by none more forcibly, or more revealingly of the colleges' *modus operandi*, than by that same Dr Powell who had introduced the college examinations at St John's:

[8] For a brief account of the abolition of tests see below, p. 136.

It would surely be a bold and dangerous expedient to take the direction of the studies of our youth from the particular colleges and the Tutors there appointed to instruct them, and to commit it to seven examiners, hired at the mean price of ten guineas yearly and chosen anew every year, who must be wholly strangers to most of the pupils, to their abilities, their previous education, the professions or stations for which they are designed; and to authorize three or four of these examiners, after a hasty secret trial, without any preparatory knowledge of them, to give a public and lasting judgment concerning the respective merits of perhaps two hundred young men, among whom there must often be some better scholars than the examiners, and some just entering into life of the highest ranks in the kingdom.

Other colleges had even more cause to fear the possible effects of subjecting to public examination the gilded sons of the aristocracy. Besides, as Dr Powell continued, 'The Tutors too, the established and experienced Tutors, must have submitted to the same direction and have changed their lectures every year, according to the fancies of these examiners, or have sent their pupils unprepared to the examinations.'[9] Deeply embedded in this protest is a view of the merits of the collegiate system which has always found, and still finds, its adherents. It is by no means always an absurd view, but from that day to this it has proved a formidable obstacle to reform, and even to quite trivial changes of a practical kind.

There were two stages to the BA. The first consisted of the disputations which had continued from medieval times. For the weakest students these had now become a travesty: one student would mount a rostrum and say 'Recte statuit Newtonus' (Newton is right), to which his opponent on the other rostrum would solemnly reply, 'Non recte statuit Newtonus' (No he wasn't). They would then change places and repeat the exercise. Alternatively they might 'huddle' and allow one student to represent several. For the academically ambitious, however, these academic 'acts' might be taken very seriously, and although at times there was a measure of collusion whereby the two participants prepared their act together, this was by no means always the case. Instances of academic espionage are recorded. For these disputations the proctors and moderators, who were in charge, paired the disputants on the basis of their tutors' reports on their ability. Some weeks' warning was given

[9] *An observation on the design of establishing annual examinations at Cambridge* (1774), cited by Winstanley, *Unreformed Cambridge*, 327–8.

26. Pembroke College early in the nineteenth century: drawing by A. C. Pugin (father of a more famous son), subsequently engraved and published by J. Storer, showing how much of a rustic character the town retained in the early nineteenth century (from the extra-illustrated copy of the second edition of Harraden's *History of Cambridge* in the University Library).

and also some freedom in the choice of the three propositions to be defended. These might be in mathematics or in moral philosophy with mathematics usually predominant but depending to some extent on the decision of the moderators. The mathematical propositions were nearly always from Newton's *Principia* or from Newtonian physics (hydrostatics, optics, and so on, 'fluxions' being an object of peculiar dread).

Largely on the basis of these disputations the candidates for the BA were divided into a great many provisional classes. In due course the whole body proceeded to the Senate House, where they were seated according to their provisional class and required to write down the answers to questions in moral philosophy and, in ever greater proportion, in mathematics called out by the examiners. The length of this ordeal (it was January and there was no heating) tended to increase over the years, but those who aimed only for 'ordinary degrees', the 'poll men', were released in the early stages. The remainder continued, falling out at different stages as advised by the examiners, for several more days, with evening sessions, usually in the examiners' rooms, where refreshments were provided. By these means, testing students of comparable ability against each other, the examiners were finally able to draw up a list of honours graduates in continuous order of merit but divided into three classes, Wranglers, Senior Optimes and Junior Optimes. Into this list, originally at the top, but often, out of respect, after the name of the Senior Wrangler, the vice-chancellor, the senior regent and each of the proctors was entitled to insert the name of one student *honoris causa*. From the 1770s these names came to be placed at the bottom of the Senior Optimes and after 1797 the anomalous exercise of this ancient right was finally abandoned.

Such was the Senate House examination as it evolved (from the proctors' ancient right to settle by private questioning the order of merit among disputants) in the middle of the eighteenth century and as it continued for many decades, with the introduction of printed question papers only in the 1820s. By this time a group of mathematicians led by George Peacock and William Whewell were successfully, if belatedly, introducing more modern algebraic concepts to Cambridge. By 1763 the examination was formally recognised as the final test of merit as against the disputations, which were finally discontinued in 1839, although not formally abolished for another thirty years. The prestige attached to being head of the whole list (the Senior Wrangler) was immense and increased as the nineteenth century advanced. It had diminished by the time the strict order of merit was abandoned in 1910 only to the extent that mathematics was no longer the only subject in which honours degrees were granted.[10]

By 1774 the university was sufficiently perturbed by the pressure of work on those aiming for high wranglerships to set up a syndicate (or committee) to consider the matter. In 1777 the examiners were forbidden to take private pupils who were in their final year, and in 1781 a grace was passed forbidding the use of private tutors by students in their last two years. As the Senate House examination grew longer and longer this ban proved unenforceable, and the period was reduced to eighteen months in 1815 and to six in 1824. No one who was a candidate for honours felt that he could do without a private tutor and, indeed, few colleges could boast the skill or emulate the intensity of the mathematical teaching of the greatest among them, William Hopkins, nor could they rival his intimate knowledge of the minds of examiners. By his own calculation, in the years 1828 to 1849, Hopkins had coached a hundred and seventy-five wranglers, of whom a hundred and eight were in the top ten, forty-four were in the top three and seventeen were Senior Wranglers. He did not vouchsafe the numbers of his pupils who had failed to be classed as wranglers. Hopkins's income as a coach was sufficient for him to maintain a very considerable household, and many fellows of colleges also supplemented their income from college dividends with (extra) fees for mathematical and other tuition.

Until the end of the first quarter of the nineteenth century mathematics provided the only route to an honours degree (although the examinations in civil law were marked in classes from 1816), but fellowships were reserved not only for those high in the list of wranglers. The introduction in 1751 of the Chancellor's Classical Medals, in 1752 of the Members'

[10] From the custom of printing the list of successful candidates on the reverse of the sheets of verses which had long been circulated on the occasion of the Bachelor's Commencement (or formal graduation) came the Cambridge term 'tripos' for an examination for an honours degree since the author of the verses, an annually selected BA, had originally declaimed them sitting, as a licensed jester like the Praevaricator, on a three-legged stool. Hence he acquired the title of 'Mr Tripos' and his verses were designated 'tripos verses'.

prizes for a Latin essay, both for BAs of the rank of Senior Optime and above, provided a field of competition for all those whose mathematics was sufficient for a second class, and some fellowships were also awarded to clearly meritorious students who had exhibited no talent at all for mathematics like Thomas Babington Macaulay, unplaced in the tripos in 1821. Since some teaching in classics continued throughout the period, becoming indeed slightly more important with the introduction of very elementary intermediate (or 'Previous') examinations in 1822 and the devising of alternative courses of study better suited to the 'poll man', there were still some openings for those of a more literary bent.

The demand for more rigorous classical teaching increased with the establishment, also in 1822, of the Classical Tripos, first examined in 1824. Until 1850 candidates for this tripos, unless they had the good fortune to be the sons of peers of the realm, had first to have obtained honours in mathematics. Putting the Classical Tripos in February offered the opportunity of sitting both triposes in the same year, an opportunity seized, among others, by Benjamin Hall Kennedy (who was to be Regius Professor of Greek in 1867 and lend his name to the familiar *Latin primer*), 28th Senior Optime and Senior Classic in 1827. In the eighteenth century the lamp of classical learning, kindled so notably in Cambridge by Richard Bentley, was taken up by the frequently convivial Richard Porson who, like Bentley, achieved, at least for a time, an international reputation based, like Bentley's, on the attempt to establish the precise original wording of ancient texts. This style of scholarship was long dominant in Cambridge classics, many questions in the early papers of the Classical Tripos calling for an explanation, rather indeed than an assessment, of Porson's proposed amendments.

Meanwhile, the torpor of the medical school had been rudely disturbed on the arrival of a gadfly in the exotic form of Sir Busick Harwood, lately returned from India with a handsome fortune, to serve first as professor of anatomy from 1785 and, concurrently from 1800, as the first Downing Professor of Medicine. Celebrated in his time as an eccentric and as a racy raconteur, he deserves, and has recently received, recognition both for his researches, notably his experiments in blood transfusion, and for his teaching. His successors in the chair of anatomy and the successors of his hated rival Sir Isaac Pennington in the Regius Chair of Physic were to ensure that, from this time, the study of medicine in

27. Sir Busick Harwood (1750–1814) in MD gown with an anatomical model. Stipple by W. H. Gardiner after Sylvester Harding, 1790.

CAMBRIDGE, FEBRUARY 23, 1805.

On THURSDAY the 28th of FEBRUARY,

B. HARWOOD, M. D.

PROFESSOR OF ANATOMY,

WILL BEGIN

A COURSE OF LECTURES

ON

COMPARATIVE ANATOMY

AND

PHYSIOLOGY,

Calculated for the purpoſe of conveying general Instruction.

IN these Lectures the Structure and Œconomy of *Quadrupeds, Birds, Fishes*, and *Amphibia* will be investigated; the corresponding Organs in the different classes of Animals compared with each other, and with those of the Human Body; Analogies explained, and the most striking Varieties accounted for. Pathological remarks on the diseases to which the several parts are obnoxious will be introduced, with observations on the nature and effects of the Medicines usually employed for their removal. The doctrine of Transfusion will be considered, and the Practice exemplified by an actual Experiment.

The Lectures will be given from One to Two o'clock each day, at the ANATOMICAL SCHOOLS, opposite Queen's College.

TERMS AS USUAL.

Gentlemen are requested to put down their names at Mr. DEIGHTON'S.

F. HODSON, PRINTER, CAMBRIDGE.

28. Notice of a course of lectures in 1805 by Busick Harwood on comparative anatomy and physiology, including a demonstration of blood transfusion, of which he was a pioneer.

Cambridge became more of a reality. Largely at the instigation of John Haviland, Regius Professor of Physic from 1817, a written examination including pathology, the practice of physic and clinical medicine, anatomy, physiology, chemistry, pharmacy, and some relevant botany was instituted in 1829. Students had also to produce certificates of attendance at the lectures of the professors in question (chemistry, anatomy and botany), who were to assist in the examination, and of the Downing Professor if he were lecturing on topics not otherwise covered. Since the MB could not be awarded until five years after matriculation, whereas residence was required for only three years, Haviland further procured a regulation in 1834 that students should further certify that, in their two years' or more absence from Cambridge, they had attended some well-known hospital and heard medical lectures. The licence to practise medicine, which the university had assumed to itself (in addition to the right granted by the 1570 statutes to license practitioners in surgery) and which had traditionally been awarded two years after the MB, was in 1841 brought forward five terms and made subject to examination by the Regius Professor and a Doctor of Medicine.

The decline in the number of students and the parallel building programmes carried out in the seventeenth and eighteenth centuries by many colleges, meant that by 1700 the necessity for fellows, however junior, to share rooms with students had long passed. It is indeed hard to envisage most eighteenth-century fellows tolerating such a notion: their lives had become increasingly gentrified and it is impossible to rid the mind of the images of them, as provided by Rowlandson and Bunbury, exulting in the more self-indulgent vices of the gentry. Nor are anecdotes lacking to support this vision. Many fellows certainly, having laboured prodigiously in the schools and the Senate House to secure their fellowship, saw little need, or indeed opportunity, for further endeavour. In the smaller colleges the offices of master, tutor and bursar, if not of dean also, might effectively be exercised by a single individual. As this became less common the burden of college work did not necessarily increase. At Downing, the sole foundation between Sidney Sussex in 1594 and Girton in 1869, and one bedevilled by the diminution of its endowment through litigation, the fellows in the early years comfortably outnumbered the students, many of whom were fellow-commoners and several of them either relations of the fellows or students of other colleges merely taking advantage of the superior accommodation offered.[11] They hardly seemed to warrant a vast amount of moral or academical supervision.

In Trinity and St John's, at the other end of the scale, the picture is different. These two colleges between them gradually increased their share of the undergraduate market from a third of the total in about 1730 to a full half by the 1790s. The competition between them was naturally fierce, especially for high wranglerships and university prizes. Their tutors were potentially responsible for a great many students, far too many, indeed, for them to know them all, at least until the number of tutors was increased (from two to three at St John's in 1860) and the useful expedient hit upon of appointing assistant tutors. College lecturers lectured and set exercises, and so they did in other colleges, sometimes at any rate. Some colleges, like Emmanuel and Trinity Hall, were at times more concerned with their undoubted aristocratic tone than with anything so vulgar as university examinations, but by the late eighteenth century the tutors of Emmanuel, and probably of most colleges, took their teaching duties seriously even if they did not direct them towards achieving success in the university examinations. There are accounts both of stimulating and of very perfunctory teaching – and of students who despised both equally. For most eighteenth-century fellows, however, teaching was something that someone else did; such duties as they recognised lay in keeping a watchful eye on the proper handling of the college estates, the proper disposition of the college livings and the proper casting of votes. In all these things they could be models of propriety. Any increase in student numbers would merely cause a degree of wear and tear to the college fabric which would probably not be met by increased income from room rents and would certainly impinge on their comforts and, terrible possibility, on their leisure. Nevertheless, uncertainly from the 1760s and emphatically from about 1800, numbers began to rise.

In the university at large, meanwhile, although the Heads remained constitutionally dominant, the custom began to develop of setting up

[11] The will, made in 1717, of Sir George Downing, who died in 1749, should have become operational in 1764 on the death without heirs of his cousin, the fourth and last baronet. It took the college five years to establish its claim in law, and a further thirty to achieve possession of what remained after legal costs had been paid. The foundation stone was not laid until May 1807 and the first undergraduates not admitted until 1819.

syndicates to manage discrete items of business. Some of these syndicates were permanent, as those that controlled the major university institutions (the Press, the Library, the Botanical Garden), supervised the ceremonial and practical activities that took place in the Senate House, or acted as trustees for the university estates. Others were set up *ad hoc* to conduct legal business, to supervise the collation and printing of the university statutes (first achieved in 1785), to acquire land for building, to prepare briefs for architects and to supervise the actual erection of buildings, including that majestic addition to the townscape and amenities the Fitzwilliam Museum. Among the members of these syndicates may be discerned many a useful man of business otherwise unknown to history.

Increasingly from 1800 onwards syndicates were established whose business bore on educational matters. Some drafted schemes for the preliminary and final examinations for poll men; others considered whom they might best spare as audiences for the professors, many of whom were now positively anxious to lecture; others again were set to consider ways of raising funds for lecture rooms, laboratories and observatories. The eyes of the nation were turning on Oxford and Cambridge, and they seemed to gaze with a cold unblinking stare. As the industrial revolution got under way Edinburgh easily outstripped the two English universities in the teaching of the essential sciences and Göttingen was both the youngest and much the most distinguished centre of learning in the territories of the House of Hanover. As yet, however, if English gentlemen preferred the Grand Tour to the fare offered by any university, English clergy preferred English universities, and that in spite of the tiny place now occupied by divinity in undergraduate reading. The now dominant clerical element in the university subscribed largely to the evangelical party, initially strongest at Magdalene, very effectively fostered by Isaac Milner at Queens' from the 1790s, but famous above all for its most charismatic, not to say histrionic, proponent, Charles Simeon, vicar of Holy Trinity (1783–1836), fellow of King's (from 1782), and author of eleven volumes of skeleton sermons. The early years of Simeon's ministry were marked by great hostility from his parishioners, who suspected him of 'Methodism', but he was in his generation almost alone in attempting to supply some practical instruction for potential ordinands and, later in his career, fathers bringing their sons up to the university are reported

29. University business. Details from a much over-painted picture, originally of the sixteenth century, that hangs in the Old Schools. These two vignettes appear to depict, (1) a meeting of the Caput, and (2) a syndicate meeting, perhaps originally a meeting of the vice-chancellor and Heads.

30. Charles Simeon preaching: part of a set of silhouettes by Auguste Edouart (1828) showing the gamut of Simeon's homiletic gestures.

to have made it their first business to seek an interview with Simeon, to effect an introduction and to seek his guidance as to a suitable tutor.

It has been estimated that between 1700 and 1800 the proportion of students from the gentry, including those destined for careers in the church, rose from 25 to 35 per cent. At the same time the social standing of those sizars who were genuinely poor students improved in many colleges, the contrast being now not between them and the pensioners, but between these two groups together and the fellow-commoners with their fancy gowns and tasselled caps and their aristocratic pretensions and diversions.[12] We should not necessarily, however, look to see a similar trend in the social origins of 'dons'. The gentleman's business with the university was typically temporary. He sojourned there awhile and then returned to whatever course of life his family had planned for him. A fellowship provided, indeed, a billet for life; but for those without a private income it was not so very cushy a billet, even if a headship was.[13] For the poorer students, however, success at the university was essential to their careers, whether these were to be pursued in Cambridge or elsewhere. Thus while such sons of the gentry as deigned to attend the university gave themselves increasingly aristocratic airs, their mentors continued to come very largely from the less privileged classes. Socially, in their style of living eighteenth-century 'dons' were aping their more affluent students, and this continued to be so into the nineteenth century when the gulf between fellows and students widened perceptibly.

As suggested above, various movements for the reform of the syllabus were gathering head from about the turn of the century. Other kinds of reform had been attempted even earlier. The 1760s had seen an attempt, soon abandoned, to allow fellows of colleges to marry, a proposal which prompted Dr Robert Plumptre, president of Queens' and himself of a mildly reforming bent, to the remark that 'if the liberty was obtained without restriction, the ruin of the University as a place of education would infallibly and speedily ensue: if restrained to non-resident fellows,

[12] For these divisions in the ranks of students see p. 62 above. Thomas Hughes in his *Tom Brown at Oxford*, however, records continued social discrimination against *batellers* or *servitors*, the equivalent of *sizars*, in mid-nineteenth-century Oxford.

[13] 'What is the prospect of a fellow of Trinity?' 'A long narrow one with a church at the end of it.' The distant prospect of Coton church to one looking down the Trinity avenue lent literal force to the observation.

the ruin would perhaps be not quite so expeditious but no less certain'. The reaction is not as absurd as it at first sounds. Given that most fellows had no definite employment that would entail their residence, the colleges might well, as Winstanley remarks, have become 'institutions for giving out-door relief on an extensive scale, and academic life revolutionised very much for the worse'.[14] The time had not yet come.

Agitation in the 1770s for the abolition of religious tests, especially for those graduating BA, was less obviously untimely and met with considerable support within the university, including that of Richard Watson, Regius Professor of Divinity and, later, bishop of Llandaff, Edmund Law, Master of Peterhouse and bishop of Carlisle, and William Paley, then tutor of Christ's. As, however, subscription by all those proceeding to degrees to the three articles (viz. to the Act of Supremacy, and to a declaration that the Book of Common Prayer and the Thirty-Nine Articles of Religion were in accordance with the word of God) had been imposed by James I and willingly enforced by the university since 1619 it seemed to the Caput that it had statutory force and that the university was powerless to abolish it on its own authority. A petition to the House of Commons in February 1772, however, resulted in the ball being returned into the university's court, with the threat that, if no action were taken internally, an Act might be introduced for reform of the university by Parliament, a threat to be evaded at all costs. Accordingly, in June 1772, graces were proposed abolishing subscription for each of the ten degrees offered by the university. They were all rejected in the Non-Regent House, those for senior degrees by very substantial majorities, but that for the BA by only eight votes. The Cambridge bishops, aware of the parliamentary interest, gathered at Lambeth to confer, and it was probably on their advice that a grace was proposed and granted later in the month substituting for the three articles the declaration by BAs that they were '*bona fide* members of the Church of England as by law established'. It was a small, and not very meaningful, concession but it proved sufficient to avert the threat of parliamentary interference, and this modified form of subscription was extended, without opposition, to bachelors of law, physic and music, and to doctors of music. The door

[14] D. A. Winstanley, *Unreformed Cambridge* (Cambridge, 1935) 301.

to full membership of the university was to remain officially shut to dissenters and others for many years yet.[15]

In theory at least the most 'liberated' college was the struggling foundation of Downing where the statutes provided for a master, a professor of the laws of England, a professor of medicine and sixteen fellows, of whom only the two who were to reside and to act as tutors were to be in holy orders. The remaining fellowships were to be held for twelve years only, and that on the condition of the holders acquiring (necessarily away from Cambridge for the most part) professional qualifications in either law or medicine. So far from serving as an object of emulation in its exemption from the thralldom of mathematics and theology, however, the college in its struggle for survival and then for recognition moved ever closer to the traditional model.[16]

The minds of the students, however, were not confined to, often indeed were not engaged with, events within the university. Wordsworth and Coleridge were not the only students to be driven to a pitch of high excitement during the early months of the French Revolution. Subsequent events cooled Wordsworth's ardour and, of course, reinforced Tory attitudes as well in Cambridge as in the nation at large. The victory of Waterloo was, in due course, celebrated (by bonfires, of course, and in the selection of topics for university prizes). Notwithstanding, the increasing confidence of the Whigs and a general stretching of political minds was neatly marked by the coalescence in 1814 of three existing student debating societies to form the Union Society.

The early history of the society is chequered. Meeting first in February 1815, it was temporarily closed down in 1817 under the vice-chancellorship of Dr James Wood, the reactionary Master of St John's, for its impudence in daring to discuss government policy in Ireland and other political issues. When the proctors arrived in mid-meeting to wield the axe, they were confronted by the young William Whewell, BA, very shortly to be a fellow of Trinity, in the chair: 'Strangers will please to withdraw', he announced, in best parliamentary style, 'and the House

[15] It was, however, possible for dissenters to attend the university as undergraduates, even if they could take no qualification away with them. See Chapter 3, note 1, p. 69.

[16] Trinity Hall, of course, also had a large, indeed a larger, complement of lay fellows all busily pursuing their legal avocations in London.

31. 'Cambridge in 1797': 'the day before Ordination' and 'the day after Ordination'. Original pen-and-ink sketches from the portrait collection of the Cambridge Antiquarian Society portrait collection deposited in the University Library (F.147).

will take the message into consideration.' Several senior members rose to the society's defence, but Dr Wood was implacable, and it was not until 1821 that the then vice-chancellor, the far-from-revolutionary Dr Wordsworth of Trinity, permitted the resumption of meetings – on the condition, which prevailed for about ten years, that no political question 'falling within a floating period of twenty years anterior to the time of discussion' was to be debated. Meeting at first in a room at the Red Lion Inn in Petty Cury the society moved several times before achieving the premises, which it now occupies only in part, behind the Round Church in 1866. From its earliest days it was to be a training ground for budding politicians, though not presuming to hold a candle to the sister society in Oxford in that respect.

Other student groups formed in the university and in individual colleges with the aim of debating a wider range of issues than appeared on the agenda of the Union. Of these one of those to survive longest was The Apostles. Founded in 1820 as the Cambridge Conversazione Society by a group of more than usually earnest-minded, if subsequently undistinguished, young men, within ten years it had attracted a galaxy of talented students, among them F. D. Maurice, James Spedding and Tennyson's friend Arthur Hallam. Numbering twelve (hence the name they adopted) the members devised a society in which no topic was to be taboo except 'Mathematics and Classics, *professionally* considered'. Members took turns to present papers for discussion and, although the membership tended to be drawn from those sympathetic to, indeed eager for, reform, every variety of opinion was admissible, it being understood only that no paper should contain sentiments or beliefs that the writer did not genuinely entertain. It was clearly intended that discussions should take place with total frankness, and the membership was carefully selected so as to avoid any consequent embarrassment, public or private. In its heydays, which have come and gone, the society has been notable for the variety of distinctions which have marked its past members, who in after-life retain honorary membership as 'Angels'. The fact of membership was not initially seen as a subject for secrecy, except perhaps from those who might prove tiresome in seeking admission for themselves. It was an episode of this kind, in the 1850s, which first drove the society underground.

Other university societies were founded with a view to furthering more specific interests, and of these particular success attended the Philosophical Society, founded in 1819, on the inspiration of Adam Sedgwick, recently elected Woodwardian Professor of Geology, and John Stevens Henslow, later professor of botany, with the characteristically enthusiastic support of E. D. Clarke, professor of mineralogy, as 'a corresponding society for the purpose of introducing subjects of natural history to the Cambridge students'. The idea was received with great enthusiasm and the society was formally founded later in the year 'as a point of concourse for scientific communications' at a public meeting advertised by a notice carrying the signatures of thirty-three individuals including six Heads, six professors and eleven tutors. It is a very distinguished list of signatures. The society flourished immediately and by 1820 was able to buy a house in Sidney Street and to embark on the accumulation of a library and a museum. In the next year a reading room was added to supply a social function, with foreign as well as English newspapers and magazines and, of course, scientific journals. In 1832 the society was chartered and adopted a code of by-laws based on those of the Royal Society. The next year it moved into yet grander premises specially built for it in All Saints' Passage. Membership, however, began to decline, partly, it was alleged, because the cost of newspapers was now so much reduced that everyone could afford their own, and in 1865 the house was sold and the museum and library taken over by the university. The library formed the nucleus of the present Scientific Periodicals Library and the society continued and continues to flourish as a prestigious one, in spite of its loss of premises. Its *Transactions* were for many years published free of cost by the University Press, which was later also to subsidise the society's other publications.

University meetings to support missionary and bible societies were held (and sometimes heckled by those who disapproved of the precise flavour of the society in question) and donations were made both by subscription and corporately to numerous worthy causes, as for example to distressed Portuguese and British prisoners in France in 1811. The university was active in petitioning against slavery, spurred on by William Wilberforce and by Thomas Clarkson of St John's; and even more active in petitioning Parliament against all attempted moves for the relief or emancipation of Roman Catholics.

When Pitt died in 1806 a single veto in the Caput prevented the presentation of a grace to consider some mark of respect to his memory. At a public meeting three days later in Trinity Lodge it was resolved that a collection be put in hand for the erection of a statue. Committees were set up in London and in Cambridge and met with startling success, raising a sum in excess of £7,400, and enabling the commissioning of the handsome statue by Nollekens that stands in the Senate House. There was enough money over in the Cambridge fund to contribute £1000 towards the endowment of the Pitt Scholarships in Classical Learning (in 1813), and in the London fund to make a very substantial subvention towards the erection of the Pitt Press (completed in 1833).[17] In the light of this Tory enthusiasm it comes as no surprise to learn that the Senate voted to petition against the Reform Bill of 1832, the regents (or residents) more decisively than the non-regents. A group of BAs *per contra* drew up a petition in favour of the Bill.

Political and religious zeal and involvement in philanthropic causes were not, however, sufficient to absorb all the leisure time of all undergraduates, although BAs should have been happy enough after the passing of a grace on 18 March 1829 permitted them to borrow books from the University Library. It was too little and too late: on 10 June 1829 the first boat race between Oxford and Cambridge was rowed at Henley. An unpromising young undergraduate named Charles Darwin took a day off from his relentless pursuit of beetles to witness the event.

It is difficult to tell whether any characteristic of the young Darwin other than his enthusiasm for beetles served to draw down upon him the kindly attention of Professors Henslow and Sedgwick. It does not appear that his tutor, John Graham, soon to be Master of Christ's and later bishop of Chester, saw in him anything but a typically idle 'poll man' destined for the church, dawdling away his Cambridge days with his horse and his gun until thrown into panic by the approaching examinations. Henslow it was, however, who made a friend of him, encouraged his collecting habit, introduced him to other collectors, sent him geologising with Adam Sedgwick and finally recommended him as naturalist on the *Beagle*. After the momentous voyage Darwin's visits to Cambridge

[17] See p. 119.

were few and short; as an institution she had done nothing for him; Henslow all that was necessary. It is only a more spectacular version of a story that could be told of many.

More closely connected with the university was the mathematician Charles Babbage who, unlike Darwin, was, although largely self-taught, notably in advance of his tutors when he entered Trinity in 1811. He soon associated himself with Herschel, Peacock and others in the foundation of the Analytical Society with the aim of promoting the integral and differential calculus, then flourishing on the continent but practically unknown in Cambridge. He migrated to Peterhouse and from there took his BA in 1814 – not having sat for honours, as he might have done, in 1813: believing that the Senior Wranglership was bound to go to Herschel he had no wish to appear second. It was an early sign of those quirks of character which were to mar his career. The next year he moved to London, where he had inherited a house, and he was relatively rarely in Cambridge thereafter. He was, indeed, Lucasian Professor from 1828 to 1839, but as such he delivered no lectures. His fame rests securely on his invention in the early 1820s of a calculating machine, the forerunner of the computer. It was widely acclaimed and he immediately set about designing a more elaborate version which, however, for all its theoretical brilliance he never managed either to build himself or to persuade others to build. His publications were very numerous, and he was a member of a vast number of scientific bodies throughout Europe, starting with the Royal Society in 1816. His life, however, drifted ever further into frustration and eccentricity, marked by the declaration of implacable war on organ-grinders who, he maintained, had robbed him of one-quarter of his potential working time.

His two associates in the Analytical Society prospered better: John Frederick William Herschel, son of the astronomer Sir William Herschel, did indeed graduate Senior Wrangler in 1813, and, after a brief dalliance with the law, was gently pushed by his father into astronomy, where he achieved outstanding success in his observations, especially of nebulae and of double stars, many of them taken at the Cape. He became a pillar both of the Royal Society and of the Astronomical Society, of which he was one of the principal founders, and achieved a general fame for his elegant expositions not only of his own speciality but also of other scientific topics.

Peacock remained in Cambridge, as a fellow of Trinity, taking a very active part in the movement for reform and in the teaching of the new style of mathematics which, as moderator, he was the first to introduce into the university examinations. From 1823 he served as tutor of Trinity, and continued so even after his election to the Lowndean chair in 1837. He resigned as tutor, but not as professor, on his appointment as dean of Ely, where he devoted his zeal and energy, and his own resources, to the restoration of the cathedral. His initials adorn the paintings in the lantern over the octagon in the centre of the cathedral.

The stirrings of change which we have described in the early nineteenth-century university were accompanied by striking architectural accomplishments: the Fitzwilliam and the Pitt Press stand out as landmarks of their generation, but there are other buildings, no less essential to the view of Cambridge in the mind's eye, which represent spectacular transformations. With the obvious exception of the chapel, virtually the whole of King's College, comprising the Gibbs Building (completed in 1731), and the whole of the south range with the flamboyant gatehouse and screen (built to Wilkins's designs between 1824 and 1828) is of this period, while the removal of the sprawling mass of the old Provost's Lodge, which previously nestled between King's Parade and the chapel threw open a view of the east end of the chapel which must previously have been much impaired. Wilkins's hand is also to be seen in his classical design for Downing (realised only in part between 1807 and 1811), the gothic New Court at Trinity (from 1823), and, with the exception of Old Court, most of what is now seen at Corpus Christi, including the chapel. Happily a proposal that Wilkins should 'gothicise' the Gibbs Building at King's was abandoned. Many of these buildings either create or take advantage of a spaciousness previously to be enjoyed, perhaps, only in the Great Court and Nevile's Court at Trinity. In this mode also, much admired since its erection, is the proud view from the south-west, across the broad expanse of 'the Walks', of St John's New Court with its Eagle Gate by Rickman and Hutchinson (1827–31).

This last prospect is one of a succession of remarkable views from 'the Backs', but the Backs themselves are also a product of this era. St John's had, in 1772, employed Lancelot (Capability) Brown on their fellows' garden and, thus encouraged, Brown presented the university in 1779 with a scheme, still extant in the University Archives, for landscaping the

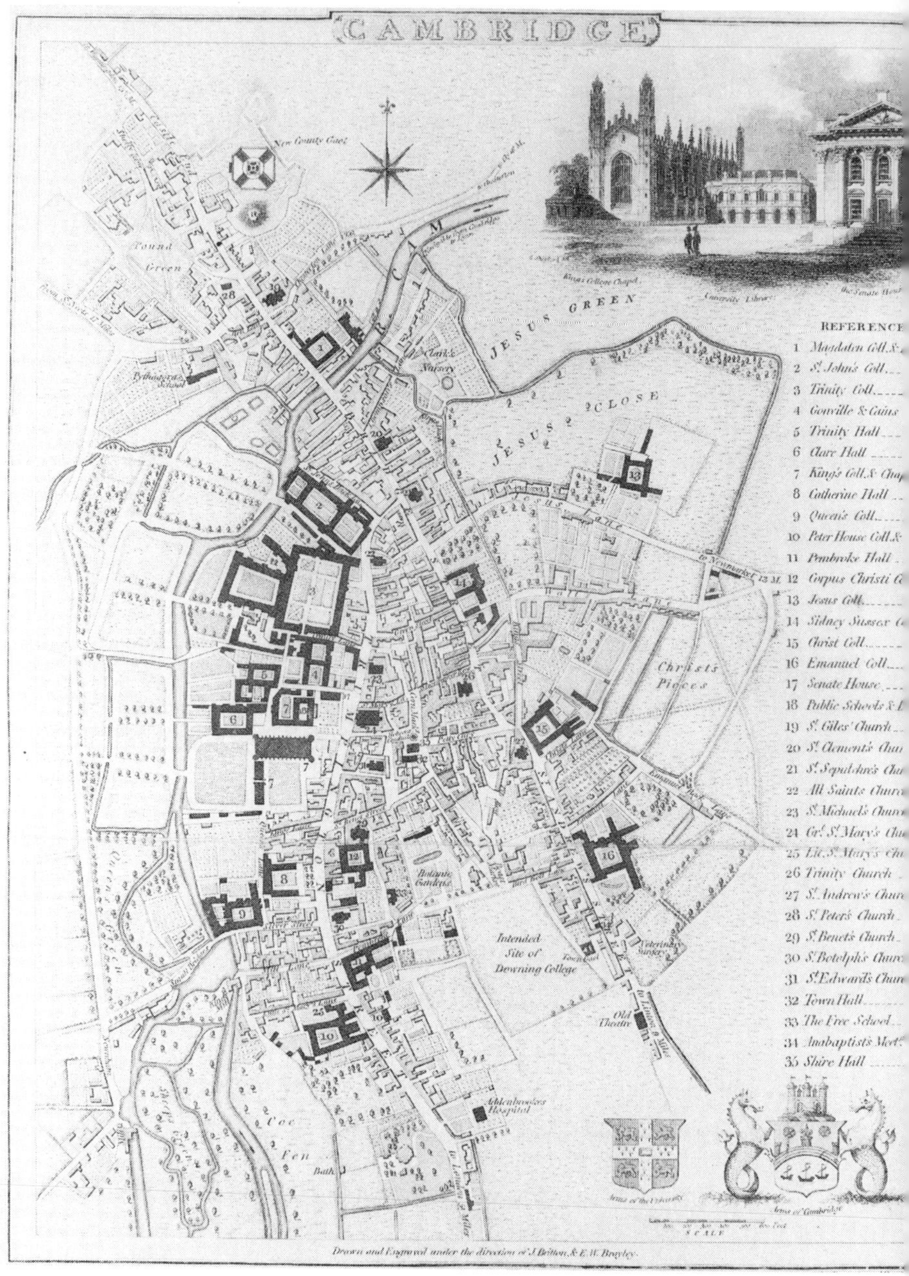

32. Map of Cambridge in 1810, engraved by J. Roper from a drawing by G. Cole, for *The beauties of England and Wales*. The map shows how, before the building of Downing, whose site is marked, nothing stood between the Old Botanic Garden (now the New Museums Site) and the open fields.

Backs. His plan is, as it were, for a park serving a massive country-house comprising all the colleges backing down to the river. It was not adopted, and the present appearance of the Backs, still imposing, but more domestic in scale, came about gradually with the turfing of the area between the Wren Library and the river in 1760, the clearing of the land between King's chapel and the river in 1771 and Wilkins's completion of King's and re-siting of its bridge between 1818 and 1828. In spite of the buildings now standing on the west side of Queens' Road it is still happily possible to summon up to the imagination the cheerful spectacle of Commencement Sunday when, from about 1805 to 1840, the newly created MAs and the Doctors in their scarlet gowns would parade on Clare Hall Piece, now the site of Clare College Memorial Court, west of the river, showing off their university and themselves to their visiting relatives.

5

From the Victorian reforms to the First World War, 1840–1914

The election to the chancellorship of Thomas Pelham, duke of Newcastle, in 1748 had been the result of much strenuous political activity by his supporters. As chancellor he had founded medals for distinction in the Classical Tripos, responded to legislative moves in his official capacity as the university's representative and visited the university at regular intervals. The duke of Grafton, who succeeded him in 1768, was elected unopposed. After 1774 he seems not to have visited the university in his official capacity, even on such occasions of high ceremony as the admission to the MA of HRH Prince William Frederick of Gloucester in 1790, an event otherwise graced by a remarkably distinguished audience. Like Newcastle, Grafton had held the highest offices of state. He was followed as chancellor by that same William Frederick, now duke of Gloucester, in 1811. His MA had been his by right – by the right of all sons of peers to proceed to that degree without previous examination after three years' residence. His Royal Highness had been a fellow-commoner of Trinity since his admission in 1787 aged twelve, and George Romney's portrait of him as a 15-year-old MA is one of the most charming in Cambridge. The duke had been elected by 470 votes against the 356 cast for his opponent the duke of Rutland; he gave a memorably lavish dinner to nearly a thousand people in Trinity cloisters on the occasion of his installation and found time twice during his tenure of office to visit the university. Probably no more was expected of him. (He is one of several royal personages laying claim to having been the original 'Silly Billy'.)

On the duke's death the university opted unanimously for the marquis of Camden, also of Trinity and now aged seventy-five. He had held high political office and was a noted supporter of worthy causes, including the public to whom he voluntarily gave in 1817 the surplus fees and emoluments arising from his office as Teller of the Exchequer – a sum amounting to more than £250,000. His successor too, the duke of

33. Prince William Frederick, 2nd Duke of Gloucester, as a 15-year-old nobleman fellow-commoner at Trinity. George Romney, 1791.

Northumberland, High Steward of the university and donor in 1842 of the Warwick Vase that stands on Senate House lawn, was elected unopposed. The pattern seemed well established.

When therefore on Northumberland's death the vice-chancellor, Henry Philpott of St Catharine's, and other Heads, following up an initiative rapidly seized by Whewell, offered the chancellorship to none other than the Prince Consort, it came as a nasty shock that the election would be contested. The prince had said that he would only stand if unopposed, but the Master and Seniors of St John's, who had already approached the earl of Powis, and had met with a gracious reply, felt that they could not ask their candidate to withdraw. The earl showed no signs of withdrawal and the prince stated formally that he could not therefore allow himself to be nominated. His supporters were in despair, feeling, probably rightly, that the election of Lord Powis would be interpreted as a gesture of defiance towards the Whig ministry and would immediately provoke parliamentary intervention in the affairs of the university. At the eleventh hour those close to the prince gave their opinion, with or without his knowledge, that in spite of his refusal to be nominated, he would, if an election nonetheless took place, not sabotage it by any statement that he would not accept office if elected. The election was closely fought, but embarrassment was saved by the victory of the prince by 954 votes to 837.[1] The installation took place, in the presence of the queen, in Cambridge. Since the previous visit of the royal couple five years earlier, in 1842, certain advances had been made: this time they were able to come by train.

As his supporters had foreseen, this was to be no figure-head chancellor. The Prince Consort was yearning for a field of activity, and it was not hard for him to see that much needed to be done if Cambridge was to be made able to rival the progress in the sciences which had been made by the universities of Germany. Many abuses indeed survived: the absence of any entrance examination, except by 1836 at Trinity, and the fact that honours could be obtained only in mathematics,[2] ensured that those with no talents in that direction had very little incentive for serious study, and the standard of the Ordinary BA was lamentably low. Several professors were very willing and able to lecture, and, indeed, in the first two decades of the century they had succeeded in attracting audiences, whether for Professor Marsh's

[1] The Earl of Powis was subsequently shot by his youngest son, albeit by accident.

[2] Although the Classical Tripos had been instituted in 1824, until 1850 it was only open to those who had already obtained mathematical honours.

theological lectures, given in the university church, or for the dramatic and eccentric perfomances of E. D. Clarke as professor of mineralogy, and this in spite of the fact that such students as they attracted were neither assessed nor rewarded. The statute of 1570, whereby men admitted to the university at the age of at least twenty-four were entitled, after ten years, to take the exercises for the BD without previous examination, not only remained on the statute book but was proving popular as never before. An attempt to modify the scandal in 1788 by demanding at least three terms' residence in the last two years proved ineffective: the BD exercises of these Ten-Year men were little more than a farce (and, indeed, attended as such by undergraduates), until in 1825 they were replaced by an examination conducted by the Regius Professor of Divinity.

Dr Haviland, shortly before his death in 1851 reported that, notwithstanding his reforms, medical studies were at a low ebb. Since 1814 termly examinations had been imposed on candidates for the LL B, but the imposition was widely regarded as a gentle one. The complete failure to provide any formal theological instruction besides the lectures of the Norrisian Professor for those destined for the church (about 50 per cent of students at this time) was a further scandal and one which was confronted by Dr Graham, as vice-chancellor, in reaction to a pamphlet published by Charles Perry, in 1841. Perry had proposed a scheme for theological lectures, and an examination, after the normal time of graduation. Dr Graham, foreseeing objections to any extension to the period of residence, proposed rather that the BA examinations should be brought forward from the tenth term to the beginning of the ninth and a voluntary theological examination set in Lent Term. It is somewhat astonishing that he should so have underestimated the volume of the howls of protest (which he had indeed expected) at the proposed reduction of the time to be devoted to mathematics. An attempt to salvage the situation by withdrawing the grace for his scheme and substituting one to appoint a syndicate to consider the matter failed in an atmosphere of near hysteria, but after some manoeuvring a scheme drawn up by Dr Turton, Regius Professor of Divinity, for a voluntary theological examination was finally approved in 1842.[3] The voluntary theological examination, thus established in principle, might yet have foundered in practice had it not been

[3] Successful candidates were also to have the option of then sitting a voluntary examination in Hebrew; but the option was never widely taken up.

for the action of Whewell who, just before resigning the vice-chancellorship in 1843, persuaded most of the bishops to require of Cambridge candidates for ordination a certificate that they had passed it. From fourteen candidates in the first year the numbers rose rapidly to two hundred and five in 1851. For ordinands, the examination was effectively no longer voluntary.

The towering figure of William Whewell, whether as a youthful leader of the reform party, as a polymath and systematiser of knowledge ('science was his *forte* and omniscience his foible'), as the great advocate of the natural sciences in the 1820s and, allegedly, the coiner of the term 'scientist', or as a formidable academic politician and, as Master of Trinity, an increasingly adamantine rock of resistance, dominates the early and middle years of the nineteenth century to the extent that there was in these years hardly an event, a movement or a development in any academic field in which his support or his opposition was not critical.

As reported above, the 'Previous' examination, taken in the fifth term, had been introduced in 1822 as an obstacle to the sort of academic idleness so elegantly enjoyed by Lord Byron in the early years of the century before exercising his right, as a nobleman, to proceed to the MA without examination. The topics for examination were the early books of Euclid and of Paley's *Moral philosophy*, and the standard was extremely elementary. Its enemies, however, maintained that it distracted serious students from their mathematical studies besides requiring college tutors 'to do the work of an under Master in a Grammar School'.[4] It was indeed an attempt to ensure that some work was demanded between matriculation and the Senate House examination of candidates for the ordinary degree, but neither this nor the reforms outlined above could be counted as anything more than gestures in the direction of raising the general academic standard of the university to a respectable level. It was clear to some at least within the university, and to very many without, that reform was inevitable. The only question was whether the university and colleges would have the will and the energy to introduce in short order reforms substantial enough to pre-empt government action.

[4] *College tuition*, by a fellow (1854). The introduction of the Previous Examination and modest reforms to the examinations for the Ordinary BA were also blamed, probably

Oxford and Cambridge had not, for centuries, been the only universities in Britain. They were now no longer the only ones in England. The University of London, offering full access to dissenters, was constituted by letters patent in 1836; by the next year the University of Durham was chartered. The Scottish universities had long demonstrated their superiority, in medicine in particular, but this fact seems only to have impinged in Cambridge upon the medical professors. London, and the comparisons it was likely soon to provoke, presented a threat obvious to all but the most complacent, and even they must have been aware that in 1837 Lord Radnor was promoting a Bill in the House of Lords for a commission of inquiry into the two ancient universities. The Bill failed. It was said that the Heads and the Visitors of colleges had full power to reform any abuses. Radnor, not pausing to enquire whether they had also the will, proposed a committee to enquire as to the reality of these powers. The marquis of Camden, Chancellor of Cambridge, and the duke of Wellington, Chancellor of Oxford, between them achieved a stay of immediate execution by maintaining that the colleges of both universities were, even then, deeply concerned with proposals for their own amelioration.

There had been nimble footwork in Cambridge to ensure that this statement would stand examination. Camden had written to the vice-chancellor, who had arranged for each college to state whether or not it was willing and able to reform its statutes. The answers have not survived, and it is likely that a refusal came at least from King's, where Provost Thackeray happily ensconced himself behind his oath, taken on admission to office, not to meddle with the statutes. Most of the colleges, however, seem to have taken a line at least mildly affirmative. Jesus, Pembroke, Emmanuel and Queens' made minor modifications; Peterhouse liberated its fellowships from restriction to men from particular counties. At Christ's the Master (Dr Graham) and ten fellows petitioned the crown for real reforms – marriage for fellows and full admission for those not members of the Church of England. It was a bold attempt; too bold for others of the fellows who successfully appealed to the Visitor to

with some truth, for a marked falling off in attendance on even such popular lecturers as Professors Sedgwick and Henslow.

put a stop to it. Trinity and St John's, after long and painful deliberations, managed to agree on nothing likely to placate critics outside the university. The university itself did no better and some members at least began to think that no reforms could be achieved without intervention from above.

Other minds were thinking along similar lines. On 23 April 1850 it was moved in Parliament that 'as all systems of academical education require from time to time some modification, from the change of external circumstances, the progress of opinion, and the intellectual improvement of the people' and as the universities had failed to move with the times, partly on account of ancient college statutes, and as 'better laws are needed to regulate the ceremony of matriculation and the granting of degrees, to diminish the exclusiveness of the university libraries, to provide for a fairer distribution of the rewards of scientific and literary merit, to extend the permission of marriage to tutors of colleges, and to facilitate the registration of electors for the universities', and as means should be found to control the 'continued extravagance of individual students', and as 'the mode of tenure of college property ought to be ameliorated, particularly in Ireland', a Royal Commission should be established to inquire into the state of the universities of Oxford, Cambridge and Dublin 'with a view to assist in the adaptation of those important institutions to the requirements of modern times'.

The motion had considerable support but not that of the prime minister, Lord John Russell, who objected to the prescriptive clause. He announced that he would indeed ask for a Royal Commission, but that such a commission should be empowered to enquire and report only. He wrote to the Prince Consort (who forwarded a copy to the vice-chancellor), explaining, surely unnecessarily, how and why the universities were in need of reform. The universities, he said, 'fully acknowledged' the expediency of making provision for the admission of modern literature and of the physical sciences to the syllabus and had already introduced 'very large reforms'. The first statement was open to question: there were plenty of Heads and others in Cambridge who saw little or no need for reform, and were alarmed at what had been achieved already: the establishment of two new triposes, in Moral and in Natural Sciences. Arrangements for both triposes were complete in 1850, and the first examinations were held in 1851. It was to be some years before the

34. 'Degree time' from John Lewis Roget's *A Cambridge scrap-book* (1859). The student's bedmaker collects her last tip on investing him with his hood. The 'spoon' refers to the wooden spoon presented to the bottom candidate in the third class of the Mathematical Tripos; the 'wedge' to the candidate in the same position in the Classical Tripos.

number of candidates in either tripos equalled the number of examiners.[5]

There was a foreseeable problem: how could the smaller colleges afford to pay teachers in the new subjects? Where would they find them? They would have to wait until there were enough graduates in the new triposes to provide potential fellows. That such problems should be addressed by a Royal Commission proved altogether unacceptable to a hundred and fifty-seven members of the Senate (including fourteen out of seventeen Heads but only twelve out of twenty-seven professors) who signed a petition to the vice-chancellor, Dr Cartmell of Christ's, urging him to offer all possible resistance. The university and colleges, they claimed,

5 From 1850 it was possible to take the Classical Tripos without having first graduated in mathematics. Candidates for the Moral Sciences and Natural Sciences triposes had until 1860 to have first graduated in arts, law or medicine.

had, and were already exercising, the powers to reform themselves; it was too soon to make judgements about the new triposes; and, besides, if the threatened commission 'to enquire into the state and revenues' of the universities were to have power to collect only information voluntarily offered, certain parties would certainly refuse to co-operate and the resulting report would therefore be distorted. The vice-chancellor concurred and wrote to the Prince Consort along these lines, adding, with reference to Lord John Russell's letter, that the proposal to overrule the wishes of founders and benefactors by removing the restriction of certain scholarships and fellowships to those from specific regions or schools would be 'an interference with the rights of property both dangerous and unprecedented'. He made very clear the university's resentment. The Prince Consort replied soothingly and sympathetically, apologising for not having had the opportunity to warn the university of the proposal before it was made, but recommending that, since the commission was inevitable and its membership was to be selected with a careful view to assuring the universities of its benignity, the university should co-operate. Any hostility, he pointed out, 'might add strength to the accusations of their enemies'.

The commissioners turned out to be John Graham, bishop of Chester and previously Master of Christ's; George Peacock, fellow of Trinity and dean of Ely; Sir John Herschel, previously a Trinity Senior Wrangler and now a sort of universal scientific *éminence grise*; Sir John Romilly, Attorney General, Master of the Rolls, and formerly a Trinity wrangler; and Adam Sedgwick, fellow of Trinity and Woodwardian Professor of Geology. Their brief was 'to enquire into the state, discipline, and revenues' of the university and colleges. Peacock and Sedgwick had both been leaders of the reform movement in Trinity, although Peacock's failure to relinquish the Lowndean chair or to fulfil his obligations as a lecturer on his elevation to the deanship might by now have marked him in the eyes of some as a more likely object than agent of reform.

Meanwhile the Statutes Revision Syndicate (set up in 1849) continued nervously with its labours and, to forestall coercion, King's College, under a new provost, on 1 May 1851 voluntarily surrendered the rights of its members to proceed to the BA without examination. When the Statutes Revision Syndicate submitted its first draft statutes in December 1851 they were found to include unexceptional and overdue rationalisations of the procedures for graduating in the higher faculties; proposals that the ranks of noblemen with special privileges of exemption from the usual exercises for degrees should be more narrowly defined; that the university should be allowed to confer on its own authority those degrees on heads of houses and deans of cathedrals for which mandates had previously been necessary; that the custom of incorporation of degrees, long since restricted to graduates from Oxford and Dublin, should be extended to those of other universities; that the levying of ancient and inequitable fees, known as 'compounders', on graduates who were possessed of real property or were incumbents of certain livings, be abolished, and the loss of funds made good by the abolition of one of the three Esquire Bedells; that resident MAs with no intention of graduating in theology be no longer required to perform Acts in that faculty; and that the Elizabethan statute for Ten-Year men proceeding to the BD be repealed.[6] In its place they put forward a scheme for the award of a Licenciate in Theology. These were sound proposals with a good prospect of success. Reforms to the examination system were not proposed as it was rightly thought that these were more properly the subject of ordinances which the university could adapt at will as the times might demand.

Other proposals were less likely to command universal assent, as that the BA course be reduced from ten terms to nine. The syndicate also proposed a new scheme for election to the Caput but no redefinition of its powers. It was on this proposal that the report came to grief as it aroused so much opposition that the vice-chancellor feared that all the graces proposed might be rejected out of malice. The syndicate was therefore reconvened and in May 1852 put forward a new proposal, that the Caput should henceforth function only as a body for approving graces for degrees, and that a new body, the Council of the Senate, should be established consisting of three members elected by the Heads, one each elected by those doctors of divinity, of medicine and of law who were not Heads, three by the professoriate (not being Heads), and three regents and three non-regents appointed by the colleges in rotation, which would take over from the Caput the business of considering and preparing all graces to be presented to the Senate.

[6] See above, p. 149.

The syndicate's proposals of December 1851 and May 1852 were never put to the vote: by May 1852 the report of the commissioners, though not yet published, was complete and had been seen by the vice-chancellor. It was argued by the syndicate that there was little point in the university voting on proposals to which the commissioners might have objections or substantive amendments, and their argument won the day, in spite of the reservations of the vice-chancellor, Prince Albert and Dr Philpott. In allowing the syndicate to jettison its report the university sacrificed the only opportunity it was to have as a corporation clearly to indicate its willingness to reform itself. In the event the commissioners' report was found to be highly complimentary of their efforts and those of some of the colleges to introduce such reforms as lay within their powers.[7]

The commissioners, however, had felt free to go much further than the syndicate in their proposals for the university's educational responsibilities, recommending that triposes be established in engineering, in modern languages and history, and in theology; that the standard of the Previous Examination be raised and sufficiently successful candidates have the option of proceeding to any tripos. Boards of Studies, such as that recently introduced for mathematics, with the duty of ensuring a measure of correspondence between the lectures of professors and the subjects for examination, were to be established in the new subjects, and a General Council of Studies set up to co-ordinate them. Candidates less successful (but not unsuccessful) in the Previous could choose to take an Ordinary BA in a range of subjects running in parallel with the triposes but at a lower level. New professorships were to be created, and a host of university lectureships which would be open to married men. The costs would be met by the colleges, whose teaching henceforth would be limited to the preparation of candidates for the Previous Examination. As for the cost of providing the necessary laboratories and museums, this might be met if the state would agree to remit the £3,000 or so which it received annually by stamp duty on matriculations and degrees (a sum included in the fees charged to students which might now be diverted to the university's use) in exchange for relief from the payments, amounting

[7] Also in 1852, in the midst of so much academical tribulation, a new syndicate had to be set up to comment on a lengthy memorial submitted to the commissioners by the town authorities, bearing on all aspects of the university's involvement with municipal affairs.

to about £1,000 annually, which it had hitherto shouldered in meeting the stipends of certain of the professors.

If the commissioners' proposals for the university were thus radical and bold, falling short only of proposing an entrance examination, the paragraphs relating to the colleges (where perhaps they foresaw more opposition) were decidedly anodyne. The fellow's lot was still to consist of celibacy and holy orders unless the individual colleges wished to rule otherwise, although the obligation in some colleges to proceed to the BD was to be removed. In the sequel celibacy was abolished at Caius and mitigated in several colleges, although it is a measure of the inherent resistance to the notion of married fellows that the enabling clause adopted at Emmanuel was not invoked until 1871. Local and hereditary restrictions were generally to be abolished, and scholarships and fellowships tied to certain schools commuted into exhibitions; but while the fellows of Peterhouse were henceforth, instead of nominating two candidates to the bishop of Ely, to elect their own master absolutely, no such freedom was held out for the fellows of Trinity, Magdalene, Jesus and Downing, all of which had masters imposed from without. The Master of Gonville and Caius, however, was no longer to be necessarily a native of the diocese of Norwich (a restriction which enquiry revealed to have been introduced not by the original founder but by Dr Caius). The fellows, eager to act in anticipation of legislation to this effect, therefore found it a sufficient disqualification of Dr George Paget, otherwise probably the most attractive candidate, that he was in fact a native of the diocese.

The commissioners' report wound to its conclusion with a stirring peroration, penned by Adam Sedgwick, who himself could not read it without tears, celebrating the virtues of the university and its members; but this was scarcely enough to render acceptable the considered and stated opinion of the commissioners that only external intervention could effect the necessary reforms. Syndicates were rapidly appointed in an attempt to avert the impending doom, one to consider provision of lecture rooms and museums, the other, the Studies Syndicate, to consider the educational proposals of the report. As governments came and went, and ultimatum followed ultimatum, the Lecture Rooms Syndicate came up with an admirable proposal for a development, which the university could by no means afford and to which the colleges declined to contribute, on the Old Botanic Garden Site. The Studies Syndicate bickered and dragged its heels and it was not until March 1854 that they suddenly published four reports proposing Boards of Studies for classics, medicine, law, theology and natural and moral sciences, and triposes in theology and in law. The standard of the Previous Examination was to be raised, but no improvements were suggested for the Ordinary BA course. The question of making financial provision for the extra teaching that would be required, however, defeated them utterly, and their sole suggestion was that two new divinity professors might have canonries at Ely appropriated to them by Parliament. Catastrophically, the Senate failed to approve the proposals for new triposes. Prince Albert expressed himself astonished, as well he might have been, given that, even as the voters mustered, the Bill for the statutory commission for Oxford was passing through Parliament.

The Bill for Cambridge, incorporating variations to the Oxford Bill suggested by the allies of the Prince Consort and with his active assistance, was finally passed in July 1856. Peacock was once more a commissioner, and his seven colleagues were again Cambridge men. In November the Caput was abolished and the first members of the Council of the Senate, clear-sighted men for the most part, elected by all resident members of the Senate. The Council was to approve all graces and to exercise the right, previously the prerogative of the Heads, to present two nominees for election to certain university offices. The Council and the governing bodies of colleges were given until 1 January 1858 to draw up or to amend statutes for the approval of the commissioners who, after that date, were to have the power to frame statutes themselves, statutes which would, however, be subject to revision if objections were raised in good faith by two-thirds of the body in question.

The Council set smartly to work on the basis of the draft drawn up by the revisers of 1854 of the statutes as they would have been had those amendments been accepted. Trapped between the commissioners and a frequently intransigent Senate they struggled to make progress, the issue of the status of the established church proving again and again one on which no compromise could be found. Inevitably time finally ran out and it was left for the commissioners to act. This they did so far as possible along lines already suggested to, if not approved by, the Senate: the Regent and Non-Regent Houses were merged; provision was made for public discussion of all graces before they were subjected to a vote; obsolete offices, such as those of taxor and scrutator, were abolished as carrying no surviving duties; ancient endowments were redirected to provide stipends for newly created professors;[8] terms were lengthened and residence for two-thirds of the term henceforth required. MAs and Doctors were no longer obliged to take their degrees in person and the decline of Commencement Sunday, already apparent by about 1840, became precipitous. The Council seldom exercised their right of protest. Statutes were drawn up for university hostels but the commissioners abandoned schemes for non-collegiate students who, however, were shortly to be seen.[9]

The colleges, predictably, fought back with greater determination in the defence of greater abuses. They, after all, boasted founders, long venerated and toasted, whose wishes, however inappropriate to the mid-nineteenth century, merited in the eyes even of many who had striven valiantly for the reform of the university defence to the last paragraph. Nor is it difficult to sympathise with those for whom their college was not only their home but their very *raison d'être* and who felt that the passing of celibacy, even with such limitations as remained, would surely presage the end of the university as they had known it, if not of the universe itself. The ideal communities of scholars which they imagined themselves to inhabit would indeed change, if not as immediately, and not so far beyond recognition as they had feared. The winds of change felt chill indeed when they whistled around the familiar courts; but these were but vernal breezes to what was to follow.

The time was not yet come when the university could settle peaceably once more to its business and to the new demands made of it. The question of religious tests refused to lie down quietly. The settlement of 1856 had removed the requirement of a declaration of faith from those proceeding to all degrees except those in divinity, but membership of the Senate was still restricted to those prepared to declare themselves *bona fide* members of the Church of England, and the same bar, though withdrawn from scholars and exhibitioners of colleges, still applied to fellows.

8 The Sadleirian lectureships were suppressed to finance the Sadleirian chair in algebra, and, after much dispute, Hulse's Christian Advocate converted to a professor with attendant alterations to the regulations for the Hulsean Preacher.

9 See pp. 170–1.

In 1860 Trinity, for the first time in fourteen years, had a Senior Wrangler, James Sterling. As he was a Presbyterian he could not be elected to a fellowship. The next year exactly the same thing happened. In 1862 there started a wearisome succession of petitions and counter-petitions, of Bills and amendments to Bills. Once again it was 'college feeling' that divided and paralysed, and it became clear that the liberation of fellowships must be enforced rather than permitted; when that was accepted there remained doubts, more in Cambridge than in Oxford, also engaged in the same battles, as to whether the heads of houses should not still be required to be members of the established church. The Bill that finally passed in 1871 removed religious restrictions from them, from fellows, from university officers and from all professors and lecturers who were not obliged by the terms of their appointment to be in holy orders. As a comfort to the defeated it was enacted that colleges must provide religious instruction to undergraduates and BAs who were members of the Church of England, and that Morning and Evening Prayer must continue to be observed daily in college chapels.

By this time the university was already bracing itself for a further commission appointed 'to inquire into the property and income belonging to, administered or enjoyed by, the Universities of Oxford and Cambridge and the colleges and halls therein . . . and . . . to report the uses to which such property and income are applied' with the purpose of ascertaining whether the colleges were indeed sufficiently healthy financially to be laid under contribution to the universities. It was a question on which the Commissioners' Report of 1874 left little room for doubt; nor did the fall of the Liberal government earlier that year presage any long delay in action. The Royal Commission of Scientific Instruction, which had reported on Oxford and Cambridge in the previous year, had not despised the efforts already made to improve the teaching of science, but had clearly indicated that much, much more remained to be done. In August 1877, after several attempts, a Statutory Commission was once more appointed with the brief to ensure that provision be made for college contributions to university funds particularly as devoted to teaching ('robbery and spoliation' in the opinion of Dr Perowne of Corpus); for the attachment of fellowships to university offices, and for the review of fellowships not so attached. Once again the university was given time (up to the end of 1878) to draft its own statutes. Once again the Council set to its ungrateful task of steering between the reactionaries and the commissioners; once again syndicates were set up to consider specific aspects of university business and teaching, and once again time ran out.

Meanwhile the commissioners made enquiries of numerous officials as to the needs and revenues of the university. When their report was finally adopted there were to be established a General Board of Studies, to correlate the work of the Special Boards in specific subject areas, and a Financial Board with functions obvious enough; terms and residence were once more defined; statutes for university officers and for professors duly framed. Readers came into existence and Doctors of Science and of Letters. The Council was responsible for suggesting the arrangement whereby each college was to have its quota of professors among its fellows, elected as occasion arose. The commissioners had proposed a more rigid scheme whereby specific chairs were to be tied to each college (as from the nature of their endowments the Downing chairs in law and medicine were already tied to the founder's college, certain of the Regius chairs to Trinity and the newly founded Dixie Professorship of Ecclesiastical History to Emmanuel), thus impinging further than necessary on the colleges' cherished freedom of choice and perhaps obliging a newly elected professor to risk exchanging a college which he venerated, or at least enjoyed, for one for which he might have felt no such emotions.

As to the colleges, their Heads were well and truly freed from the requirement of holy orders and some of the fellows in some of the colleges were freed from the obligation to celibacy (a freedom which, though available to the colleges in theory since 1860, had not been fully taken up except at Caius). Fellowships not held conjointly with a university or college office were to be tenable for a maximum of seven years. Reactionaries continued to resent these dangerous innovations, but it was the taxation of the colleges that caused the greatest furore, its effect memorably likened by Dr Phelps, Master of Sidney, 'to that of an explosive shell thrown into a besieged fort in close proximity to the powder magazine'. On the advice of the Council, there had been substituted for the original proposal of a fixed tax based on each college's current income one calculated on a percentage basis (with a maximum of £30,000 finally fixed in 1896), with a proviso that, with the advice of the Financial Board, the chancellor should be empowered to reduce the contributions. Even with these modifications the colleges were in fact to encounter genuine difficulties with the deepening of the agricultural depression which ensued soon after the assessment. The university was, however, at last to have the means to introduce some of those educational reforms so long looked for, and was accordingly to assume a far more powerful position *vis-à-vis* the colleges than it had enjoyed for many centuries.

The only new tripos, as such, established between 1850 and 1870 was that of law (from 1870 to 1875 'Law and History'), in which there had been classed examinations admitting to the LL B since 1816. The 1870s saw the final splitting of Law and History into independent triposes and the establishment of honours degrees also in Theology (in which there had been examinations leading to an ordinary degree since 1856), in Semitic Languages (1878) and in Indian Languages (1879–92). By 1914 Semitic Languages had been absorbed into Oriental Languages (1895) and new triposes had been set up in Medieval and Modern Languages (including English), first examined in 1886, in Mechanical Sciences (1894) and in Economics (1905). None of these new triposes, however, had as dramatic an effect on the academic preoccupations of Cambridge as the vast expansion of the physical and natural sciences in the latter part of the nineteenth century. In 1882, when the division of the tripos into two parts was first fully operational, 60 candidates passed Part I and 6 Part II of the Natural Sciences Tripos. By 1900 it had become the most popular of the triposes: 136 candidates passed Part I and 25 Part II, about 20 per cent more than the equivalent figures for classics and about twice those of mathematics.

Since the munificent endowment of the Cavendish Laboratory by the duke of Devonshire in 1870, two extensions to the building had been added by 1908, and under the leadership of the first three professors, James Clerk Maxwell (1871–9), Lord Rayleigh (1879–84) and J. J. Thomson (1885–1919), physics in Cambridge had very rapidly attained, and was to continue to maintain, an international reputation. Sir George Liveing, who lived to be ninety-seven, only to be slain in 1924 by a Girtonian on a bicycle, defended the chair of chemistry for forty-seven years, faithfully if without distinction. His elementary lectures were enjoyed largely for his occasional exasperation with his attendants, although he took great pains with those advanced students who had the courage to approach him and, very significantly, with plans for the new laboratory. Fireworks in chemistry had been provided earlier by James

35. J. J. Thomson delivering a lecture on a Braun cathode-ray tube in Cambridge in the 1890s.

Dewar, long Liveing's collaborator in spectroscopic research, and Jacksonian Professor from 1874. Dewar, however, on acquiring quarters at the Royal Institution in London, where the facilities were better, became noted in Cambridge chiefly for his absence. Sir William Pope, coming from Manchester to succeed Liveing, gave vent to blunt utterances on the facilities and administrative arrangements available on his arrival in 1908 and immediately set about acquiring the funds for a new laboratory.

In medicine Sir George Paget, Regius Professor from 1872 to 1892, fought strenuously and successfully, both within the university and with the General Medical Council, to establish his school on a professional footing. His ambitions for a clinical school were not to be achieved, but he established diplomas, open to practitioners not necessarily from Cambridge, of which the most important was probably that in Sanitary Science or public health.

The long tenure (1873–1917) of Sedgwick's successor in the Woodwardian chair, Thomas McKenny Hughes, initiated a period when

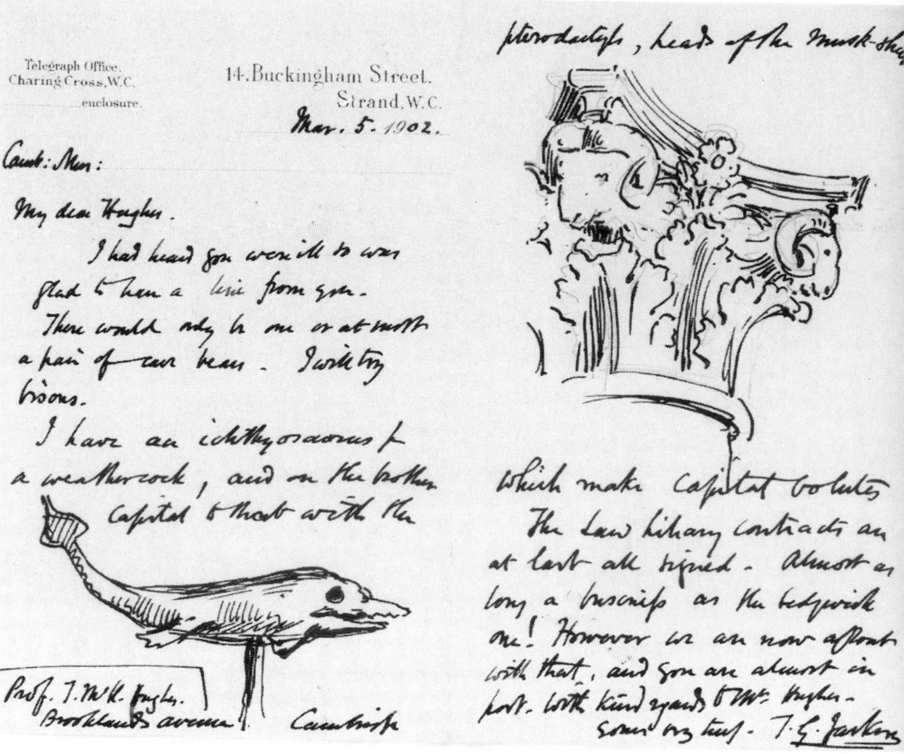

Telegraph Office.
Charing Cross, W.C.
........enclosure.

14. Buckingham Street.
Strand, W.C.
Mar. 5. 1902.

Camb: Mus:

My dear Hughes.

I had heard you were ill & was glad to have a line from you.
There would only be one or at most a pair of cave bears. I will try bisons.
I have an ichthyosaurus for a weathercock, and on the brother capital to that with the pterodactyls, heads of the musk-sheep which make capital volutes.
The Law Library contracts are at last all signed. Almost as long a business as the Sedgwick one! However we are now afloat with that, and you are almost in port. With kind regards to Mrs Hughes.
Yours very truly. T. G. Jackson

Prof. T. McK. Hughes.
Brooklands avenue.
Cambridge

36. Sedgwick Museum of Geology: letter from the architect, T. G. Jackson, to Professor T. McKenny Hughes, discussing the sculptural details: 'There would only be one or at most a pair of cave bears [at the foot of the external stair]. I will try bisons. I have an ichthyosaurus for a weathercock, and on the brother capital to that with pterodactyls, heads of the musk-sheep which make capital volutes' (5 March 1902).

Cambridge geologists were to be found in universities, geological surveys and museums in every corner of the empire and beyond. Sir Michael Foster (1883–1903) in physiology, Alfred Newton in zoology (1866–1907), George Murray Humphry (1866–83) and Alexander Macalister (1883–1920) in anatomy, F. M. Balfour (1882) too briefly in animal morphology and A. C. Seward (1906–36) in botany lent lustre to the chairs in the biological sciences. Their successors were not to disgrace them.

Several of these professors had been active in their field before their professorships came into being. Foster, who was a graduate of London, was a gift to the university from Trinity College, which, although he was debarred by his Nonconformity from the fellowship, created for him in 1870 the post of Praelector in Physiology. On the repeal of the Test Acts in 1871 he was elected a fellow and in 1883 the university showed its appreciation of his enormous talents, evident not so much in his publications as in his teaching and in the reputation which enabled him to bring to Cambridge many distinguished colleagues, including (Sir) Frederick Gowland Hopkins, by creating the professorship for him.

It is the way of scientists to attract others to their own particular lines of research or to enquiries that bear upon them; they shine amidst a constellation. Others in Cambridge shed a more lonely light because the studies they particularly pursued were not seen to relate to any generally recognised field of studies. Among these we may single out Robert Willis, a pioneer in studying from the viewpoint of an engineer the structure of medieval buildings, justly celebrated with his multifariously busy nephew, John Willis Clark,[10] for the *Architectural history of the University of Cambridge and of the colleges of Cambridge and Eton* published in four volumes in 1886. Happy the university that in the absence of a chair in engineering (until 1875) or in architecture (until 1956) had been endowed with the flexibly defined Jacksonian Professorship of Natural Experimental Philosophy. Willis used it from 1837 to 1875 to teach engineering.

With the introduction of new fields of study the peculiar character of the Cambridge mathematical course seemed less defensible: the first part of the tripos was altogether too demanding, while the fierce competition for high wranglerships was calculated to dissuade the most able from the pursuit of horizons less regularly scanned by the examiners. Not without some nostalgic regrets therefore, the practice of placing the successful candidates in strict order of merit was abandoned. The last Senior Wrangler was classed in 1909 and the three classes, still under the ancient names of Wranglers, Senior Optimes and Junior Optimes, were henceforth published in alphabetical order.

The rise of science within the university is manifest by the laboratories

[10] Fellow of Trinity; Superintendent of the Museum of Zoology and Comparative Anatomy, 1866–92; Registrary, 1891–1910; but also patron of the ADC; Secretary of the Museums and Lecture Rooms Syndicate; and author of pioneering and still valuable works on the history of libraries.

and museums, many of late nineteenth-century date, jostling each other for space on the Old Botanic Garden or New Museums Site and of the Downing Site, while to the west of Cambridge the Observatory built in 1822 was augmented by the New Equatorial Building of 1896, the Huggins and McClean Building of 1909 and the Solar Physics, Spectroheliograph and Siderostat Houses in 1912–13. The laboratories required, of course, their complement of laboratory assistants. Originally hired personally by the professors, the inequalities of their terms of employment were somewhat smoothed out as they came to be added to the university's payroll. In the last decade of the century they set up the 'New Museums Club', a vigorous body concerning itself with the welfare, social activities and education of its members, organising on the one hand elaborate *conversaziones*, concerts and cricket matches in which they demonstrated respectively their scientific, vocal and athletic skills. It survives today, having evolved, painfully for some at the time, into the Association of Cambridge University Assistants, the trades union of the assistant staff.

In the humanities the figures of Henry Sidgwick and of Frederic William Maitland stand as examples of teachers who, in different ways, set new standards of rigour and, indeed, of excitement in their respective fields. Probably few now read Sidgwick's works on ethics and on political economy, although they were eagerly studied in their time. He served with distinction as Knightbridge Professor of Moral Philosophy from 1883 to 1900, but he was also active constantly in university politics, both formally, as a respected member of the Council of the Senate and, from 1882, secretary of the General Board of Studies, and informally as an indefatigable advocate of the admission to the university of women and of dissenters. He was a man of outstanding intellectual honesty whose resignation of his Trinity fellowship in 1869 on grounds of religious doubts had a profound impact on the movement for the abolition of tests, a measure, in part, of the veneration and affection which he universally inspired.

The works of Sidgwick's pupil, protégé and fellow Apostle, Maitland, on the other hand, remain standard texts to this day. After taking first place in the Moral Sciences Tripos Maitland spent ten years at Lincoln's Inn and there developed the interest in legal history which was to dictate his future career. In 1884 Sidgwick, from his own pocket, financed a readership in law enabling Maitland to return to Cambridge and in 1888 he was elected Downing Professor of the Laws of England. Unlike Sidgwick, Maitland was a solitary (albeit happily married) figure, both socially and intellectually. It was not until after his death that his works came to serve as the foundation on which arose a distinguished school of medieval historians in Cambridge and elsewhere.

These two figures seem peculiarly rooted in Cambridge, in the sense that it is somehow hard to imagine them elsewhere. The same is true of Leslie Stephen, a committed fellow of Trinity Hall, notable for his precipitate flight from a traditional collegiate life into agnosticism on the publication of Darwin's *Origin of species*, for his extravagantly enthusiastic immersion up to that time in the world of rowing, and for his many delightful satires of university life. Recent biographies testify to the continued attraction of his character. His great monument is the *Dictionary of National Biography*.

Other Cambridge luminaries of the late nineteenth and early twentieth centuries had more conventional academic careers, and were celebrated in their generations. Brooke Foss Westcott in divinity is still remembered with respect, as is also the acute textual critic F. J. A. Hort, although perhaps his greatest labour was one that courted anonymity, namely his patient exertions as one of the principal authors and organisers of the Revised Version of the Bible. Less memorable now for his scholarship, but a much-loved and venerated, if not an entirely consistent, advocate of reform, was their colleague J. B. Lightfoot, always ready to enter the lists. Mandell Creighton and H. M. Gwatkin in succession, meanwhile, served with distinction the newly founded Dixie chair of ecclesiastical history.

Richard Claverhouse Jebb, succeeding Benjamin Hall Kennedy as Regius Professor of Greek, produced in such time as was not devoted to the adornment of his person or the representation of the university in Parliament, editions of the plays of Sophocles which, in varying degrees, are still to be found in the hands of students. William Sterndale Bennett and Sir Charles Villiers Stanford, both by their distinction as composers and by their commitment to the study and performance of music within the university, gave abiding stature to a discipline which had previously enjoyed only a fitful existence in Cambridge.

Others ploughed new fields. The etymological dictionary of Walter Skeat senior, first professor of Anglo-Saxon (1878–1912), remains a standard work of reference. Sir Thomas Wade, as first professor of Chinese, prepared the way for a distinguished succession. Sir Henry Maine, having abandoned the Regius Professorship of Civil Law, which he had occupied from 1847 to 1854, for the Corpus Professorship at Oxford, returned in his glory in 1887 to follow Sir William Vernon Harcourt as the second occupant of the Whewell Professorship of International Law for the last year of his life.

As subjects for teaching and research multiplied and facilities for both improved, academic careers began to appear more feasible, even desirable. The commissioners of 1850–2 had aimed at precisely this. Good teachers should be encouraged to stay in the university, and to that end tutors (by which, presumably, they meant all teaching fellows) should be permitted to marry. They were not, in fact, pioneers in this; the suggestion had first been made in 1766. Heads, and such professors as could afford to forgo fellowship dividends, had long been free to marry; fellows had to wait until their individual colleges took the necessary decision to relax the requirement of celibacy. Thus, although the first married fellow is recorded as early as 1861, it was not until the 1880s that the opportunity became general. The homogeneous style of architecture of many of the residential streets to the east and north of central Cambridge bears witness to the increasing need for the accommodation of wives and children in the last decade of the nineteenth century. The inevitable corollary was that, as more and more fellows started to live outside college, common rooms gradually became less frequented of an evening and an intimate knowledge of college affairs less general. While in many colleges fellows continued to dine regularly, some were nonetheless to have to introduce rotas of fellows who were to spend the night in college, and two houses for married fellows were built within the precincts of Jesus College in 1885, so as to ensure that some control other than the master's might be exercised over the nightly boisterousness of the young.

The social life of the university outside college walls also changed. Early in the nineteenth century there was one social circle of the Heads and their wives, and another, only sporadically overlapping, of the professors and their wives. There were also a few fellows who, though unmarried, were nonetheless essentially domesticated, like Joseph Romilly, fellow of Trinity and, from 1832 to 1862, registrary, who lived at home with his sisters and had a foot in both camps. As matrimony became general the fragile edifices of the academic hierarchy tended to crumble over domestic dinner tables.

It was also inevitable that, as academic specialisation increased, so too did mobility and the consequent desire of individuals for national and international recognition. To this end the Council had prompted the Statutory Commissioners to introduce statutes for doctorates in science and in letters, to be awarded on the basis of published works, and a differentiation of doctoral gowns was devised.[11] Naturally the older men, both those still in Cambridge and those who had taken posts elsewhere, saw themselves as the most distinguished representatives of their chosen fields, and many of them applied for the new degrees and could not but be appraised by their juniors, who, by and large, took a lenient view of outmoded learning. The eminent rapidly acquired remarkable skill in reporting on candidates, as Richard Jebb:

> Mr Verrall's editions of the *Medea* and the *Septem contra Thebas* clearly constitute, in my opinion, a sufficient ground for granting him the Degree of Doctor in Letters. Both these books may be regarded as valuable additions to the literature of their subjects. They are marked by learning, scholarship, and literary skill. They are also distinguished by a verbal ingenuity which is often most striking. This ingenuity is frequently exercised, as it seems to me, at the expense of sober judgment, and of a due regard for what is probable, or even conceivable, in literature and in language. But it contributes to give Mr Verrall's work what might perhaps be named as its peculiar merit, – a certain intellectual freshness, which is stimulating and suggestive, even when the particular subtleties which are laid before us fail to win our belief. It may be noticed that in the *Medea* the editor's acuteness is chiefly concerned with amending the text, and in the *Septem*, with showing how the traditional text can be defended by a new interpretation; and the same kind of ingenuity is shown in both processes. Its characteristic is that it deals more with the word than with the sentence or context as illustrated by the spirit of Greek idiom. Hence the general impression which we receive is sometimes one that surprises or interests us rather than persuades. A modern mind, of much acumen, and richly endowed with the gifts of the advocate, seems to treat the material with more keenness, perhaps, than sympathy; yet with unquestionable power; and therefore with an instructiveness of the larger sort; because, by its qualities and by their defects, it makes us think wherein the antique differs from the modern; and so helps us to appreciate the antique better. Again, this αὐθάδεια [wilfulness] of subtlety sometimes hits the mark, or suggests

[11] The Council had, in fact, also expressed a wish for statutes for a B.Sc. and an M.Sc., but in this they did not prevail.

the right way; and then the gain is direct. There can be no sort of doubt, I venture to think, about this Degree.

In the following year Verrall was to dedicate to Jebb his edition of the *Agamemnon*, as unconsulted now as his *Medea* and his *Septem contra Thebas*; but on his election in 1911 as first Edward VII Professor of English his lectures were widely relished as star performances.

As the university began to feel that it had to a large extent put its own house in order, it ventured to look over its walls and to examine the condition of those who were, or should have been, clamouring to get in. They fell into three main groups: those who could not afford to come; those who were too ill-prepared to come; and finally those who were forbidden to come, viz. Roman Catholics and women.[12]

The days when sizars had maintained themselves in colleges by acting as servants were long since past: their status, but also their living costs, had increased, and although some argued that college fees were not in fact exorbitant there was some force in the retort that, even granting as much, a genuinely poor student could not compete with the life-style normal to college students and that social pressure on him to conform with it might well prove disastrous. The answer seemed to lie in some new kind of institution which would cater for him and his kind alone and it was with a view to meeting this need that, after the university's objections had deterred the commissioners from making the same allowance at Cambridge as at Oxford for a class of 'non-collegiate' students in the 1850s, a Bill was introduced in Parliament and, after the university's objections had been answered, enacted in 1869 providing for a 'Censor', with the general duties of a tutor, and a Board for Non-Collegiate Students. The university did not react generously, but grudgingly bound itself to guarantee any deficit in the accounts of the board to a maximum of £100 per annum. In the event they were called upon for only £38, all in the first two years. This was the more remarkable as the scheme in fact ran into all the problems which the feeble-hearted had envisaged: the students led lonely lives, scattered in lodgings about the town, but with the inconvenience of having to sign an attendance register five times a week. Accounts of attempts to foster some *esprit de corps* by hiring rooms

[12] For the nature of the bar on Roman Catholics, see below, p. 174.

at 31 Trumpington Street where the men could meet, and by encouraging the formation of sporting clubs and a debating society, are redolent of that forced jollity which so ill conceals grim desperation. Non-collegiate students who did manifest ability promptly turned collegiate: those who had more than average abilities, whether academic or sporting, were lured to the more congenial communities of the colleges by offers of scholarships or exhibitions; those who could scrape together the cash braced themselves to pay college fees. There was indeed a danger that those who remained would be seen as the rump of the student body. The board suggested a change of name to something less depressingly negative, but no one seemed to care.

Censors and board nevertheless persevered. By 1887, with the help of a loan of £1,000 from the university, they were in a position to buy the freeholds of numbers 31 and 32 Trumpington Street. Further sums, some from the pockets of the first three Censors themselves, were then scraped together to pay for the necessary reconstruction work, and in October 1892 the opening of Fitzwilliam House was celebrated with a grand dinner. William Fiddian Reddaway, the fourth Censor, by his energy, determination and faith succeeded not only in raising the spirits and the pride of 'his' students but also in equipping them with a playing-field (in 1908) and a chapel (in 1913) as well as further residential accommodation on and near the site. Fitzwilliam House set off on what was to prove a long trail leading to full collegiate status.

The failure of two of the next three such attempts may be attributed partly to the eccentricities of their progenitors. In 1873 Joseph Brereton, an inveterate founder of schools, set up County College, on the premises now occupied by Homerton College, for students who were to be younger than most undergraduates and subjected to a discipline more appropriate to schoolboys. It soon changed its name to Cavendish College, in acknowledgement of a sizeable contribution by the chancellor, the duke of Devonshire, but few other substantial benefactions were found and in 1892 it collapsed, as Brereton's foundations were apt to, from lack of funds. In 1884 a scarcely less eccentric individual, William Ayerst, set up an eponymous hostel originally near Parker's Piece. It was ostensibly a godly foundation, but strict discipline was not seen to be observed there and Ayerst was frequently charged with failure to observe the spirit of the statute for hostel keepers. He finally moved his establishment into premises on Mount Pleasant just in time to close down, in 1896, again for lack of funds.

Both of these ventures, aiming to cater for the widely bruited needs of poorer students, might perhaps, under judicious management, have hoped for support from within the university. The foundation of Selwyn, in 1882, an establishment emphatically identified with the Church of England and modelled on Keble College, Oxford, with the implicit aim of providing for impoverished ordinands, and with a master bound to be in holy orders, aroused vigorous protests from those who had so recently fought for the abolition of religious tests. By the same token it was no doubt welcome to many of those who had fought for their retention. Be that as it may, in June 1882 the Senate approved a grace which established a new status for public hostels, whose students were all to reside on the premises, but were otherwise on the same footing as other undergraduates; the principal, however, was not to rank as a head of house and so be eligible to the vice-chancellorship. Selwyn opened its doors in October 1882 and in February following achieved official recognition as a public hostel, a status which it enjoyed until promoted to the category of 'Approved Foundation' concocted in the statutes of 1926 and very marginally mitigating the restrictions as to residence.

Selwyn was not the only source of comfort to those who deplored the loosening of the formal bonds between the university and the church in England. In January 1881, in Cambridge but independently of the university, Ridley Hall and the Clergy Training School, now Westcott House, had opened their doors to their first students, graduates seeking ordination within the established church. The Clergy Training School, founded largely by the efforts of Professors Lightfoot and Westcott, who had, after initial co-operation, dissociated themselves from the 'Ridleians' because they found their doctrinal basis too narrow, was the more intimately associated with the university in practice as its Council included all the divinity professors being clergymen of the Church of England. Earlier in their foundations, but to appear later on the Cambridge scene, were Cheshunt College, originally founded by Lady Huntingdon and established in Breconshire as a training college for six students expelled for Methodism from St Edmund Hall, Oxford, and their successors, and Westminster College, a Presbyterian foundation of 1844, rootless until it acquired a house in London in 1864. Cheshunt moved from Brecon to Cheshunt in Hertfordshire in 1792, and to Cambridge in 1906, its constitution no longer tying it to a single denomination. Westminster College arrived in Cambridge in 1899 thanks to the munificence of those remarkable twins Mrs Gibson and Mrs Lewis (the 'Giblews'), the discoverers in 1892 of the Sinai palimpsest of the Old Testament.

Just as the churches were looking for ways of making use of the universities' interest and facilities, so too were school-teachers seeking to improve their professional standing. This was to be achieved in two ways: a system of public examination which would crown the teachers' efforts by the award of school certificates to their pupils and the creation of training courses carrying recognised qualifications for the teachers themselves. The first of these aims had been addressed since 1857 when a syndicate was established to arrange examinations for school-children, but both aims were later to converge to some extent in what was soon to become known as the University Extension Movement, set up to provide lectures in centres all over the country and, in due course, to award its own certificates.

Interest in Cambridge in the training of teachers centred on the flamboyant, petulant and in many ways ludicrous figure of Oscar Browning, previously a master at Eton, where he had come under a shadow, partly on suspicion of having too close an association with the young George Nathaniel Curzon. Browning, however, was always a toady, and no precise accusations were laid against him, although his departure from Eton was not voluntary. Despite the endless anecdotes about Browning's social antics in King's he had proved on his return to Cambridge in 1876 to be an effective gadfly in promoting the two causes which he particularly advocated: the recognition of history as an academic discipline and the provision in Cambridge of a training college for teachers. The year 1879 saw the establishment of the Teachers' Training Syndicate, with Browning as secretary, and with the task of arranging lectures and examinations for student teachers, and from 1891, with the foundation of the Day Training College, teachers' training under the aegis of the university was offered both to primary and to secondary teachers from outside the university, and as a supplementary course for those who had already completed or were still studying for the BA. After Browning had been persuaded to resign from the training college and, moreover, to stop meddling with it, teachers' training for men flourished in Cambridge. Women were by now served by the independent Women's Training College, established in 1885, and admirably served by its first principal, Elizabeth Phillips Hughes of Newnham, fresh from the only first class in Moral Sciences in 1884 and a second in History the following year. The college was later to honour her by changing its undoubtedly unromantic name to Hughes Hall.

The existing schemes for school examinations and new proposals for extension lectures were adopted with enthusiasm by a young fellow of Trinity, James Stuart, later to be Cambridge's first professor of mechanism and applied mechanics, and MP successively for Hackney, for Hoxton and for Sunderland. His energy was prodigious in organising memorials and conferences, and his financial contributions to the success of the Local Lectures Syndicate were considerable. Stuart's aims for university extension were supported by his wife, Laura Colman, whom he married in 1878. She and her sister, pillars of Quaker philanthropy financed by mustard, had long been active in reforming movements, but by the time of his marriage Stuart had been obliged, through ill health, to resign the secretaryship of the syndicate and, in spite of his continued support, its early years were years of struggle. Both the scheme for school examinations and the scheme for local lectures were alternately forwarded and complicated by negotiations with Oxford, where precisely similar schemes were afoot. From the successful centres for local lectures organised from Cambridge were to arise the university colleges of Sheffield, Liverpool and Nottingham and support was also offered to the existing colleges at Newcastle and Birmingham. From these beginnings evolved the Board of Extra-Mural Studies, now the Board of Continuing Education.

The passage of Roman Catholics and, especially, of women was to be less smooth. So far as the university was concerned catholics had, along with dissenters, been admissible as members and as potential graduates (but not as officers) since 1856. From 1870 religious tests had been confined only to heads of houses and graduates in theology. No catholics, however, had arrived, the reason being that a rescript emanating from the congregation *de propaganda fide* in 1867 had, without actually forbidding attendance at protestant universities, objected to it on moral grounds which could scarcely be ignored. The challenge was taken up by Baron Anatole von Hügel, who had been brought to Cambridge in 1883 by the Cambridge Antiquarian Society when it was constrained to follow the example of the Philosophical Society by handing over its collections to the university. Von Hügel was to be the curator of the resultant Museum of Ethnology[13] and to labour patiently for the opening of Cambridge to his fellow catholics. Having secured the backing of the duke of Norfolk and the support of a number of members of the university, notable among them Henry Jackson, Regius Professor of Greek from 1906 and most knowing of dons, he succeeded, albeit not at the first attempt, in persuading the university to allow him in 1896 to open (at the expense of the duke) a house in Cambridge for catholic students from St Edmund's College, Old Hall, at Ware, under the tutelage of their vice-president Fr Nolan. (To those who uttered shrill cries about seminaries, Jackson modestly enquired how then Selwyn should be defined.) An attempt to have what was soon known as St Edmund's House adopted as a public hostel (like Selwyn) within the university was rejected by 471 votes to 218 in 1898. In the event this proved less than a disaster since the application would have bound the institution to articles of association that would seriously have cramped its style. As it was, the students came under the aegis of the Non-Collegiate Students Board and their premises were recognised by the Lodging Houses Syndicate. The chosen house was the one lately vacated as Ayerst Hostel, and it is sad to relate that von Hügel arrived to take possession just too late to prevent the defacement by a group of absurd evangelicals of the legend 'to the glory of God' above the door. Henceforth the serious struggles of the house were to be with the more conservative elements of the catholic hierarchy.

For full admission to the university women were to wait much longer, until 1948, and the prospect of opening the door for them, even a crack, was viewed with the wildest terror. The first positive approaches to the university were made in 1863 by Miss Emily Davies with a proposal, canvassed among the local centres, that the university's local examinations should be open to girls. The university went so far as to allow

[13] From 1913 renamed 'the Museum of Archaeology and of Ethnology', now 'of Archaeology and Anthropology'.

that the examiners might, in a private capacity, mark along with the boys' papers any submitted from girls' schools. Eighty-three candidates were found ready for the ordeal and were found wanting, relative to the boys, only in arithmetic. Thus encouraged, Miss Davies and her allies assembled a petition with some 1,200 signatures requesting that the Cambridge Local Examinations be formally opened to girls. A syndicate was duly assembled to consider the proposition and its report, in favour of it, was accepted by fifty-five votes to fifty-one. In the years immediately following, the Schools Inquiry Commission brought to the attention of the nation the generally deplorable level of education for girls, while Miss Davies, with her allies in the National Association for the Promotion of Social Science, set up numerous committees thoughout the country to press for the establishment of a college for women, and by 1869 the first five students were admitted to what was later to be Girton College but was, for the time being, Benslow House at Hitchin. The choice of Hitchin was dictated by Miss Davies's uncertainty as to whether her cause was likelier to succeed in Cambridge or in London.

Meanwhile, in the north of England Miss Anne Jemima Clough, sister of the poet Arthur Hugh Clough, set about organising lectures for girls in the larger cities. On the advice of Mrs Josephine Butler she selected as her itinerant lecturer James Stuart, soon to be Cambridge's chief proponent of the Extension Lecture, whose successful fulfilment of the task led to the formation of the North of England Council for Promoting the Higher Education of Women. At its first meeting, in 1867, the Council gave vocal support to Miss Davies's proposed college; by 1868 it had prepared, aided and abetted by Henry Jackson, Henry Sidgwick and other Cambridge well-wishers, a petition that the university institute an advanced examination for girls of eighteen or so years of age. Mrs Butler carried the petition to Cambridge and easily disarmed most of the opposition. A syndicate soon reported in favour of the idea and so successful were they that within two years the examinations were open to boys also. Encouraged by these successes, Henry Sidgwick in 1871 acquired and furnished number 74 Regent Street and installed there Miss Clough and the first five students of what was to become Newnham College. In 1873 Miss Davies and her flock were ready to move to their imposing buildings at Girton; the Newnhamites, after a succession of temporary expedients, settled on their present site in 1875.

37. Girton College Fire Brigade, 1887.

The women who fought so hard for admission to higher education were themselves divided as to the best tactics. Miss Davies of Girton was inclined to batter at the door, Miss Clough of Newnham to tap persistently; the one aiming from the first for a status for women precisely on a par with that for men, the other willing for forgo what she saw as matters indifferent in order to achieve the goal of education. Students of Girton were to sit precisely the same examinations as the men; Newnhamites could proceed to the tripos examinations as soon as they were formally opened to women, with little real opposition, in 1881 without having first submitted to the Previous Examination. Initially those who had fought inside the walls for the admission of women continued their services by providing, and persuading their friends to provide, lectures specifically for them; gradually, however, university lecturers and professors consented to their attendance at their normal lectures, even if, like

Sir Arthur Quiller-Couch, they habitually included them in the general salutation of 'Gentlemen'.

Gradually, also, and more gradually at Girton than at Newnham, the women were able to forsake the laboratories which they had had to provide for themselves and to join their fellow students in the university laboratories. Attempts to admit them to full membership of the university in 1887 and 1897 were, however, voted out (and in 1897 followed by a deplorable assault on the gate of Newnham). Not much dismayed, women continued to pursue their studies, sometimes with notable success. When Agnata Ramsay, of Girton, was awarded marks above the Senior Classic of 1887, *Punch*, usually hostile to the cause, printed a full-page complimentary cartoon; H. M. Butler, Master of Trinity, on the other hand, a consistent proponent of the admission of women, now aged fifty-five and later to become the very picture of a superannuated cherub, promptly married her. In 1890 Philippa Fawcett of Newnham was above the Senior Wrangler. The results of the Mathematical Tripos were, by tradition, read aloud, men first, then women, great excitement still attending the announcement of the name of the Senior Wrangler. George Forrest Browne, Senior Proctor at the time, has left a vivid account of the confusion of the reader of the list, accustomed to announcing women's positions as, say, 'between the fifteenth and the sixteenth wrangler', of the obvious solution proposed – 'above the Senior Wrangler' – and of the pandemonium that ensued. The friends of the man who was Senior Wrangler of that year in name alone still spoke many years later of their (and his) emotions.

The appearance of women students, few and closeted as they were, had little impact on the social life of the average undergraduate. This, from much earlier in the century, had been centred rather on oars, and bats and boots. The first cricket match between the two universities was played in 1827, and the first boat race rowed in 1829. Number four in the easily triumphant Oxford boat was Charles Wordsworth of Christ Church, and he it was also who, taking seven Cambridge wickets in 1827, ensured an easy victory for Oxford. Cricket became an annual fixture from 1838, the boat race not until 1856. Other games were to follow: rackets in 1855, real tennis in 1859, shooting in 1862, athletics in 1864, rugby football in 1872, chess in 1873, bicycling and soccer in 1874, polo and golf in 1878 and so on. Billiards, in 1860, was early in the field, and met with less enthusiastic support

38. 'Honour to Agnata Frances Ramsay' – Senior Classic in all but name. Cartoon from *Punch*, of 2 July 1887.

from those in authority than rowing and the other sports fostered at the public schools in a strong tradition of muscular Christianity. In these, encouraged, sometimes to a ludicrous extent, by Heads and fellows, every college had its teams and its boats. Large green spaces were bought up as playing fields (except by Jesus, which already occupied one), and the river was rapidly bordered by the ranks of college boathouses. Boat clubs had been founded at Trinity and St John's in 1825. College played against college all the year round; dons too took to, or failed to forsake, the river. The advent of Prince Albert Victor at Cambridge precipitated the addition of hockey to the canon, although he never got his 'blue'. An agreeable custom arose whereby the 'lab. boys' challenged their professors to an annual cricket match.

Encounters on playing fields and in boats must have proved the more alluring at a time when accommodation in colleges could no longer keep

39. Consternation at the imminent extinction of the greater part of the Downing student body, from *Scrawls* by 'XIT', 1881.

pace with the rising numbers of students (see Figure 2), many of whom now lived in small groups or solitarily in lodgings licensed by the university. The use of lodging houses, later often owned by colleges, goes back to the late eighteenth century. Registers of lodgings survive from the 1840s and it soon became the custom for printed lists, first of applicants for lodging-house licences, and then of those actually licensed, to be issued at regular intervals. Strict rules for lodging-house keepers were drawn up, not least that they were to report first thing in the morning the names of any young gentlemen who had not returned to their lodgings by the prescribed hour. The vice-chancellor's licence to let rooms was, however, eagerly sought by many who found the extra income useful and the hours compatible with other work in the colleges or elsewhere.

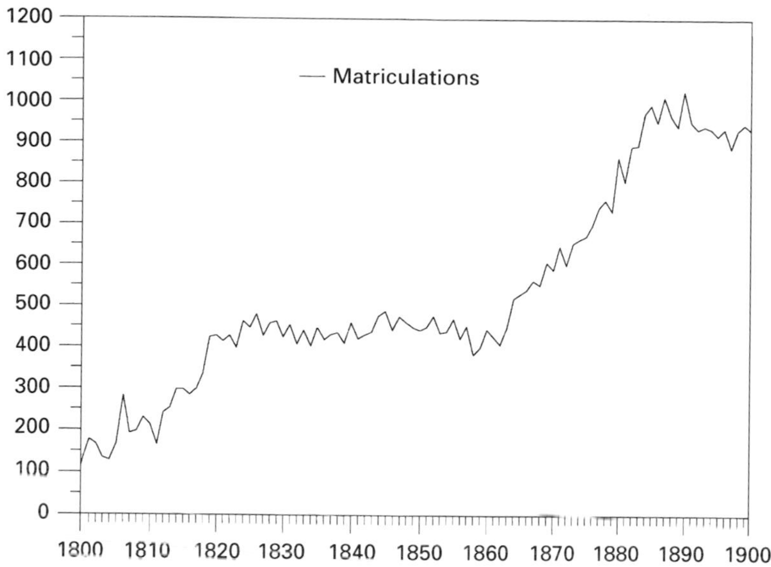

Figure 2. Matriculations 1800–1900

The syndicate set up to consider the memorial submitted by the town authorities to the Royal Commission[14] had failed in its negotiations and, at the suggestion of Lord Palmerston, previously MP for the university, and now Home Secretary, Sir John Patteson was appointed in 1855 to arbitrate on the matters in dispute, the very same matters which had been in dispute from at least the fourteenth century. His award, which was embodied in an Act of Parliament in the following year, was based on a correspondingly vast body of evidence submitted by both parties and addressed both the symbols and the realities of the relative standing of the two corporations. That mighty bugbear to the town, the Magna Congregatio or Black Assembly,[15] which had been imprudently revived by the obdurate Dr Wood, Master of St John's, in 1817 was finally laid to rest. College buildings, excluding their chapels and libraries, and university buildings, with the exceptions of the Senate House, the University Library, museums, laboratories and lecture rooms, were in future

[14] See note 8 above.
[15] See p. 9.

to be liable to parochial rates, though this burden was partly offset by a reduction of the university's contribution to the paving, lighting and cleansing of the town from two-fifths to one-quarter of the total.

With respect to trade, the university's supervision of weights and measures, and of markets and fairs was abolished; alehouses were no longer to be licensed by the vice-chancellor, although he might appeal to the magistrates for the revocation of the licences of those incurring his displeasure. The right to issue wine-licences was, however, retained, as was, to the greater vexation of the town, the university's power to discommune tradesmen for allowing excessive credit to undergraduates and for conniving with them to flout university regulations. The sanction of discommuning was seen as essential for the protection of the morals as well as the pockets of students, and the argument served also for the retention of the vice-chancellor's right to license theatres in the town and its suburbs; other occasional entertainments were to be licensed jointly by him and by the mayor. The vice-chancellor's court, which had long since fallen into disuse, was formally deprived of its jurisdiction in cases where only one party was a member of the university. The Watch Committee to supervise the policing of the town was to have five representatives of the university to nine of the town, under the chairmanship of the mayor. Finally, to the indignation of many on the part of the town, the proctors' right to arrest prostitutes remained inviolate.

Suspected prostitutes, once taken in charge by the proctors, were subject to committal by the vice-chancellor, after the most cursory and informal examination, to the Spinning House, usually for a matter of days rather than weeks. The conditions there, even after the improvements instigated under Palmerston in the 1850s, were often very bleak, although some attempt was made to provide medical treatment when necessary. Some proctors elected to exercise their powers more rigorously than others, but it is a little surprising that, notwithstanding a number of challenges and much resort to counsel's opinion in the second half of the century, what was widely regarded as a rule of summary and arbitrary power remained in force until the celebrated cases of Jane Elsden in 1891 and of Daisy Hopkins in 1894 attracted a degree of national attention of a kind that the university authorities can hardly have savoured. Jane Elsden's solicitor at the Assizes failed to prove that his client, who was charged with prison-breaking, had been subject to wrongful arrest, and

Daisy Hopkins, though she won her case on a technicality, failed in a subsequent attempt to sue the university authorities for wrongful imprisonment. Rather than incur any further publicity, and perhaps recognising some justice in at least the less hysterical criticisms levelled at it, the university, after the Hopkins case, agreed voluntarily in 1894 to an Act abolishing its ancient right to arrest and expel 'lewd women' and, in the same breath, its right to license theatres. There was popular rejoicing that the respectable women of Cambridge could now walk the streets without fear of proctorial harassment. That said, a perusal of the three stout volumes recording committals to the Spinning House from 1823 to 1894 reveals striking testimony of the temptations offered by the presence of so many young men to young women from the surrounding countryside with no very brilliant prospects of lawful employment.

Much though the university had been exercised from the 1860s by the question of the admission of women, a matter of far more interest to its constituency at large (i.e. the MAs in the ranks of the Senate) was the question of 'compulsory Greek': should it be possible for a man to graduate without having attained that modicum of Greek which was necessary to pass the Previous Examination? The question was raised in 1871 and the abolition finally carried in 1916. The huge numbers of votes cast on either side in the course of the struggle, reaching their zenith in the massive 1,559 to 1,052 in 1905, well reflect the extent to which the university was still seen by its past, and many of its present, members as an institution feeding and fed by the major public schools with the prime function of educating 'gentlemen' (defined by a circular argument as the products of these same schools) and the clergy, with their need to study the New Testament in Greek. They also demonstrate the force of the opposition. The vicious circle whereby the schools shaped their curriculum to meet the university's requirements, and the university raised its requirements to meet the attainments of boys from successful schools was one which proved extremely hard to break. Some indeed would doubt whether it has yet been achieved.

Meanwhile the reforming process which was enabling the university to take its place among the more active universities in Europe was paralleled by the increasingly high profile assumed by its roving ambassador, the University Press. The early adoption of the stereotype process, greatly facilitating the economic production of multiple issues of popular texts, had enabled Cambridge to produce the first stereotype Bible, and this just as the demand for a world-wide circulation was being fostered by the British and Foreign Bible Society and the Society for the Propagation of Christian Knowledge. However, such was the constitution of the Press and such the expenditure on buildings and on machinery that it was some years before any financial benefit was realised. Printers came and went. J. W. Parker, printer from 1836 to 1854, oversaw the introduction of steam presses, and the production of a great many books by Cambridge authors, both in the arts and the sciences, which were to serve as standard texts, but it was open to him, whenever he saw fit, to choose to use the Press to publish works not for the Press Syndicate but on his own account, just as his early predecessors had done. The problems arising from such an arrangement were exposed in the replies to the commissioners and from 1854, almost until the end of the century, the Press was run by a partnership between the university and one or more members of the Clay family, still active as printers. The copious records surviving from these decades show that the workings of both the printing and publishing sides of the business were now fully accessible to the Syndics, but as the volume of business and the speed of communications increased, it was inevitable that executive decisions had frequently to be made on the spot by whichever Clay was in the office rather than by the Syndics. A proliferation of Sub-Syndicates appointed to handle specific items, whether of business or of specific types of books, proved inadequate as a check, and in December 1891, with a formal acknowledgement of the long service to the Press of the Clay family and with the acquiescence of the current representative, the university for the first time moved to take the Press fully under its own control by appointing one of their own number, R. T. Wright, as full-time secretary to the Syndics.

The University Library similarly evolved during this period into one recognisably a forebear of the national, and indeed international, institution which it is today. As recounted in the previous chapter, the site was, after many delays, greatly expanded by the erection behind the Senate House of the Cockerell Building, all that remained of a grandiose plan for a new building to cover both the old and the new sites. As hopes that the university would ever be able to afford anything on the scale of Cockerell's original proposal evaporated, new ranges were built in

1864–8 and 1890–1 on the site of the Old Court of King's College, acquired to that end in 1829. Thanks to the noble bequest from John Manistre of the reversion of a trust of £5,000, John Lodge, Librarian from 1828 to 1845, had been an active purchaser both at book sales, notably those of J. F. van de Velde, University Librarian of Louvain, in 1833, and of Richard Heber in 1834, and from the major London suppliers of continental and scientific books. Under his successor, Joseph Power, Librarian from 1845 to 1864, there appeared the first volumes of the printed catalogue of the Library's manuscripts and also a catalogue of printed books in the still familiar form of slips pasted into large volumes and allowing space for additions. Power's successor, J. E. B. Mayor, whose tempestuous term of office terminated after three years, employed his unquestioned irascibility and energy to good, if uncomfortable, effect both in modernising the administration of the Library and in defending it against those, some of them Syndics, who sought to restrict its funds. In Henry Bradshaw (1867–86) the Library was blessed with a scholar willing and able to acquire many notable additions to the stock of rare books, sometimes at his own expense, and one whose contributions to the science of bibliography, still valuable today, greatly increased both the international standing of the Library and knowledge of its holdings.

While the proliferation of laboratories took place largely on two sites hidden from the casual passer-by, other additions to the Cambridge scene made a decided impact on the streetscape, as for example the Divinity School in St John's Street with its statues commemorating its heroic past erected in 1877. Elsewhere Sir Alfred Waterhouse was encouraged to indulge in further Gothic posturing, most visibly with his grandiose addition to Gonville and Caius in strange juxtaposition to the Senate House. At the same time enterprising colleges developed their land surrounding the centre of the town with streets of residential accommodation, both for the increasing number of college and university employees and for their married fellows. The street names indicate the builders: Glisson, Harvey, Guest and Willis of Gonville and Caius, Mawson and Tenison of Corpus Christi as, later, Bentley, Porson and Newton of Trinity, to name but a few.

Many students still left Cambridge without an honours degree, some of them to attain academic distinction in later life, having as undergraduates pursued subjects available as components of the ordinary degree but as yet without triposes of their own.[16] As subjects proliferated to produce a far larger variety of academic groupings within colleges, so clubs were founded to foster bonds of common interest outside the curriculum, whether in music, drama, politics, literature, or, above all, in sports. The performing arts, however, were not far behind, with the foundation of the Cambridge University Musical Society in 1843–4, of the Amateur Dramatic Club in 1851, the production of the first Greek play in 1882, performances by Footlights from 1883 and by the Marlowe Society from 1907. Gradually it became harder, though never impossible, to devote three years to total idleness both mental and physical.

[16] Between 1851 and 1906 44.4 per cent of the men took honours degrees, 32.9 per cent took pass degrees and 22.7 per cent none at all.

40. The passing of the old order: the Master of Peterhouse (Sir A. W. Ward, 1837–1924), wearing a mourning rosette on his square for the funeral of Dr Atkinson, the only Master of Clare elected between the battle of Waterloo (1815) and the first battle of Ypres (1915), greets the Master of Trinity (Dr H. M. Butler, 1833–1918) outside the Senate House.

6

Cambridge since the First World War

The cheerfully noisy, crowded colleges of the early twentieth century were reduced, by the outbreak of the First World War, to echoing shadows of their former selves with fewer than half the usual number of men in residence in October 1914. Then their place was taken by soldiers, some billeted in colleges, others encamped in the fields around the town. Rupert Brooke expressed and personified the romantic idealism of so many who were to die in the trenches, while W. H. R. Rivers, Director of the newly established Psychological Laboratory, won golden opinions for his treatment of the shell-shocked and the disillusioned. Senior officers dined at high tables; Nevile's Court at Trinity was transformed into a field hospital later transferred to King's and Clare cricket ground, where the University Library now stands. Special short courses were devised, some of them practical, others makeshift substitutes for the normal courses. College war memorials record the appalling tally of the dead, not all of them British. Of those who came up after the war many had seen active service; they were anxious to get their degrees and be gone. A gulf divided them from the boys fresh from school. Others, on the other hand, made serious attempts to break all previous records for rowdiness in an attempt to blot out the horrors of their war years.

The task of carrying on the business of the university and of making necessary decisions had during these years devolved more and more on the full-time administrators, the registrary and the Secretary of the Financial Board, obliging them to devise the machinery to cope with their increasing work-load. The registrary was John Neville Keynes, a distinguished logician and father of John Maynard Keynes, the economist. When the university filled up again after the war the machinery stayed in place; from now on the university was to have a 'civil service' recognised in the new statutes of 1926.

Many Cambridge scientists, although far fewer than were to be called upon in the Second War, had been involved in war work. The government began to look at the universities with new eyes. At the same time the scientists, even in Cambridge with its strong tradition of 'string and sealing wax', found themselves more and more hampered in their research by the want of equipment beyond the means of the university. In spite of warning cries about compromising academic freedom the university had had to look more and more to the government for funding both for equipment and for stipends. Agriculture, since 1893, and forestry, since 1907, had always been dependent on state funding. They were not, however, regarded as subjects central to the university, and without that funding would probably not have been provided at all. The great debate as between the necessity of seeking financial support from the state and the threat to academic freedom which this might entail was prompted by the proposal of the Special Board for Medicine to seek a grant from the Board of Education, a proposal finally approved in March 1914. It is hard to see how, in practical terms, it could have been long resisted. In 1919 the University Grants Committee was set up to advise the government on the distribution of parliamentary grants to universities. These had hitherto been *ad hoc*, but even when the Secretary of the UGC was to announce, in April 1922, that Cambridge's grant would hitherto be on a more permanent footing, the financial position of the university remained grave.

Developments of this kind were the concern of the Oxford and Cambridge Commission set up in November 1919 (often known, after its chairman, as the Asquith Commission) and were embodied in the new statutes issued by their successors, the Statutory Commissioners, in 1926. Several of these statutes, according to a now familiar pattern, reflected proposals which the university had considered, but not adopted, in earlier years. The Special Board for Economics had, for example, in 1920 unsuccessfully proposed that all their students' fees, previously allotted course for course, should be paid into a single fund from which lecturers should be paid; a scheme which would have given the faculty greater control over the structure of its courses. The commissioners proposed just such a scheme, university-wide, with the further motive of ensuring, with the help of Treasury contributions to pensions, that the university would be able to offer more attractive stipends and so to retain the services of the most able teachers and, by releasing them from an excessive burden of college teaching, to allow them time for research. With a view to the integration of college and university life, or at least as a small rampart against their disintegration, a system of reserved fellowships was devised, with certain university posts carrying automatic entitlement to fellowships at certain colleges. The Cambridge colleges on this occasion proved more willing to forgo their control of teaching than those of Oxford, where university teachers continued and continue to be appointed very largely by colleges, with the result that at Cambridge many university teachers were to be left without fellowships. University teaching posts were to be open to women, but membership of the university was not.

Alterations were also made to the constitutions of the central administrative bodies, the Council of the Senate, the General Board and the Financial Board, streamlining them and, as a consequence, tending to make them more remote. The registrary was at last to receive some supporting staff. One of the assistant registraries was designated Secretary of the General Board[1] and the office of Treasurer was established. As for the mass of senior members, the merging of the Regent and Non-Regent Houses effected by the commissioners of 1856 was virtually reversed: the Regent House, consisting of all university teaching and administrative officers, all members of faculties and all fellows of colleges, was alone to have the responsibility for approving graces and for electing to the central bodies. The intention of the commissioners that the Regent House should consist only of those actually engaged in the day-to-day running of the university was to be undermined by the courteous custom of faculties of extending membership to those who had retired. The title of 'Senate' was henceforth reserved for the whole body of MAs who wished to keep their names on the college books, and its powers were limited to a very few ritual activities, such as the election of the chancellor and the High Steward and approving the graces for addresses to the crown and to other universities. In theory

[1] 'Secretary General of the Faculties' from 1933.

they had also a part to play in the event of the Regent House being divided in the framing of statutes, but this theory was never put to the test.

The greater part of the report of the Asquith Commissioners was, according to their brief, concerned with matters financial and in particular with investigating college endowments in order to ensure that as much money as possible was being made available to endow scholarships to assist the less wealthy. To this endeavour we are indebted for the curiously obscure form in which college accounts are statutorily drawn up, designed as it is not to reveal the overall financial position but rather to show the allocation of resources between different internal funds statutorily defined as to the uses to which they may be put. A less complicated decision was that in future the award of scholarship emoluments should be subject to a means test. An entrance examination was now made compulsory on all colleges, and nothing could be done to escape the fact that those candidates whose parents had been able to afford expensive schooling of the sort that closely followed, if it did not indeed provoke, an ever-rising standard in the examinations, would naturally tend to perform better in them than those from less privileged backgrounds, and this notwithstanding the elimination of compulsory Greek from the Previous Examination at the sixth attempt in 1919.[2] Scholarships, therefore, continued to be awarded very largely to the products of the public schools, but their recipients, if of ample means, now enjoyed only such subsidiary privileges as a better choice of rooms and a distinctive gown, while the cash was reserved for more deserving cases. Not much more deserving, however. The cost of a Cambridge education remained very high, and even had they so wished it would scarcely have been possible for most colleges to offer substantial numbers of 'free' places to such students of modest means as could overcome the hurdle of the entrance examination. Part of the answer was found in the realisation over the years of a scheme propounded at this time for the support of students by external funds: state scholarships and local authority grants. Meanwhile the colleges, in unstable groupings, vied

[2] The first attempt had been in 1873, and the proposal was raised, only to fail again, in 1880, 1891, 1905 and 1906.

with one another, and especially with Oxford, so to time their entrance examinations as to capture the 'best' candidates.

The anomalous position of women was one on which the commissioners had offered words but no radical statutes. A grace to admit women to the titles of degrees had been defeated in 1897 by 1,707 votes to 661; in 1916 they had been admitted to the examinations for the MB from which they had previously been excluded. Oxford had admitted women to all degrees in 1920,[3] but when the matter was again raised in Cambridge, under the shadow of the commission, hopes were once more to be dashed. A syndicate produced two alternative reports. One, Report B, proposing a separate women's university, was easily defeated by 146 votes to 50, the low totals reflecting the perceived implausibility of the scheme. Report A, proposing full membership of the university, was catastrophically defeated by 904 votes to 712. The Council was embarrassed, but not deterred, and promptly prepared, for a formal vote, draft statutes enacting (1) that, given a limit of five-hundred on the total number of women students, all of whom were to be members of Girton or Newnham or the equivalent and none of whom were to be admitted members of the Senate, women should be admitted to (almost) full membership of the university; or, failing that, that (2) women should be admitted to the titles of degrees. The poll was taken in October 1921 and the recommendation for full membership failed by 694 votes to 908. A clerical member of Corpus gave vent to cries of exultation – 'Now go and tell Girton and Newnham' – taken with great literalness by a mob of undergraduates who proceeded to inflict serious damage on the gates of Newnham. The fall-back proposal succeeded by 1,011 votes to 369, allowing women to supplicate for the right to use the titles of the degrees for which they were qualified. Perhaps the commissioners thought discretion in this instance to be the better part of valour: they left the matter in the hands of the university, and it was not until after the Second World War had once more demonstrated to the country at large, and even to the university, the value of the female work-force that the university was reminded that that was where the matter rested. The report of the syndicate set up in 1947 recommending the admission of women to full membership of the university met no real opposition and the new statutes received

[3] Except for the BD and the DD for which they had to wait until 1935.

the Royal Assent in May 1948 and, being by some oversight undated, took immediate effect. The women on the point of taking their final examinations could expect to graduate fully and in person in June. Gracefully, however, they agreed to defer formal graduation until January 1949: the honour of being the first woman to graduate at Cambridge was reserved for the queen, now (1996) the Queen Mother, who proceeded in person to the degree of Doctor of Laws in October 1948.

It was the establishment of faculty boards, which were henceforth to include a wider representation of those teaching, and the allocation to the boards and to departments of funds more or less at their disposal, which most changed the character of the university after 1926. Some resented the change, regretting the diminished influence of the colleges, and felt, from their place in the humanities, that it was yet another reflection of the increasing dominance of science, which they opposed to culture. The faculties were not long to enjoy control of their own purses. From 1933 all fees were paid into a central fund which, after making disbursements to each faculty and department, committed the remainder to two funds for major developments in arts and science subjects respectively. The government grant at this time made up about half the total income of the university, but with the increase in the number of university teachers, and therefore of stipends, and the high cost of scientific research by the late 1930s, the university was in no affluent state.

It had, however, between the wars managed to attract some sizeable benefactions. In 1919 £210,000 was received from British oil companies to endow the School of Chemistry (enabling it to dislodge engineering to its present site), and from Mr and Mrs Molteno came the endowment for an Institute of Parasitology. The next year saw funds forthcoming from the Council of Scientific and Industrial Research for the building and endowment of the Low Temperature Research Station and this was closely followed by a gift of £165,000 from the trustees of Sir William Dunn for a chair, a readership and an institute of biochemistry. The School of Agriculture was extended, a new School of Pathology built, largely from funds offered by the Rockefeller Foundation. Property was acquired in Lensfield Road for the Scott Polar Research Institute and in Downing Place for the School of Geography. Even the arts subjects benefited when lecture rooms were built for them in Mill Lane in 1933. Most spectacular of all was the offer in 1928 of the International Education

Board (founded by John D. Rockefeller) of no less than £700,000 not only for agriculture and the biological and physical sciences but also for a new University Library on condition that the university raise another £229,000 in addition to the £250,000 which had been amassed by the Cambridge University Association, set up in 1899 to raise the funds so greatly needed by the university in all departments.

For the securing of the Rockefeller benefaction the credit is largely due to Sir Hugh Ker Anderson, Master of Caius, whose skills in negotiation had already been employed as leader of the 1919 Cambridge Commissioners. By June 1930 it was possible for Stanley Baldwin, on his installation as chancellor, to announce that enough money had been raised for the University Press to be able to guarantee the remainder. The Press was investing more shrewdly than it could have guessed: the new University Library, opened in 1934, was, as the largest open-access library in Europe, to act as a magnet for scholars from all over the world and with the other new buildings and departments mentioned above, and with similar developments also in colloid science, in geology, in zoology, physiology and botany Cambridge was at last in a position to claim international status in reality as well as in name.

Buildings, however, are not enough. Geology could trace its academic respectability right back to the election of Adam Sedgwick (totally ignorant of the subject though he had been at the time) in 1818, and the chairs of astronomy had had distinguished occupants for almost as long, but when, for instance, Sir William Pope was persuaded in 1908, rather against his better judgement, to come to Cambridge and assume responsibility for what passed for the School of Chemistry, he had, as he had foreseen, to commit himself to herculean labours to drag it into the twentieth century. Fortunately, perhaps, he was a born tyrant. Not so (Sir) Frederick Gowland Hopkins, a modest man, who had worked his way up the academic ladder from the post of hospital chemist at Guy's in London, became a protégé of Sir Michael Foster, and was over and over again to break new ground in biochemistry, most famously with his discovery of vitamins. Inevitably he attracted a team of fellow workers as devoted as they were to be distinguished.

In the eyes of the world at large, however, the brightest of Cambridge's constellations between the wars was that which twinkled from the Cavendish. Since its endowment by the chancellor, the duke of Devonshire, in 1870 the Cavendish Chair of Experimental Physics had been graced by a series of remarkable men. James Clerk Maxwell, the first holder, with his work on electromagnetic fields, and Lord Rayleigh (1879–84), who was awarded the Nobel prize for a range of achievements including those relating to electrical measurement and whose contributions to the Cavendish included substantial financial ones, had been succeeded by J. J. Thomson, the discoverer of the electron, elected to the chair in 1884, while still in his twenties, and to the Mastership of Trinity in 1918, a post which he held until his death in 1940. C. T. R. Wilson, with his cloud-chamber, was but one of Thomson's many pupils to achieve fame in his field; and when Thomson resigned the chair in 1919 it was no surprise that his replacement should be found among his old pupils. Ernest Rutherford had worked with Thomson on the electron, and had since departed via Montreal to Manchester, where, with Charles Darwin, grandson of the first Charles Darwin and later Master of Christ's, he triumphantly disintegrated the nucleus of the atom. Sir Joseph Larmor, the Lucasian Professor, took active steps to retrieve him for Cambridge. Whether in Manchester or in Cambridge, students and fellow scientists flocked to Rutherford: Peter Kapitza, Niels Bohr, P. A. M. Dirac, James Chadwick, Patrick Blackett and John Cockcroft among them, all, including Kapitza, who returned abruptly to Russia, Nobel prize-winners. It was for Kapitza that the Mond Laboratory, now housing aerial photography and computer terminals, was built and equipped, and at Kapitza's request that it was adorned with Eric Gill's sprightly crocodile, with reference to Kapitza's nickname for Rutherford.

It was among the pure scientists, probably, conscious as they were of their international standing, that the need was most strongly felt for some more telling inducement for overseas researchers to come to Cambridge than the right to take a tripos after two years, or the award of a BA for a dissertation. Despite some stiff-necked opposition from those that scorned, or perhaps feared, comparison with German and American universities, the Ph.D. degree, to be awarded on a dissertation after three years' residence, was introduced in 1919.

The Medical School spent much time, between the wars, deliberating on the desirability of a clinical school in Cambridge and wrestling with the General Medical Council. The case for a clinical school did not prevail and the university diplomas in tropical medicine, radiology, and

41. The Cockcroft/Walton particle accelerator, being operated by Ernest Walton in 1932. For their development of this device Cockcroft and Walton shared the Nobel prize for physics in 1951.

public health ('Sanitary Science') which had been established in the later part of the nineteenth century as courses for qualified practitioners, were abandoned in the 1930s. A tradition had grown up that the Regius Professor, at least, would spend much, probably most, of his time as a consultant in London and descend only periodically on the university to pontificate: an arrangement which was not sacrificed entirely without a struggle. There was no medical tripos. Many students, however, took pride in a system which required them rather to take the first part of the Natural Sciences Tripos (concentrating, obviously, on those subjects which offered exemptions from the MB examinations) and then to go out into the world, to London, to Birmingham, to great cities with catchments far more densely populated than Cambridge's for their clinical training before returning to Cambridge to sit their final examinations. In Cambridge they studied their science 'pure', and were privileged to have as lecturers such men as E. D. Adrian, Joseph Needham and Joseph Barcroft.

The humanities too produced their luminaries: F. W. Maitland, carrying a lamp lit by Henry Sidgwick and fuelled with agnosticism and a keen but never oppressive moral earnestness, had died before the First War, leaving an influence felt as much by historians as by his fellow lawyers, eminent both in legal history and in constitutional law. A. E. Housman had come to Cambridge from London in 1911, a sharper individual in every way than his predecessors, to impose a rigour on classical scholarship, and on small talk, of which tales are too many to recount. History, which had found the great majority of its early proponents in King's, still represented until 1922 by G. W. Prothero and until 1946 by Sir John Clapham, infiltrated the university more widely, inspiring the generations responsible for the great series of Cambridge collaborative histories instigated by Lord Acton. Acton himself had been of very great significance to the Cambridge school. He occupied the Regius Chair only from 1895 to 1902 and published little, but he left behind him a tradition of awareness of the work of contemporary continental historians and a library of largely continental books to supply what would otherwise have been a woeful deficit in the holdings of the University Library. His distinguished successors in the Cambridge History School have been so many that objection will surely be taken if, of the generation between the wars, only Herbert Butterfield, Michael Oakeshott, Michael Postan and Eileen Power are mentioned.

In economics the name of John Maynard Keynes must stand first, although Keynes held no university office, operating rather from King's, where he served as second bursar from 1919 and first bursar from 1924, and from Bloomsbury. Although ever willing to assert his admiration of Alfred Marshall, the founder of the faculty, Keynes drew deeply on other influences in Cambridge, on G. E. Moore of the *Principia ethica* and on Bertrand Russell of the *Principia mathematica*, his Apostolic mentors, in particular. And indeed, Marshall too, and his subject, had had their roots in the moral sciences faculty. Of Keynes and of Keynes's Circus more has been written than can easily be summarised. His activities as a member of the university Bursars' Committee, however, deserve a brief mention: he notably increased the revenues of his own college and was generous in his advice to other colleges in the matter of share dealings. It is impossible not to wonder what elegant formula correlated his loyalties and the timing of his advice to other colleges. While Keynes spent much of his working life in London, another of Marshall's pupils, A. C. Pigou, succeeded to the chair of political economy, having received his early training in classics and in history. He was remarkable for his brilliance as a lecturer, but is probably now best remembered for his *Economics of wealth.*

Moore and Russell, in philosophy, and G. H. Hardy in mathematics, each of them in search of unifying truths, constructed paths along which few, perhaps, could follow them to the end, but they were party also to a philosophical discourse, involving among others William Johnson, the logician, C. D. Broad, Frank Ramsay and the eccentric C. K. Ogden, which attracted many beyond their immediate fields and lent a sharpness and excitement to debate on all manner of topics. The élite of many disciplines met regularly at the Heretics, a society established in 1909, with a membership of declared agnostics, where philosophical and anthropological arguments were deployed over a vast range of subjects. These, their friends and disciples, constituted an exceptionally alert, enquiring and analytical audience to greet the phenomenon of Wittgenstein on his return to Cambridge in 1929, and, first, the development of logical positivism and, later, an efflorescence of linguistic or semantic philosophy.

An enthusiastic member of the Heretics was Jane Ellen Harrison, a pioneer in the study of Greek religion, mentor and friend of Francis Cornford, first Laurence Professor of Ancient Philosophy, still a major authority for students of Plato, an ardent friend of the Working Men's College in London, and author of the enduringly diverting and instructive *Microcosmographia academica, being a guide for the young academic politician*, first published in 1908. Both are typical of their generation to the extent that they are alive not only to the theories propounded by Sir J. G. Frazer in *The golden bough*, first published in 1890, and elaborated in a succession of detailed studies up to his death in Cambridge in 1941, but also to the work of A. C. Haddon. Haddon, trained as a zoologist, came almost by chance to anthropology, but his expedition to the Torres Straits, New Guinea and Sarawak in 1898–9 bore fruit when his appointment to a lectureship in Cambridge and a fellowship at Christ's in 1901, enabled him to devote his time fully to working on his material and, very significantly, to make a second expedition to the Straits in 1914. His *Reports*, and the collections which he amassed, not only set social anthropology on a sound academic basis but alerted a wide audience to its implications.

In these years too the School of English was established, orotundly, by the first two Edward VII Professors, A. W. Verrall and Sir Arthur Quiller-Couch, more sharply by their juniors I. A. Richards, Mansfield Forbes, William Empson and, almost too enduringly, by F. R. Leavis and his wife, Queenie, née Roth, whose papers in *Scrutiny*, in particular, had an electrifying effect on literary scholarship far beyond the bounds of Cambridge or of English literature. H. M. Chadwick and Nora Chadwick meanwhile brought their philological, archaeological and historical skills, to say nothing of their literary talents, to bear on the field of Old English, opening the field of Anglo-Saxon studies both to undergraduates and to the wider world.

The poets of the First World War, first or last, came to reject in sorrow and in anger the romantic heroism that took its inspiration from classical models ('Stand in the trench Achilles, Flame-capped, and shout for me').[4] While the instinct of most students when the General Strike broke out in 1926 was to identify with the authorities (especially when offered the

[4] Patrick Shaw-Stewart, 'Dulce et decorum est'.

fulfilment of boyhood fantasies of driving trains and trams) rather than with the desperate poor, the immediately succeeding generations were to draw their inspiration rather from the romantic ideals of communism. Many sought to realise those ideals in Spain. Others, seeing what happened in Spain, lost, or at least modified, their ideals, but Hitler's rise to power and the appearance in Cambridge, as elsewhere, of Jewish refugees ensured that there was no general shift away from the left. Marxism became for many the only respectable intellectual creed. Interest in things Russian continued and was fostered by a vociferous group of scientists, including J. G. Crowther, J. D. Bernal and Joseph Needham, and by the philosopher Ludwig Wittgenstein, all of whom had a profound influence extending far beyond their immediate academic spheres, so that it was as natural for the Soviet Union to seek sympathisers in Cambridge as it was, on the approach of the Second War, for the government to look there for experts on Russia. The retrospective implication of the Apostles in the 'spy scandals' (Burgess and Blunt were both members) to some extent ignores the fact that the beliefs of those implicated were those of many of their contemporaries, and that dons were not lacking to beat the communist drum. Other opinions, of course, continued to find adherents both among the Apostles and in the university at large.

The Second World War did not dispeople Cambridge in the same way as the First: the undergraduates disappeared less suddenly, and it was possible for many to start their courses. Some completed them immediately; for others, who had intended to return and complete them later, but who found the prospect less alluring when they were finally free to do so, the university ingeniously designed a practical course in military studies which they were deemed, either by active service, or by other contributions to the war machine, to have completed, thus qualifying for an ordinary degree. Short courses were again designed, specialist ones for the signal corps, the RAF (who descended on the university in force, taking billets in nine colleges) and for the Navy; more dilettante ones for soldiers quartered in Cambridge who thought that a little education would help to pass the time. American forces were specially catered for in the months between the end of the war in Europe and their return to the States in the delightfully named 'Bull College' – so called for no other reason than that it was situated in the Bull Hotel.

Nor was this the only invasion: government departments moved into Trinity, Caius, Corpus and Sidney. Also from London, to be housed in Peterhouse, King's, St Catharine's and elsewhere, came portions of London University: the London School of Economics, Bedford College, St Bartholomew's medical school and the School of Oriental Studies with their teaching staff. Cambridge dons disappeared in large numbers, to Whitehall, to Bletchley and to other establishments around the country. Those who were already proficient in many languages were sent to learn more, notably Japanese; some of them brought their expertise back with them. Those that remained (143 out of 370 lecturers and demonstrators in 1942), apart from taking their part in the teaching and the increasingly difficult administration of a university peopled by

> Cadets (five types), State Bursars (three types), State Scholars, ex-service applicants, the medically unfit and conscientious objectors, [along with] the more normal members of the different age groups . . . split up into the various war-time courses of study, many of [them] subject to rigid limitation, either through restriction of space, the regulations of the Recruiting Board, or, in the case of medical students, by edicts of the Ministry of Health[5]

were also obliged to organise air-raid precautions and to take their turn at fire-watching. Andrew Gow, who from 1939 to 1944 composed a circular letter for his ex-pupils and others describing day-to-day life in Cambridge, was to report that more fires had been caused by the war-time visitors than by the fifteen bombs that fell on the town.[6]

Even before the end of the war some of the difficulties lying ahead had been foreseen: as the teaching staff returned the shortage of accommodation, of available fellowships and of adequate remuneration would prove pressing problems. The last was solved, for the time being, by the approval by the Treasury and the UGC of a new scale; the others remain to this day. Numbers, both of undergraduates and particularly of post-graduates, were rising and many of the lodgings in the city had either been taken up by civil servants or simply withdrawn from the market. The question was asked whether the influx of post-graduates could and should be incorporated in the existing colleges. Dr Hele, as

[5] J. A. Venn, as vice-chancellor, in the *Reporter* for 1943–4, 131; cited by Roach, 307.
[6] A. S. F. Gow, *Letters from Cambridge* (London, 1945) 255.

vice-chancellor in 1944 and 1945, spoke of a graduate club, or, better, a graduate college.

By 1953 the university had managed, with the help of the new quinquennial grant from the UGC, to fill all its established posts, but little surplus could be foreseen in the funds of the university after well-earned increases in the salaries of the assistant staff and the completion of a new chemistry laboratory. The 1950s did, however, see a new engineering laboratory opened in Trumpington Street, and a new Veterinary School off Madingley Road. A handsome benefaction of £250,000 from Mr Harold Samuel was secured for the Department of Estate Management. Plans were drawn up and construction started on the buildings on the Sidgwick Site to provide offices, libraries and lecture rooms for the arts faculties.

Once again the financial relations between the university and the colleges came up for review and, in accordance with a syndicate report approved in February 1951, the existing arrangement was to some extent reversed. The sums deducted from university stipends on account of college emoluments were to be returned to the colleges (with the partial exception of the four wealthiest, Trinity, St John's, King's and Caius), but only after the colleges between them had contributed to the university a sum increased from £45,000 to £95,000. Apart from the shift of financial dominance from the colleges to the university thus enabled by the UGC grant, the notional distinction between the colleges as teaching units and the university as a research unit was largely modified. The reserved fellowships introduced in 1926 were abolished and the university was in a position to play Robin Hood, redistributing the surpluses of the richest colleges to the poorest. It was hoped that this arrangement would facilitate the election to fellowships of university teachers and bring university and colleges closer together, but the vast increases in university teachers in these years rendered the hope vain. Between 1938 and 1954 the number of teaching staff increased by 82 per cent and of research students by 164 per cent.[7] Nearly half the 800 or so teaching staff were without fellowships (see Figure 3 for the escalation of this problem in the years following).

There was little that the existing colleges could do to cater for such

[7] For a list of post-graduate courses offered between 1875 and 1995 see Appendix 4, and for a chart of their increasing numbers, Figure 4, p. 213.

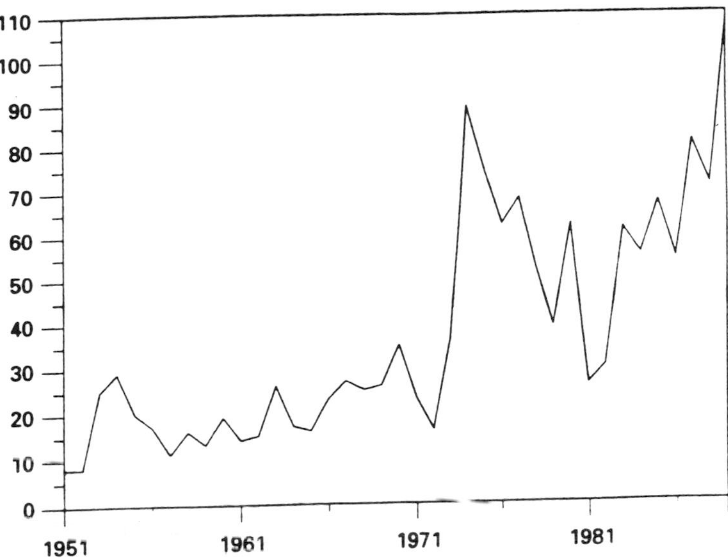

Figure 3. Matriculands (i.e. new staff) with no college, 1951–89

numbers. Many of them, with the passing of years, doubled their fellowships, but there still remained many university staff, especially in those subjects studied only by post-graduates, and in administrative posts, including librarians, museum curators and, later, computer officers, for whom no place had been found. The alternatives seemed to lie either in a large-scale abandonment of the collegiate system, or in its enlargement. In 1958 the foundation was announced of a new college as a monument to the achievements of Winston Churchill. The idea had been fostered at one end by Sir John Colville, Churchill's private secretary, and by Lord Cherwell, who had had occasion during and after the war to lament the shortage of technologists, and at the other end by Lord Todd, by now Master of Christ's and immensely eminent both as an organic chemist endowed with as much toughness as his predecessor Pope (and like Pope finding plenty of scope for its exercise) and, later, as the chairman of the Royal Commission on Medical Education. Todd introduced to Churchill in the course of discussions Sir John Cockcroft, the nuclear physicist who had inherited the mantle of his teacher Rutherford, and it was Cockcroft whom Churchill appointed the first Master. Churchill

College was to be a centre, above all, for science and technology and was to foster links with industry; it also incorporated an archive centre to house many of Sir Winston's papers. These in their turn attracted the deposit of the records of many of Churchill's war-time colleagues, and, in a parallel development, those of a number of eminent scientists. The foundation was on a princely scale both in terms of the space which it occupied and in its establishment with, initially, sixty fellows and five hundred and forty students, a high proportion of them post-graduate.

It was not long before other colleges followed, most of them, like Churchill, to display variations, greater or lesser, from the established model. Churchill, however, was not the first post-war college. New Hall, promoted largely by members and supporters of the existing women's colleges under the banner of Dame Myra Curtis, principal of Newnham, opened officially in October 1954 with sixteen undergraduates. It was, apart from its entrance examination, which was initally by essay only, conventional in all but its size, which remained modest for some years. Starting life in premises in Silver Street (The Hermitage and the Old Granary) and endowed by funds raised from many sources, including the existing colleges, it was able, largely thanks to benefactions from the Wolfson and Nuffield Foundations, to move into almost completed buildings on its present site late in 1964. Even before Dame Myra started marshalling her committees another group of women academics had formed a Dining Group out of which they hoped that a new college would somehow spontaneously evolve and so, miraculously and not without setbacks, it did as Lucy Cavendish College in 1965. Such diners as had not seceded to New Hall became fellows. Chiefly for financial reasons the delay between the admission of the first fellows and graduate students and the first undergraduates was rather longer than usual, but in 1970 candidates for the degree of B.Ed. were admitted and, in 1971, permission was at last granted for the admission of undergraduates. From its beginnings the college has made itself especially responsible for the admission of mature students: women who have had no earlier opportunity to read for a degree.

The shortage of fellowships and of accommodation for graduate students continued to be felt, and urgently, and in 1960 a syndicate was set up under Lord Bridges to report, once more, on the relationship between the university and the colleges. Its report issued in the Graduate Centre,[8] built between 1964 and 1967, which with its cafeteria, restaurant, bar, television rooms, games rooms and meeting rooms was designed to provide at least some of the amenities of communal living of which so many staff, and in practice no small proportion of graduate students, were deprived. Unlike nearly all colleges, moreover, the Graduate Centre was equipped to cope with small children and so fulfilled the needs of the many research students and staff who had nowhere else in the centre of Cambridge to meet their young families. Several members of the Bridges Syndicate had, however, like Dr Hele in the 1940s, another gleam in their eye: that of a graduate college. Michael McCrum and Frank Young drafted an appendix to the syndicate's report indicating the shape that such a creature might assume. Their vision lingered in the minds of, among others, the bursars of Trinity, St John's, and Caius and King's who, travelling often together to London deep in discussion of the Estate Act meetings for which they were bound, were obliged to find other topics for the journey back. No one knows who bribed the signalman, but he successfully delayed the train for long enough one day in 1962 for the four of them to resolve on an approach to their colleges along the lines of a draft prepared by John Bradfield of Trinity. King's withdrew later from this particular endeavour, but Bradfield, Trevor Thomas of St John's, strongly supported by his predecessor, now the Master, John Boys-Smith, and E. P. ('Sam') Weller of Caius kept their colleges up to the mark. The original proposal was for a college for fellows only, a sort of Cambridge All Souls, but it was soon suggested, by Lord Adrian, Master of Trinity, that the brew would be improved with the admixture of research students. He was quite right: the new college, opened in 1965, was quite soon to gather to itself the largest body of graduate students in the university. Frank Young was appointed the first Master, St John's agreed to sell to the Trustees The Hermitage, lately the home of New Hall, the Darwin family gladly consented to lease to them their house, Newnham Grange, with the Old Granary, in Silver Street, and to this kindness added the gift of their name. Darwin admits only graduate

[8] Now the 'University Centre', but retaining a strong trace of its origins in its familiar title, the 'Grad Pad'.

students and, receiving an application from a woman before it had been fully determined to confine membership to men, tumbled happily almost at once into being the first mixed-sex college in Cambridge. A precedent already existed in Oxford, in the form of Linacre College, founded for graduates of both sexes in 1962.[9]

Almost simultaneously the university had taken the initiative which was to lead to the foundation of another college in 1965, also designed to answer the needs highlighted by the Bridges Syndicate. This was University College, renamed Wolfson College in 1973 in response to the subventions from the Wolfson Foundation, which largely funded its extensive buildings. The prime purpose of the college was, again, to provide fellowships for teaching officers, and thirty, out of a maximum of sixty, fellowships were to be reserved for this purpose, to be allotted in order of seniority, the remaining fellows being freely elected. The student body is unusual in that, while it comprises mostly graduate students, there is allowance also for some mature undergraduates. The college has also associated itself with, and often organises, a variety of short courses in association with industry, the Home Office and so on, and so serves as a congenial Cambridge base for a great variety of people with no official university standing. Meanwhile the vice-chairman of the Bridges Syndicate, Lord Ashby, Master of Clare and previously Vice-Chancellor of the Queen's University, Belfast, had been urging on his governing body to consider what the college could do, and with the assistance of the senior tutor, John Northam, and of Richard Eden, later professor of energy studies, formulated a scheme for yet a third graduate college, for which it revived its own ancient name of Clare Hall. The original endowment by the college was supplemented by the Old Dominion Foundation and the Ford Foundation and it opened in 1966 with Brian Pippard, shortly to be Cavendish Professor, as first president. The hospitality which Clare Hall offers to visiting scholars of all kinds is the admiration of other colleges.

Nor were the ranks of the colleges increased only by new foundations. Also in the *annus mirabilis* 1965 the status of 'Approved Society' (the first step on the path to becoming a college) was granted to St Edmund's

[9] Ten years after this King's and Churchill were the first Cambridge colleges to admit women as undergraduate (and graduate) students, an initiative followed more or less gradually by all the existing men's colleges culminating with Magdalene in 1987.

House, now St Edmund's College, henceforth, while maintaining a catholic nucleus, to admit fellows, graduate students (and some mature undergraduates) of all religious persuasions and of none; and to Hughes Hall, founded in 1885 as a teachers' training college for women, which has since admitted as fellows and as graduate students representatives of other disciplines, men as well as women. Rather later, in 1977, and after some debate, Homerton, the other Cambridge teachers' training college for women, was also adopted by the university, not only in recognition of its excellent tradition, but also with the aims of extending to it some protection against government threats to its standing, and of rationalising and so strengthening the rather complex relations between the Cambridge bodies concerned with teaching and research in education. All Homerton students continue to work for qualifications in education, making it unique in Cambridge as a college devoted to a single, if many-faceted, discipline.

More dramatically, 1977 also saw the admission of the first students to the wholly new foundation of Robinson College, the munificent endowment of a Cambridge business man, David Robinson, a noble benefaction and one that benefited the entire university since it came at a time when government pressure to increase student numbers would have placed an intolerable burden on the already stretched resources of many colleges. The foundation was undertaken in close collaboration with Gonville and Caius College.

By the 1960s, as a result of changes following on the Education Act of 1944 and the availability of realistic grants from local authorities and other bodies, the composition of the undergraduate body had become somewhat less relentlessly middle-class. At the same time the postgraduate students now flooding into British universities from all quarters of the globe alerted their contemporaries to ideas and to movements from further afield, notably from the United States and from Europe. Somewhat paradoxically, with the relaxation of such constraints on students as the obligation to wear a gown in the streets after dusk there developed between junior and senior members of the university a sense of 'them and us' which had been less marked before. The mass of Cambridge students were, however, rather slow than otherwise in attempting to emulate the student uprising of Paris in 1968, but there was one serious riot in February 1970 when a Greek dinner, sponsored by the Greek

Tourist Board, in the Garden House Hotel was picketed by protesters against the regime of the Greek colonels. The police were seriously under-represented and the picket degenerated into an assault on people and on property giving rise to regret from many of the participants – and to lengthy post-mortems.

Two years later, provoked by the decision of the General Board not to ratify a proposal by the Faculty Board of Economics to substitute a dissertation for a written paper, a large group of students occupied the University Combination Room in the Old Schools. The invaders were good-tempered on the whole, and what little damage was done was credibly attributed to camp-followers from other institutions remaining after the main body had decamped. Happily, however, the authorities took a sufficiently dim view of the proceedings to set up a Court of Inquiry under Lord Devlin, the High Steward, who duly presented a written report surveying the scope already allowed for student participation in university decision-making and suggesting several areas in which further participation might be encouraged, or at least allowed. In the event, as many had predicted, most students showed little relish for the dubious excitements of committee rooms. The Devlin Report is in itself a wonderfully perceptive, judicious and elegant document, and is further supported by a transcript of the hearings and the great bulk of the written evidence submitted to the court. These, deposited in the University Archives for all to see, have been curiously neglected. Between them they present a vivid prospect of every conceivable view of the university and its functioning.

In contrast to these domestic preoccupations the international activities of the university as represented by the Press were on the dawn of a vast expansion. In the years up to 1971 the division of the Press's operations between Cambridge and London and the somewhat Byzantine relationship between the printing and the publishing divisions had brought it rather beyond the brink of financial collapse, leaving no individual with the scope to take decisive remedial action. With a revised management structure and the appointment of Geoffrey Cass as, initially, managing director of the Publishing Division, and then as chief executive, all this was to change. Following a detailed analysis of the Press's nature and history, entailing much labour in the University Archives, Cass successfully obtained official recognition of the Press's charitable status, freeing it from the burden of tax. In the years following, the London premises were closed and all the publishing and warehousing operations brought back to Cambridge so that by 1981 the whole of the Press's publishing staff in the United Kingdom was housed in the imposing buildings newly constructed for them in Shaftesbury Road and opened in that year by Her Majesty the Queen. Taking advantage of new markets, including that for textbooks for the teaching of English as a foreign language, and of new printing technology and new electronic media, and working through its branches in the United States and Australia, and its promotional offices in Asia, Africa, Latin America and the Middle East, as well as in Europe, the Press now (1996) boasts over twenty thousand authors in ninety-eight countries.

No less impressive is the output of the Local Examinations Syndicate with a permanent staff in Cambridge of over six hundred and fifty and an international market, recognised in 1992 by the Queen's Award for Export Achievement, such that of the more than 1 million candidates examined every year over 60 per cent are overseas. Eight million question papers are yearly printed at, and distributed from, the Syndicate's Harvey Road premises. Of the income generated a proportion can be made available for other purposes of the university as it was, for instance, in assisting in the acquisition of the Royal Commonwealth Library, brought to the University Library in 1993.

The achievements in research in the university since the Second World War are too many to be handled in so short a compass without grievous omissions. Suffice it to say that the move of the Cavendish to its new site spectacularly failed to stem the flow of Nobel prizes to Cambridge. In the old Cavendish in 1953 James Watson and Francis Crick unravelled the structure of DNA, while Fred Sanger, in the Department of Biochemistry, won his first Nobel prize in 1958 for determining the specific sequence of the amino-acid blocks which form the protein insulin. When Max Perutz (who shared with John Kendrew the Nobel prize for chemistry for their work on the atomic structure of the protein molecule) established the Medical Research Council Laboratory of Molecular Biology on a site adjacent to New Addenbrooke's, both the personnel and the techniques were largely drawn from the Cavendish. In the MRC laboratory Nobel laureates are becoming almost commonplace, with Fred

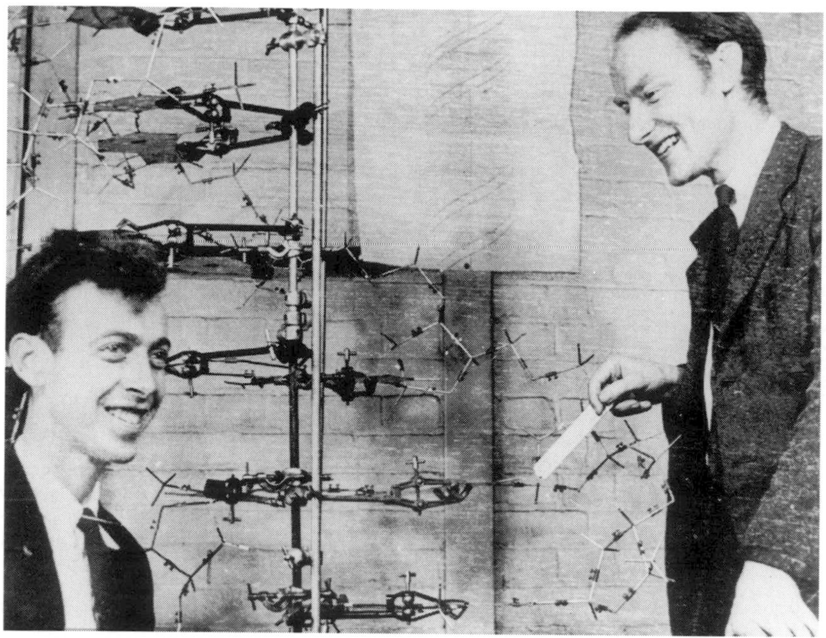

42. James Watson and Francis Crick with their DNA model in the 1950s.

Sanger again in 1980, for discovering how to interpret the information encoded in DNA; Aaron Klug in 1982 for solving complex structures such as those for viruses and RNA molecules; and César Milstein in 1984 for finding a method of producing unlimited supplies of monoclonal antibodies.[10]

The inevitable alliance of mathematics and physics, embodied so brilliantly in Newton, has also flourished prodigiously in Cambridge in the twentieth century. Paul Dirac, Newton's successor in the Lucasian Chair of Mathematics from 1932 to 1969, was one of the earliest proponents of quantum theory, now basic to chemistry and molecular biology, as well as to physics; while the present incumbent of the chair, Stephen Hawking, must surely be the best known cosmographer,

[10] A full list of Nobel prizes awarded for work done in Cambridge would include the names of many now working in other parts of the world. The list at Appendix 6 excludes several whose work in Cambridge was not demonstrably the source of the award.

if not indeed the best known scientist, of his generation with his constantly advancing theories as to the astonishing qualities of 'black holes' and their significance for our understanding of the nature of our universe. In an area where modern developments impinge on all our lives it was in Cambridge, in May 1949, that the world's first stored program computer, the 'EDSAC' (Electronic Delay Storage Automatic Computer), built by Maurice Wilkes first ran as a complete system. Today the GRANTA backbone network provides high-bandwidth connectivity between all university and college sites.

Such developments – and one could name many more, notably in chemistry, in engineering, and in the biological sciences – have made Cambridge a Mecca for all those concerned to advance the boundaries of the physical and medical sciences, and must be largely responsible for the arrival in and around the city of such independent institutions as the British Antarctic Survey, the Royal Greenwich Observatory and the European Bioinformatics Centre.

Advances in the humanities are seldom as dramatic as in the sciences, and less prone to manifest themselves in concrete and glass, or even bricks and mortar. An exceptional counter-example, however, may be found in the herculean labours of the polymath Dr Joseph Needham, the first volume of whose *Science and civilisation in China* appeared in 1954 to be followed, by the time of his death in 1995, by a further fifteen volumes. The international team engaged on the colossal enterprise to illuminate so vast a topic is now housed in the Needham Research Institute in Sylvester Road. More recent developments, the product of massive benefactions, are the Judge Institute of Management Studies, endowed in 1990 by Mr (now Sir) Paul Judge and by Guinness plc, and the McDonald Institute of Archaeological Research, the gift of the late Dr D. M. McDonald.

A comprehensive treatment of developments in research in Cambridge in the last four decades is beyond the scope of this volume. The reader is referred to Professor Brooke's account in volume IV of the *History of the University of Cambridge* (1993).

In the 1960s and 1970s the university had become increasingly aware of the world outside. The Robbins Report of 1963 not only set the nation on the path of attempting to provide higher education for all those qualified, triggering an expansion of most of the institutions destined to purvey

43. The old Addenbrooke's Hospital now restored as a home for the Judge Institute of Management Studies.

it, but also laid increasing emphasis on grants paid directly to the universities rather than to the fee-paying students. The two forms of funding co-exist but in such a way that the pressure to increase fees, especially to overseas students, has become well-nigh impossible to resist. Minimum fees are, indeed, now dictated by government. The first proposal put to the Regent House in the 1980s for 'full-cost fees' for overseas students was successfully resisted. It was an idealistic vote but one that could not be repeated: the university could not afford to lose the government grants that would otherwise have been withdrawn. Instead it set itself, very successfully, to raise funds specifically to finance those overseas students, especially from the third world and the old commonwealth, for whom the fees would otherwise have been prohibitive. For many universities overseas students are now big business, and big business is nothing if not competitive. It is largely for this reason that courses have proliferated in the last decades with the introduction not only of new subjects but of

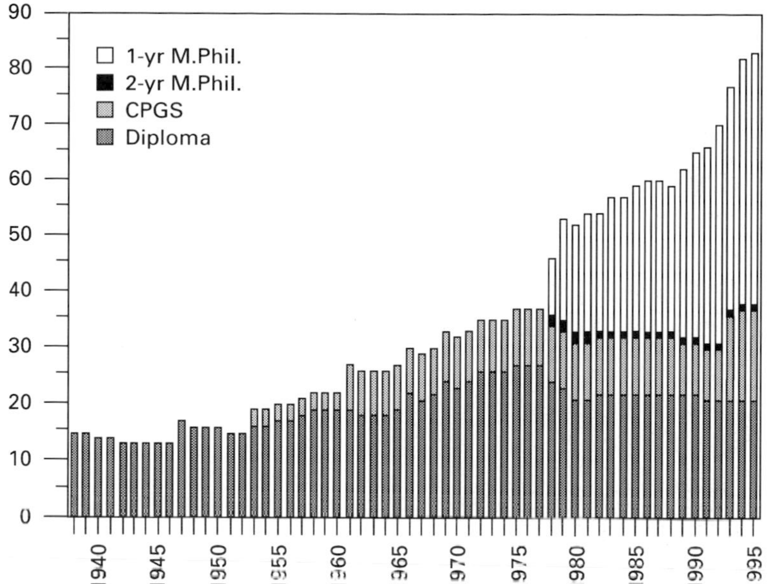

Figure 4. Numbers of post-graduate taught courses, 1938–95

new degrees (see Figure 4). M.Phils., awarded in numerous subjects after one or two years, offer the equivalent of the Masters' degrees familiar in the States and elsewhere. They have also proved serviceable as probationary exercises for those intending to study for a Ph.D., but a trap appeared. Certain of the Research Councils responsible for award of fees began to demand an M.Phil. as a qualification for candidacy for the Ph.D. course: the necessary period of study was therefore extended by one year, but many authorities still award a grant, as before, for three years only. This battle continues.

For those with only one year to spare a variety of diploma courses were devised,[11] and, most recently, schemes have been set afoot for the award of degrees based on part-time study: an MBA in business administration complements the optional papers in business studies available for several years to those reading engineering. Similar plans have been propounded by the Department of Education, and the Board for Continuing Education, previously the Extra-Mural Board, from its

[11] See Figure 4 and Appendix 4.

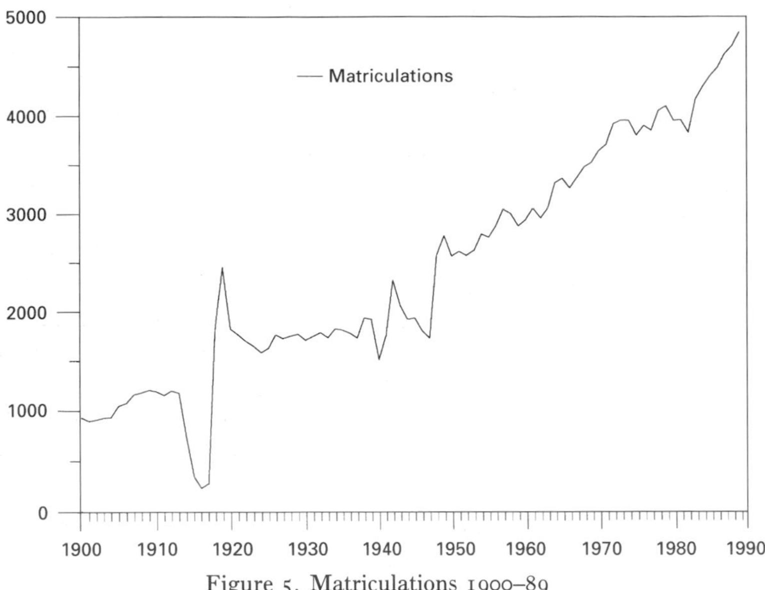

Figure 5. Matriculations 1900–89

headquarters in Madingley Hall now proposes the option of university qualifications to the many students for whom, over the years, it has provided both local courses and summer schools in Cambridge. It is a welcome corrective to the pressures on the university to view itself increasingly as a research establishment and one which, with its commitment to the collegiate model and therefore to the demanding of college as well as university fees, *must* be seen as a 'centre of excellence' in order to ensure its share both of the competitive market in students and of available grants.

Many of the changes charted in the preceding pages appear to us now, looking down the wrong end of the telescope, as quite moderate. When we look at the last fifty years or so, now using the microscope, we may at first get the same impression. To be sure there are now more students, both undergraduate and, particularly, post-graduate, studying more subjects for more degrees in more colleges. Just over 1,100 students matriculated in 1911, some 4,700 in 1989 (see Figure 5). In December 1993 there were 14,585 full-time students at Cambridge, 3,969 of them post-graduates. Even more significantly for the organisation of the university has been the corresponding increase in its staff. When the 1926 statutes were drawn up the Regent House numbered some 600 persons; the current figure is around 3,300. John Roach, writing in the 1950s, noted that after 1919 far fewer members of the university took an active part in discussions of university policy than had done before the war. This trend has continued, partly no doubt because of the increasing pressure of work and the wider geographical distribution of departments and faculties, but partly also as a result of the universal phenomenon that the larger a body the less closely its members are inclined to identify with it. The inevitable result is that more and more decisions come to be taken by those few who are members either of the permanent administration or of the central bodies: Council, General Board and Finance Committee. The democratic processes can easily become too unwieldy to operate efficiently while those who cherish them very properly resent any attempt to undermine them.

It was to address such problems that a Memorial was submitted in November 1987 which suggested, in line with the UGC's criticisms of the response drawn up by the university's central bodies to the report of the Steering Committee for Efficiency Studies in Universities (the Jarratt Report), that 'the lack of efficient procedures for policy making places the university at a disadvantage when dealing with requests from the Government, the UGC, and other external sources'. The same Memorial, in what might appear to be a contradictory spirit, also lamented 'the absence of satisfactory means by which the Regent House [could] fulfil the normal rôle of a Governing Body'. In response to the Memorial the university appointed a syndicate under the chairmanship of Sir Douglas Wass

> to consider in the light of changing circumstances, the government of the University with particular reference to (a) the tenure, powers, and duties of the vice-chancellor; (b) the functions of the central bodies and the relationship between them; (c) the relationship between the central bodies, the Councils of the Schools, the Faculty Boards, and other authorities; (d) the rule of the Regent House; (e) the inter-relationship between University and College policy.

It was not the first time since the Second World War that the university had attempted such an exercise. A succession of committees from 1961 had culminated in the publication in 1967 of the 'Grave Report' advocating, among other things, abolition of the remaining powers of the Senate, the subordination of the General Board and the Financial Board to the Council of the Senate, a revision of the membership of the Regent House, with many of its powers delegated to the Council, and the extension of the term of the vice-chancellorship to three years. The Council pondered these things and startled the university with sporadic reports upon them, the ninth and last in December 1986. Many of the Grave Committee's recommendations, however, sank into oblivion.

The Wass Syndicate reported in May 1989 and strongly urged that its recommendations should be accepted *en bloc*. Since, however, some of its suggestions commended themselves more readily to the university at large than others, it was decided that it would be more practicable to submit what were regarded as the 'core recommendations' for approval in the first instance, followed by more detailed proposals in groups with, in some cases, the very result feared by the syndicate. Parts of their proposed structure have been unpicked and their objects nullified. Briefly, the syndicate aimed to impose a more pyramidal structure on the university, very much on the lines of the Grave Report, subjecting the General Board and the Financial Board to the Council, to whom also would be delegated many of the powers of the Regent House. Alongside these measures, designed to minimise duplication and to streamline the decision-making process by giving the Council enhanced executive powers, a greater degree of autonomy was granted to faculties and departments in the distribution of the funds allocated to them. Not surprisingly, much of the ensuing debate has concerned the defining of the categories of the eligible and of the electors, with a general shift away from the spirit of the syndicate's recommendations towards the defence of the residual powers of the Regent House.

Substantially, however, the syndicate's scheme has come into place with the Council (no longer the 'Council of the Senate') established as the chief executive body, with its own Executive Committee and Consultative Committee (with membership not necessarily confined to members of the university) and with the General Board and the Finance Committee (no longer the 'Financial Board') reporting to it. The Council in turn reports annually to the Regent House and a Board of Scrutiny is established with the particular duty of examining that report and alerting the Regent House to any possible causes of contention.

More visible to the harassed and apolitical academic than these substantial constitutional changes is the total remodelling of the office of vice-chancellor. As we have seen, from 1587 the office had always been held by a head of house,[12] normally for a period of two years. It was a system which helped to weave together the strands of college and university interest, and which provided the vice-chancellor with a ready-made household for his hospitable functions. Many Heads also had substantial duties in the university, as professors and heads of departments, and for such it was scarcely possible to require of them more than a semi-passive fulfilment of the university's chief office, with its heavy obligations of ceremonial and hospitable functions, of membership of national bodies, such as the Committee of Vice-Chancellors and Principals, and of the chairmanship of many university bodies. One so situated could hardly be equipped to take an active or an innovative rôle in the context of a far larger and more complex university and one which was called upon with increasing frequency to react to changes in government policy. Henceforth, therefore, the vice-chancellor is to be no more a head of house,[13] but to devote his whole time to the office, serving for five years, with a possible extension to seven, charged not only with representing the university on formal occasions, and taking his accustomed part in the university's rituals, but with supervision of the whole machinery of university government. He may, however, appoint up to three pro-vice-chancellors to assist him in his public functions. The vice-chancellor is now no longer subject to the formality of election by the Regent House but is appointed by the Council. The shock waves that might have been occasioned on the first such appointment were happily stilled by the appointment of Professor Sir David Williams, already in post as vice-chancellor under the old dispensation.

The relationship of the university and the colleges is ineluctably problematic: the university may propose courses but it has no control over the admission by the colleges of the students who are to take them, hence, in large part, the UGC's recent threat to close the Veterinary School. Where once the university received quinquennial grants from the UGC it is now required, by the HEFCE, successor to the UGC's successor the UFC, to make quinquennial projections and to wait each year to learn

[12] See p. 57.

[13] Even the question of whether he was to be eligible to a professorial fellowship, without stipend, at any college was the object of a ballot, the Regent House finding in favour.

(a)

44. The Cambridge Law Faculty building, by Sir Norman Foster and Partners, (a) under construction and (b) completed.

its allocation. One of the Wass Syndicate's recommendations which is still under discussion is that the Colleges Committee, at which representatives of all the colleges meet to discuss university business as it bears on college interests and to settle the distribution of funds raised from the wealthier colleges and bestowed on the poorer ones, should be given delegatory powers, enabling it to make executive decisions with reference back to the colleges. Unquestionably the autonomy still claimed by the colleges, much diminished though it has been, must limit the university's freedom of action. Many colleges, especially the newer ones, could not survive without their fee income. Few in Cambridge, probably, would deny that, for those undergraduates at least who know how to make use of them, the colleges enhance almost every aspect of their university

(b)

careers, both educationally and socially. College facilities are also a bait for academic staff and, very probably, a help in retaining the services of many who might otherwise be tempted to move away. For post-graduate students, many of them married and working long hours at their laboratories, the case is less obvious, despite the earnest endeavours, especially of the graduate colleges, to provide facilities for intellectual as well as social activities. Such colleges shiver under the threat of the research councils to cease paying college fees. The threat is not to them alone: if post-graduate students were to be allowed non-collegiate status, then they would soon drift away from the older-established colleges, so destroying the continuum of experience which is so vital to their character.

It should not be supposed, however, that, from the university's point

45. Work at the MRC Cambridge Centre for Brain Repair.

of view, the colleges are merely a nuisance. Many endowments of chairs and of institutes have taken root from loyalties fostered by the colleges, and the richer colleges have launched initiatives of immediate benefit to the whole university and to the city around it. Notable among them are the Science Park established by Trinity in 1973 on the inspiration of Dr John Bradfield, attracting innovative enterprises to the city and facilitating exchanges between the university and industry vital to them both. Other colleges have been quick to follow suit, notably St John's, with its Innovation Park opened in November 1987. Trinity again inaugurated in 1992 the Isaac Newton Institute as a mathematical hotbed opening its doors to scholars from all over the world. King's has used its research institute as a seedbed for various branches of study which have since taken root both in the university at large and beyond.

Probably there has been no generation in the university which has not thought that it lived in 'interesting times', that the nature of the university had altered radically in the course of the previous century. One phenomenon of the present century is certainly unprecedented. In 1900, of some 20,000 university students in Great Britain one-third were at Cambridge or Oxford. By 1980 the total numbered about a quarter of a million of whom less than 8 per cent were at Oxbridge. Similarly, in 1900 40 per cent of 2,000 university teachers and administrators were at Oxbridge against 7.5 per cent of 40,000 in 1980. Numerically Oxford and Cambridge together no longer comprise a significant proportion of the total provision of university education in Britain. They remain the best-known universities in England and would probably have done so for many years by virtue of their antiquity alone, that and the beauty of their buildings: the very images of Arcadia. There will always be some who will hanker for Arcadia, but academics, on the whole, are a pragmatical breed and surveys of academic staff by A. H. Halsey in 1964 and 1976 show that the proportion whose first preference would be a university lectureship and fellowship of a Cambridge college, as against a chair at Sussex, a professorial headship of department at Leeds or a readership at London, all better remunerated, rose in that period from 33 to 35 per cent, heading the league.

Undoubtedly the perceived social advantages of a collegiate university are among the inducements which help Cambridge to retain its distinguished staff, but a further survey by Halsey in 1989, asking academics country-wide to name the university with the strongest department in their subject, shows Oxford with 1,920 points and Cambridge with 1,902 easily outranking the next comer at 678 points. An impartial observer considering the academic status of Oxford, Cambridge, London, Edinburgh and Glasgow in the 1890s would scarcely have predicted such a result. Supposing, however, as government is increasingly inclined to suppose, that academics are not the best judges of their own business, we may fall back both on the result of the government's own assessments of research in universities since 1992, in which, consistently, Cambridge has been found, in the words of *The Times*, to be 'simply the world's best university', and on the assessment of teaching by the Higher Education Funding Council in 1994, in which Cambridge and Oxford again headed the list. Pessimists and cynics, of which every institution needs a few, might observe that this is a precarious position, with 'only one way to go from here'. Precarious it may be, but it is a position which Cambridge is determined to defend.

Appendix 1
Foundations of Colleges

Only those colleges and hostels are included which survive in some form today.

1280–4	**Peterhouse**, originally 'the College of the scholars of the Bishop of Ely', alternatively known at different times as St Peter's College
1317	The King's Hall, refounded 1337, absorbed into Trinity College in 1546
1321	University Hall, incorporating hostels dating from *c.* 1200, and refounded in 1326 as Clare Hall, q.v.
1324	Michaelhouse, absorbed into Trinity College in 1546
1326–46	Clare Hall, later known as **Clare College**
1347	Pembroke Hall (the College, House or Hall of Valence Mary), later known as **Pembroke College**
1348/9	Gonville Hall, refounded in 1351 (as the Hall of the Annunciation of the Blessed Virgin Mary), incorporating from 1393 Physwick Hostel (absorbed into Trinity College in 1546); and again refounded in 1557 as **Gonville and Caius College** ('founded in honour of the Annunciation of the Blessed Virgin Mary')
1349/50	**Trinity Hall** (the College of the Scholars of the Holy Trinity of Norwich)
1352	**Corpus Christi College** (the College of Corpus Christi and the Blessed Virgin Mary), long known as St Benet's, or Benet College
1428	Buckingham College, refounded in 1542 as Magdalene College
1439	Godshouse, refounded in 1505 as Christ's College, q.v.
1441	**King's College** (the Royal College of St Mary and St Nicholas)
1446–8	**Queens' College** (the Queens' College of St Margaret and St Bernard), refounded 1465
1473	Catharine Hall, known since 1860 as **St Catharine's College**
1496	**Jesus College** (the College of the Blessed Virgin Mary, St John the Evangelist, and the Glorious Virgin St Radegund)
1505	**Christ's College**, incorporating Godshouse, above
1509–11	**St John's College** (the College of St John the Evangelist)
1542	**Magdalene College** in continuation of Buckingham College, above

1546 **Trinity College** (the College of the Holy and Undivided Trinity), incorporating the King's Hall (1317), Michaelhouse (1324) and Physwick Hostel (1393)

1584 **Emmanuel College**

1594–6 **Sidney Sussex College** (Lady Frances Sidney Sussex College)

1731 **Homerton College** (as a training college for Nonconformist ministers. A teachers' training college since 1852, it moved to Cambridge in 1895 but was not adopted by the university until 1977)

1800 **Downing College** (as a result of a bequest of 1717)

1869 **Girton College** (in Hitchin until 1872)

1871 **Newnham College**

1882 Selwyn Hostel, from 1923 known as **Selwyn College**; full collegiate status from 1957

1885 **Hughes Hall**, originally the Cambridge Training College for Women, 'approved foundation', 1985

1892 Fitzwilliam House, housing non-collegiate students, initiated in 1869; from 1966 **Fitzwilliam College**

1896 St Edmund's House, from 1965 **St Edmund's College**, 'approved foundation' from 1975

1954 **New Hall**

1960 **Churchill College**

1964 **Darwin College**

1965 **Lucy Cavendish College**

1965 University College, from 1973 **Wolfson College**

1966 **Clare Hall**

1977 **Robinson College**, 'approved foundation' from 1985

APPENDIX 2
MATRICULATIONS 1544–1989

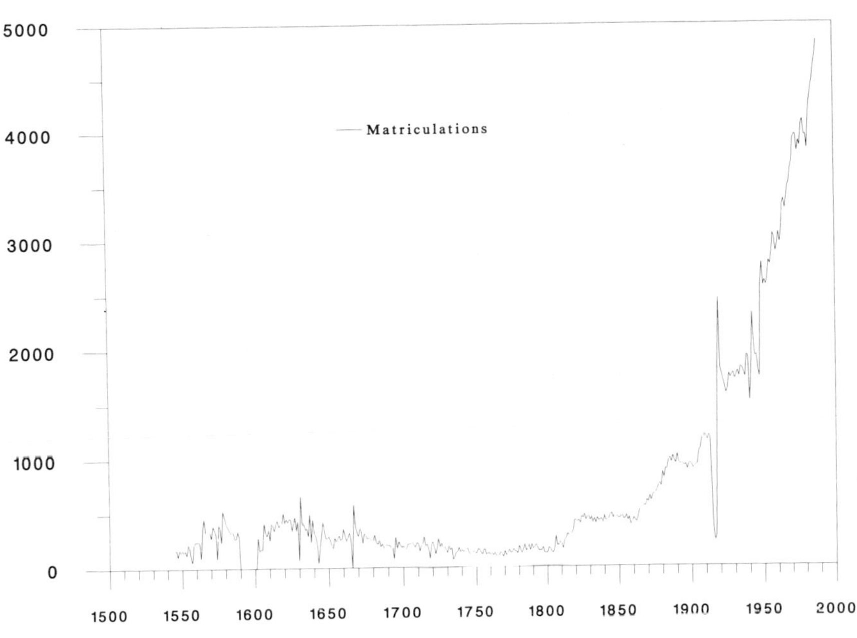

(No records for 1590 to 1600)

APPENDIX 3
TRIPOSES: DATES OF FIRST CLASS-LISTS

1748	Mathematics
1824	Classics
1851	Moral Sciences [to 1969]
	Natural Sciences
1858	Law [to 1869; examinations from 1816]
1870	Law and History [to 1874]
1874	Theology [examinations from 1856; Theological and Religious Studies from 1970]
1875	Law
	History
1878	Semitic Languages [to 1894]
1879	Indian Languages [to 1892]
1886	Medieval and Modern Languages [to 1916]
1894	Mechanical Sciences [to 1970]
1895	Oriental Languages [to 1957]
1905	Economics
1917	Modern and Medieval Languages [previously Medieval and Modern Languages]
1919	English
1920	Geography
1921	Anthropology [to 1927; actually established in 1915]
1928	Archaeology and Anthropology
1948	Music
1950	Chemical Engineering
1958	Oriental Studies
	Anglo-Saxon [previously part of Archaeology and Anthropology]
1961	Architecture and Fine Arts [to 1970]
1963	Electrical Sciences [to 1986; previously part of Mechanical Sciences]
1964	Agriculture [to 1971]
1965	Land Economy

1969	Medical Sciences [to 1991]
1970	Philosophy [previously Moral Sciences]
	Engineering [previously Mechanical Sciences]
1971	Anglo-Saxon, Norse and Celtic [previously Anglo-Saxon]
	Architecture } [previously Architecture and Fine Arts]
	History of Art }
	Social and Political Sciences
1972	Computer Science
	Theological and Religious Studies [previously Theology]
1980	Education
	Production Engineering [to 1988]
1987	Electrical and Information Sciences [previously Electrical Sciences]
	Management Studies
1989	Manufacturing Engineering [previously Production Engineering]
1992	Medical and Veterinary Sciences [previously Medical Sciences]
1999?	Education

APPENDIX 4
DIPLOMAS (NOT ALL OF THEM DESIGNED FOR GRADUATES OF CAMBRIDGE) AND TAUGHT COURSES FOR POST-GRADUATES, 1875–1995

Date	Diploma	Certificate of Postgraduate Study
1875	Public Health[1]	
1894	Agriculture[2]	
1904	Tropical Medicine[1]	
1907	Geography[3]	
1912	Forestry[4]	
	Anthropology[5]	
1919	Medical Radiology and Electrology[6]	
	Psychological Medicine[7]	
1921	Classical Archaeology	
	Hygiene[1]	
1922	Education	
1925	Coal Mining[8]	
1929	Architecture	
?–1929	Horticulture	
1936	General Archaeology[9]	
	Oriental Languages[10]	
1938	(Comparative) Legal Studies	
	Economics	
1947	International Law	
	Agricultural Science[11]	
	Mathematical Statistics	
	Estate Management[12]	
1953	Numerical Analysis and Automatic Computing[13]	Biochemistry[14]
		Chemistry
		Metallurgy[15]
1955	Slavonic Studies[16]	
1957	Roman Law[17]	
1958	Oriental Studies[18]	Physics

Date	Diploma	Certificate of Postgraduate Study
1961	Criminology[19]	Chemical Engineering Engineering Social Anthropology Physical Anthropology Prehistoric Archaeology

1. Rescinded in 1932.
2. 'Agricultural Studies' from 1966.
3. Rescinded in 1940.
4. Rescinded in 1935.
5. Replaced in 1961 by Certificates in Social Anthropology, Physical Anthropology and Prehistoric Archaeology.
6. Rescinded in 1942.
7. Rescinded in 1927.
8. In collaboration with Birmingham University; rescinded in 1951.
9. Rescinded in 1948.
10. Converted to Oriental Studies after 1957.
11. Converted to Agricultural Studies from 1966, and back again to Agricultural Science in 1969.
12. Rescinded in 1966. No candidates are listed until after 1955.
13. 'Computer Science' from 1966.
14. Rescinded in 1989.
15. Materials Science and Metallurgy from 1980.
16. Rescinded in 1970.
17. Rescinded in 1967.
18. Rescinded in 1962.
19. Converted to a one-year M.Phil. from 1978.

Date	Diploma	Certificate of Postgraduate Study	2-year M.Phil.	1-year M.Phil.
1965	English Studies[1]			
1966	Agricultural Studies[2]			
	Computer Science			
	Development Economics[3]			
	Linguistics[4]			
1967	Historical Studies			
1968	Nutrition[5]			
1969	Agricultural Science[6]	Pharmacology[4]		
1971	Applied Biology[4]			
	History & Philosophy of Science[4]			
	Land Economy[7]			
1972	Latin-American Studies			
	Theology[8]			
1975	Polar Studies[9]	Genetics[10]		
1978			Philosophy[11]	Applied Biology[12]
			Theology	Biochemistry[13]
				Control Engineering and Operational Research[14]
				Criminology
				Development Studies[10]
				History & Philosophy of Science
				Linguistics
				Materials Technology
				Pharmacology[12]
				Plant Breeding[15]

Date	Diploma	Certificate of Postgraduate Study	2-year M.Phil.	1-year M.Phil.
1979				Archaeology Biological Anthropology Economics International Relations Land Economy Latin-American Studies Social Anthropology Soil Mechanics[16]
1980				Quaternary Research
1981				Education Polar Studies
1982	Development Studies			History of Medicine
1983				Economics & Politics of Development Musical Composition Musicology
1985				Architecture[17] Oriental Studies
1986				Computer Speech & Language Processing Physics
1989		Biological Science		Finance Medieval and Renaissance Literature Philosophy Psychopathology Social & Political Theory

Date	Diploma	Certificate of Postgraduate Study	2-year M.Phil.	1-year M.Phil.
1990				Biological Science Economics of Developing Countries Medieval History Sociology and Politics of Development
1991				English & Applied Linguistics Microelectronic Engineering & Semiconductor Physics
1992				Chemistry Environment & Development Geographical Information Systems & Remote Sensing Management Studies
1993		Anglo-Saxon, Norse & Celtic Archaeology English History Legal Studies Theology & Religious Studies		Economic Theory and Econometrics Epidemiology

Date	Diploma	Certificate of Postgraduate Study	2-year M.Phil.	1-year M.Phil.
1994		History of Art		Archaeological Science Classics Environmental Design in Architecture European Literature History & Philosophy of Architecture
1995				Political Thought & Intellectual History

1. In abeyance since 1971.
2. Rescinded in 1967 and re-instated as Agricultural Science in 1969.
3. Rescinded in 1978 on the creation of the one-year M.Phil. in Development Studies.
4. Rescinded in 1977 and replaced by a one-year M.Phil.
5. In abeyance since 1979.
6. Rescinded in 1971.
7. Converted to a one-year M.Phil. from 1979.
8. Ceased to be a Graduate Student qualification from 1991.
9. Rescinded in 1980.
10. Rescinded in 1989.
11. Discontinued after 1981 intake.
12. Discontinued after 1988 intake.
13. Discontinued on the introduction of Biological Science in 1989.
14. Suspended after 1985 intake.
15. Discontinued after 1992 intake.
16. No candidates in 1988–9; course suspended.
17. From 1994 separated into History and Philosophy of Architecture and Environmental Design in Architecture.

Appendix 5
Extracts from an unofficial guide to the organisation and procedures of the University of Cambridge, by G. B. Skelsey, Senior Assistant Registrary (1995)

1. The Chancellor is an eminent public figure elected by the Senate, as the constitutional head of the University. The Chancellor continues to have important statutory duties, and is also available to advise, as a respected and experienced individual detached from current local controversies, on points at issue, sometimes of great sensitivity and delicacy, and to support the day-to-day work of the Vice-Chancellor and Colleges, especially perhaps in their external relations.

The Chancellor's principal public responsibility in modern times has been the conferment of Honorary Degrees at an imposing annual ceremony, but it will be clear that this is a small aspect of his or her continuous overall involvement with the University in all its aspects.

[From 1977 to the present (1996) the Chancellor has been HRH The Prince Philip, The Duke of Edinburgh.]

2. The Vice-Chancellor is now explicitly the full-time resident head of the University and is its principal academic and administrative officer. He or she is appointed by the Council for a period of up to seven years, and the office may no longer be held in plurality with the headship of a college or any other University post.

The main tasks of the Vice-Chancellor are to provide leadership, academic as well as administrative, to the whole of the University; to represent its members both in the local community and externally; to guide and monitor the work of his subordinate chief officers and their staffs in relation to the University's overall mission and to the fulfilment of policies established by the various governing and legislative bodies referred to below; and – a matter of increasing importance – to head the development campaign on which the future health of the University vitally depends. He or she also has important ceremonial duties, chairs personally or appoints deputies to chair most University committees, and serves as a member of many national and international bodies. There is a Pro-Vice-Chancellor and a number of Deputy Vice-Chancellors to whom specific duties and areas of responsibility are delegated.

The Vice-Chancellor has a small personal secretariat which also oversees directly the central press and public relations activity of the University and other aspects of its external relations, including ceremonies.

3. The Regent House is the primary governing body and electoral constituency of the University. It principally comprises the current teaching and administrative staff of both the University and the thirty-one Cambridge Colleges, including most holders of University Offices, administrative as well as academic, and College fellows. There are, at present, over 3,000 members. [The Senate, which consists of the several hundred thousand holders of the MA or higher degrees, was formerly the principal legislative authority of the University and controlled its affairs. It now retains mainly electoral responsibilities, for instance in electing the Chancellor.]

The process of making and amending the regulations which govern most matters of University business involves the Regent House through its effective control of Graces and Reports.

A Grace is a motion for debate and decision, presented to the Regent House, in almost all cases by the Council. It is published in the University's weekly journal, *Cambridge University Reporter*, and, for most minor matters, a footnote of explanation will be appended to it. Appointments made by the Regent House to many University bodies are also 'made by Grace'. If no objection is raised by a specified number of members within ten days, the Regent House is deemed to have approved the Grace.

More complex matters and proposals are presented in the form of a Report, again published in *Reporter*, with extended, reasoned recommendations. Such a Report is first put up for Discussion, that is, public debate in the Senate House. The remarks made at the Discussion are then considered by the body responsible for originating the recommendations, who advise the Council on the response to be contained in a statement or Notice, also published in *Reporter* and replying to the Discussion. Such a Notice normally ends by re-submitting the proposals to the Regent House in the form of a further Grace, amended, if necessary, in the light of the remarks that have been made. The procedure then allows either for approval without dissent or, if requested, for a Ballot of members of the Regent House in person. (It should be stressed that this is not an empty formality. There have been very many modern examples of successful opposition to legislative proposals, although the great majority are approved.) Provision exists, in some circumstances, for voting to be by postal ballot rather than in person.

The Regent House also has important electoral responsibilities in appointing members to a wide range of University bodies, and has the right of approving all degrees conferred by the University, including honorary degrees.

4. The Council (formerly called the 'Council of the Senate') is the principal executive and policy-making body of the University. It has overall responsibility for the administration of the University, for defining its mission, for planning its work, and for the management of its resources. It deals with relations between the University and the Colleges, conducts negotiations with outside bodies on many matters (other than those relating directly to the educational and research programme of the University, which are dealt with by the General Board) and

is responsible for the appointment or nomination of certain members of internal and external Committees, and for many student matters, apart, of course, from the selection of entrants, which is a College concern.

The Council has an Executive Committee which meets more frequently and deals with the more routine items of business. The Registrary, as he or she is termed at Cambridge, is Secretary of the Council, with an office, the Registry, which deals with business of the Council as well as the conduct of examinations and the maintenance of student records. The Registrary is head of the University's administrative service.

5. The General Board of the Faculties. The principal duty of the General Board (as it is abbreviated, in distinction to the former 'Special Boards' or Faculty Boards) is to advise the University on educational policy and to control the resources necessary for the proper implementation of that policy. It is responsible for maintaining a high standard of teaching and research, and for ensuring that University teaching officers satisfactorily perform their duties and fulfil their conditions of appointment. In recent times it has become heavily involved in national programmes of assessment and evaluation of teaching, research and personal quality, and with important initiatives in the area of equal opportunities.

Many aspects of the General Board's work must pass through the legislative machinery of the Regent House described above, although it now has certain delegated responsibilities, for example in respect of examination regulations. The Secretary General of the Faculties is Secretary of the General Board, and his or her office deals with the administrative work associated with the duties of the Board, including training and personnel functions for academic staff.

6. The Finance Committee. The Council has many standing committees, amongst them those dealing with functional matters on the Council's behalf such as student matters, but amongst the most important committees with executive responsibilities is the Finance Committee (known until recently as the Financial Board). Its main responsibilities are to account to the Council for the receipts and payments of the University and all its Departments and subsidiaries; to budget and advise the Council on trends in University income and expenditure; to control the University's investments; and to maintain and care for all University sites and buildings.

The Treasurer – the Cambridge equivalent of a Finance Officer in most respects – acts as Secretary to the Finance Committee, and is the Council's principal financial officer and professional adviser on financial matters.

7. The Board of Scrutiny. The more extended powers delegated to the two principal executive bodies – Council and General Board – have been balanced in the University's new constitution by re-affirmation of the role of the Regent House as the ultimate governing body of the University. It is acknowledged as the body to which the Council and other bodies are explicitly accountable, and to enforce this accountability the Council now submits an Annual Report to the

Regent House which, with the Annual Estimates and Accounts, is subject to examination and public review on behalf of the Regent House by a new body, the Board of Scrutiny. This Board consists of the Proctors and Pro-Proctors and eight elected members of the Regent House who may not include those holding University administrative offices or serving as members of the central bodies.

8. The Councils of the Schools. The term 'School' in Cambridge occasionally means a building, such as the Music School, but more usually indicates an administrative grouping of related subjects. In this sense there are six Schools: of Physical Sciences; of Biological Sciences, including Veterinary Medicine; of Technology; of the Arts and Humanities; of Humanities and Social Sciences; and of Clinical Medicine. Each of these bodies covers a specified group of Faculties. Except for Clinical Medicine, each has an elected supervisory body – the Councils of the Schools – which acts as a co-ordinating organisation and filters much academic business before its transmission to the General Board.

9. Faculties and Syndicates. Teaching and research in Cambridge is organised between a number of Faculties (currently Archaeology and Anthropology, Architecture and History of Art, Biology 'A', Biology 'B', Classics, Clinical Medicine, Clinical Veterinary Medicine, Divinity, Earth Sciences and Geography, Economics and Politics, Education, Engineering, English, History, Law, Mathematics, Modern and Medieval Languages, Music, Oriental Studies, Philosophy, Physics and Chemistry, and Social and Political Sciences). In addition, certain bodies entitled Syndicates also have responsibilities for teaching and research and exercise powers similar in effect to those of Faculty Boards. These twenty-four Faculties and Syndicates cover the whole of the academic programme in the University, each being responsible for a broad subject area.

The term 'Syndicate' is also used for bodies responsible for the supervision of work in areas other than teaching and research, such as the Library Syndicate, the Fitzwilliam Museum Syndicate, the Careers Service Syndicate, and the Athletics Syndicate; others, such as the Press Syndicate and the Local Examinations Syndicate, preside over some of the University's most important ancillary institutions. (Syndicates are also appointed by the Regent House from time to time to consider and report on specific current issues.)

The Faculties have different organisational sub-structures which partly reflect their history and partly their operational needs. It is normal in the scientific Faculties for the work to be organised in Departments. Administratively there is great convenience in dividing the work of a large Faculty into separate Departments but it carries the danger that the academic programme may become too compartmentalised. The Councils of the Schools play an important role in ensuring that the natural academic links between different Faculties are maintained and developed.

Each Faculty is governed by a Faculty Board which is responsible to the General Board of the Faculties for the provision of adequate teaching and facilities for research.

10. Departments. Most scientific Faculties are divided into Departments, of which there are about sixty under the supervision of the General Board of the Faculties. Each Department has a Head, who is in most cases a Professor or other teaching officer in the Department appointed for five years at a time by the Faculty Board. The term 'Department' is also used of some academic subdivisions in the Arts and Humanities, but these institutions are not generally as administratively autonomous as they are in the scientific Faculties. There is also a small number of Sub-Departments, which are distinct divisions of scientific departments.

11. Other Institutions. In general terms, Syndicates or Boards of Management, rather than Faculties, are established as organisational units when the subject has a clear need for support from a number of existing Faculties within the University. For example, Chemical Engineering will draw its undergraduates from either the Natural Sciences or from Engineering; Land Economy may receive them from Law, Economics and Politics, Geography, and a few from the Natural Sciences. A more recent innovation in the University is the establishment of Centres of Studies, such as the Centre for South Asian Studies. These are all controlled by Committees of Management which consist of teaching officers drawn from the Faculties with a main interest in these areas.

Another institution with important academic responsibilities is the Board of Continuing Education, based at Madingley Hall, which looks after continuing education within the University, much of which involves close Faculty participation, together with extra-mural studies.

12. Staff. University teaching is undertaken by Professors, Readers, Lecturers and Assistant Lecturers, and there are also numerous grades of research personnel and of academically-related staff working in libraries, museums and the university administration. Essential supporting functions in all these areas are carried out by the University's assistant staff. The Assistant Staff Office, jointly responsible to the Council and the General Board, looks after personnel needs in relation to them, under the management of the Personnel Officer. Personnel functions for academic staff are carried out directly by the General Board.

APPENDIX 6
NOBEL PRIZE-WINNERS AND MEMBERS OF THE ORDER OF MERIT

The ensuing list contains the names of those whose working lives were spent largely in Cambridge or whose prizes were awarded for work demonstrably done while they were at Cambridge. It would extend to some eighty names if one were to include all Nobel Laureates who have, at one time or another, studied or worked in the university. The list of OMs is less scrupulously exclusive.

NOBEL PRIZES

1906 J. J. Thomson (Physics)
1915 William and Lawrence Bragg (Physics)
1922 A. V. Hill (Physiology/Medicine)
1927 Charles Wilson (Physics)
1929 (Sir) Frederick Gowland Hopkins (Physiology/Medicine)
1932 E. D. Adrian, with C. S. Sherrington, previously of Cambridge (Physiology/Medicine)
1933 P. A. M. Dirac (Physics)
1935 James Chadwick (Physics)
1937 G. P. Thomson (Physics)
1947 Edward Appleton (Physics)
1948 Patrick Blackett (Physics)
1957 (Lord) Alexander Todd (Chemistry)
1958 Fred Sanger (Chemistry)
1962 Max Perutz and (Sir) John Kendrew (Chemistry)
Francis Crick and James Watson (Physiology/Medicine)
1963 (Sir) Alan Hodgkin and (Sir) Andrew Huxley (Physiology/Medicine)
1967 Sir George Porter and Professor Ronald Norrish (Chemistry)

1973 Brian Josephson (Physics)
1974 Sir Martin Ryle and Antony Hewish (Physics)
1977 James Meade (Economics)
1980 Fred Sanger, again (Chemistry)
1982 Aaron Klug (Chemistry)
1984 César Milstein (Physiology/Medicine)

ORDER OF MERIT

1902 Lord Rayleigh (J. W. Strutt), Cavendish Professor, chancellor
Lord Kelvin (William Thomson), physicist
1905 Richard Claverhouse Jebb, Regius Professor of Greek
1908 Henry Jackson, Regius Professor of Greek
1911 Sir George Otto Trevelyan, politician
1912 Sir J. J. Thomson, Cavendish Professor
1916 Lord Balfour (A. J. Balfour), politician, Chancellor
1924 Sir Charles Scott Sherrington, physiologist
1925 Sir James Frazer, anthropologist
Sir Ernest Rutherford, Cavendish Professor
1927 Sir Charles Algernon Parsons, engineer
1930 George Macaulay Trevelyan, historian
Montague Rhodes James, antiquary and Provost of King's
1931 Sir William Henry Bragg, physicist, Director of the Royal Institution
1935 Sir Frederick Gowland Hopkins, professor of biochemistry
Ralph Vaughan Williams, composer
1938 Sir Arthur Stanley Eddington, astrophysicist
1939 Sir James Jeans, mathematician
1942 Lord Adrian (E. D. Adrian), physiologist, chancellor
1944 Sir Henry Dale, physiologist and pharmacologist
1945 Alfred North Whitehead, mathematician and philosopher
1947 Jan Christian Smuts, statesman, chancellor
1949 Lord Russell (Bertrand Russell), philosopher
1951 George E. Moore, philosopher
1957 Sir John Cockcroft, physicist
1963 George Peabody Gooch, historian

1965	Dorothy Hodgkin, chemist
	Lord Florey (Howard Walter Florey), pathologist
	Lord Louis Mountbatten, statesman
1967	Lord Blackett (Patrick Maynard Stuart Blackett), physicist and strategist
1969	E. M. Forster, novelist
	Lord Penney, physicist
	Sir Geoffrey Ingram Taylor, physicist, mathematician and engineer
1973	Paul Adrien Maurice Dirac, physicist
	Sir Alan Hodgkin, physiologist
1976	Baron Hinton of Bankside (Christopher Hinton), engineer
1977	Lord Todd (Alexander Todd), chemist
1983	The Revd Professor W. O. Chadwick, historian
	Sir Andrew Huxley, physicist
1986	Frederick Sanger, biochemist
1988	Max Perutz, molecular biologist
1992	Sir Michael Atiyah, mathematician

Glossary

This glossary aims only to elucidate terms actually used in the text; for a more extensive, and far more entertaining, glossary of Cambridge terms the reader is referred to Frank Stubbings's *Bedders, bulldogs and bedells*, to be found in the list of suggested further reading.

ACTS: academical exercises, anciently in the form of disputations or sermons.

BA: Bachelor of Arts; the most junior of the university's degrees.

BD: Bachelor of Divinity, in earlier records often appearing as STB (Sanctae Theologiae Baccalaureus).

BEDELLS: permanent officials appointed to assist in the conduct of the university's business as emissaries and guardians of ceremonial. The Esquire Bedells, long since reduced in number from three to two, retain their ceremonial functions. The Yeoman Bedell, or Dog Bedell, whose more modest errands included the serving of warrants on those summoned to the university courts, has been partly replaced by the University Marshal.

BLACK ASSEMBLY: see Magna Congregatio.

BLACK-HOOD HOUSE: from the custom of non-regent masters wearing their hoods reversed at **Congregations**, the Non-Regent House.

BLUE: one selected to play in certain sports in the annual match against Oxford; strictly not the person but the distinctive blazer and scarf worn only by those so honoured.

BULL: a written mandate of the pope.

BULLDOG: see university constables.

CAPUT: a body originally elected *ad hoc*, but from 1570 until 1856 annually, to oversee all graces prior to their presentation to the Regent House.

CENSOR: the 'master' of the non-collegiate students and of their hostel, Fitzwilliam House.

CHANCELLOR: the university's principal officer, originally elected annually, later for life. See Appendix 5.

CHANTRY: an endowment for the maintenance of priests to pray for the souls of its founder and/or their kin; a building or part of a building set aside for this purpose.

COLLEGE: an endowed, self-governing community of scholars; also the buildings provided for them comprising at least a dining-hall and residential accommodation with, as time passed, a chapel and a library.

COMMENCEMENT: the ceremony of admission to the degree of master or doctor, for many centuries the chief academic festival of the year.

CONGREGATION: a meeting of the Regent House for voting on graces, including those for the conferment of degrees.

COUNCIL OF THE SENATE: a body created in 1856 as successor to the **Caput** charged with preparing business for the **Regent House** and with limited executive powers. See Appendix 5.

DD: Doctor of Divinity, in earlier records often appearing as STP (Sanctae Theologiae Professor – with no reference to the holding of a teaching post).

DEAN: a fellow of a college with responsibility either for the conduct of the college chapel or for the maintenance of discipline, seldom for both. In recent years the term has been sparingly introduced in the sense familiar from the United States of one with administrative responsibility in a given area of the university's academic activities.

DISCOMMUNE: penalise a tradesman (usually for allowing excessive credit to an undergraduate) by forbidding junior members to patronise his establishment for a fixed period of time.

DISPUTATIONS: formal and stylised debates forming part of the exercises for degrees up to the nineteenth century; their performance became increasingly ritualistic.

DIVIDENDS: payments made to fellows of colleges out of whatever surplus was found to be available at the annual audit of the college's accounts.

EXEQUIES: masses for the souls of the deceased.

EXERCISES: the hurdles to be publicly negotiated before admission to a degree; they might, according to the faculty, the standing of the candidate and the date, include disputations, written examinations, the submission and defence of a dissertation, the preaching of sermons and other demonstrations of practical competence.

FACULTY: originally used to designate in broad terms a subject in which teaching was available and degrees were conferred (arts, divinity, law, medicine) and now used more specifically and less consistently to describe the assorted individuals annually listed as having more or less involvement in teaching in a subject or group of subjects, the persons appointed to the Faculty Board whose duties include the organising of teaching, or even the building in which a faculty is housed. See Appendix 5.

FELLOW: a senior member of a college, supported to a greater or lesser extent by the college's endowment and nowadays often required upon election to undertake academic or administrative duties within the college.

FELLOW-COMMONER: an affluent, usually aristocratic, student granted among other privileges that of sharing with the fellows of a college the amenities of the high table.

GRACE: a proposal put to the vote in the **Regent** (and/or **Non-Regent**) House.

HEFCE: Higher Education Funding Council for England.

HALLS: used, confusingly, of hostels, of the dining hall of colleges, and as part of the title of certain fully-fledged colleges (e.g. New Hall, Trinity Hall). In this last sense the term was commonly attached to institutions now universally called 'colleges', notably Pembroke Hall and Clare Hall. The present college, Clare Hall, thus represents a reuse of the old title of its founding institution.

HEAD OF HOUSE: the head of a college, usually termed '**Master**' but sometimes '**Provost**' as at King's, '**President**' as at Queens', Clare Hall, Wolfson and Lucy Cavendish, '**Principal**' as at Newnham, '**Mistress**' as at Girton, or '**Warden**' as at Robinson.

HOSTELS: halls of residence, usually unendowed, and varying greatly in size, wealth and permanence, the precursors of the colleges which, as corporate institutions, absorbed or replaced them. In the nineteenth century 'hostel' or 'house' was the term adopted for institutions, such as Selwyn, established on a less grandiose model than the traditional colleges but with a more or less conscious aspiration to collegiate status at some future date.

HOUSE: see hostel.

INCEPTION: graduation as a master or doctor in one of the ancient faculties.

LIBERAL ARTS: the subjects comprised by the **trivium** and the **quadrivium**.

MA: Master of Arts.

MAGNA CONGREGATIO OR BLACK ASSEMBLY: the annual ceremony at which, for many centuries, the town authorities were obliged to swear obedience to those of the university.

MANDATE DEGREES: degrees conferred in response to instructions issued by the crown or, on the occasion of royal visits, by the chancellor.

MATRICULATION: registration as a member of the university, at one time extended to college and university servants as well as to students and, still, to teachers from elsewhere. For many centuries matriculation was conditional on the taking of oaths of allegiance to the crown and of assent to the established religion.

MISTRESS: the head of Girton College.

NON-REGENT HOUSE: the assembly of non-regents – Masters of Arts and Bachelors of Divinity, Law and Medicine of such standing as to be no longer statutorily obliged to lecture, and Doctors in the superior **faculties**. The Non-Regent House could veto decisions of the **Regent House**.

OLD SCHOOLS: the buildings now occupied chiefly by the central administrative offices named from their having incorporated within them the earliest lecture rooms built by the university; see **school**.

PENSIONER: a student paying fees to his or her college for teaching and for board and lodging. See also **sizar** and **scholar**.

PRAEVARICATOR OR VARIER: the author and performer of a set piece at **Commencements**; his verses, ostensibly a 'variation' on a topic for disputation, were a vehicle for the display of wit and, not infrequently, great scurrility.

PRESIDENT: in most colleges a synonym for Vice-Master, but a synonym for 'Master' at Queens', Clare Hall, Wolfson and Lucy Cavendish College.

PRINCIPAL: the head of Newnham College; also used for the heads of the medieval hostels.

PROCTORS: normally used for the two university officers, in early years known sometimes as rectors, appointed annually to represent the interests of the regent masters, and to maintain discipline. Their early responsibilities for the university finances devolved increasingly on the **vice-chancellor**. The term was also used of those practising as advocates in the university courts.

PROVOST: the head of King's College.

OPTIME, SENIOR or JUNIOR: one placed in, respectively, the second or third class in the Mathematical Tripos, from the moderator's judgement, 'Optime disputasti' you have argued very well.

ORDINANCES: regulations made by the university autonomously for the conduct of business.

QUADRIVIUM: the subjects comprising the second part of the arts course: arithmetic, music, geometry and astronomy. These, with the three philosophies (moral, natural and metaphysical), formed the basis of the MA course.

REGENT HOUSE: the assembly of regent masters, the ultimate executive body of the university; its composition and powers have varied widely over the centuries. See also **Non-Regent House**. The term 'Regent House' is still sometimes applied to the University Combination Room situated in the room in the Old Schools where the Regent House met before the Senate House was built. See Appendix 5.

REGENTS OR REGENT MASTERS: Masters of Arts with responsibilities for teaching – 'serving their regency'; the members of the Regent House.

REGISTRARY: an officer originally appointed to compile and maintain the records of the university, now the secretary to the Council, the chief executive and policy-making body; the head of the university's permanent 'civil service'. See Appendix 5.

SCHOLAR: the general term for all members of the university ('The Chancellor, Master and Scholars of the University of Cambridge'); in the context of colleges one supported by funds forming part of the college endowment; also used of those holding one of the many prize scholarships awarded, in a variety of forms and a multitude of subjects, by both the university and the colleges.

SCHOOL: originally used, usually in the plural, of lecture rooms assigned to different faculties, then both of a building and of the academic discipline fostered within it; nowadays also used of groupings of academic subjects.

SCRUTATORS: MAs, at one time annually elected, charged with the counting of votes.

SENATE: a body consisting of all MAs of the university with electoral and legislative functions now almost non-existent. See Appendix 5.

SIZAR: a student originally financing his studies by undertaking more or less menial tasks within his college and, as time went on, increasingly likely to receive small grants from the college without being 'on the foundation'; see also **scholar** and **pensioner**.

SPINNING HOUSE: a house of correction to which women suspected of prostitution were committed under the vice-chancellor's jurisdiction.

STATUTES: regulations for the conduct of university business, subject from an early date to confirmation or enforcement by the crown.

STB and STP: the old forms of the BD and DD degrees – Sanctae Theologiae Baccalaureus/Professor. The term 'Professor' in this context does not designate the holder of a university teaching post except to the extent that all newly created Doctors had, in theory, a statutory duty to undertake a short, fixed period of teaching within the university and were, by tradition, qualified to teach in universities elsewhere.

STUDIUM: medieval term for any school with formal facilities for advanced study. A *studium generale* originally differed from a *studium particulare* in attracting an international rather than a local clientele, but came to signify a school with at least two faculties for advanced study.

SYNDICATE: a committee appointed by the university either to exercise a supervisory management role, as in the cases of the Press and Library syndicates, or to consider and to propose remedies for a perceived problem.

TAXORS: MAs, elected annually to exercise the university's right to the supervision of weights and measures and generally to interfere in the conduct of the trade in victuals in Cambridge. They were abolished in the 1850s.

TRIPOS: see p. 126, n. 10.

TRIVIUM: the subjects comprising the first part of the arts course: grammar, rhetoric and logic.

VICE-CHANCELLOR: the Chancellor's deputy, from the late fifteenth century until the late 1980s elected annually, usually for two years in succession, and usually a head of house. The chief executive officer of the university. See Appendix 5.

UGC: University Grants Committee, set up in 1919 to control the distribution of government funding to universities.

UNDERGRADUATE: a matriculated student below the degree of BA.

UNIVERSITY CONSTABLES: part-time officers, usually employees of the university or colleges, appointed to assist the proctors in their disciplinary and ceremonial functions; popularly known, in the days when, accompanying the proctors, they prowled the streets on the watch for peccant undergraduates, as 'bulldogs'.

UNIVERSITY MARSHAL: a university officer exercising some of the duties of the extinct office of Yeoman Bedell and with particular responsibility for the university constables and for all functions connected with the Senate House.

VARIER: see **praevaricator**.

WARDEN: the head of the King's Hall and, in recent years, of Robinson College.

WRANGLER: one placed in the first class in the Mathematical Tripos, the Senior Wrangler being the man with the highest marks.

FURTHER READING

OFFICIAL AND SEMI-OFFICIAL SOURCES

Lists of university officers and of degrees conferred were compiled, if sporadically, from the sixteenth century; the first attempt at an annual handbook, however, was launched by G. Mackenzie as a private venture in 1796 as the *Cambridge University Calendar.* After the first few years it regularly recorded the academic calendar, in the form of an almanac; current officers; members of committees, faculties, etc.; appointments; university and college patronage; and tripos lists, catalogues of prizewinners, etc., for the previous year. For colleges it gave: the present establishments and all known living members, as well as a cumulative list of all the members of the university (with full forenames given in college lists to 1950/1). Examination papers for the previous year were for many years also included, with mathematics problems from the tripos and Smith's prize question papers from 1807 to 1882 and Classics Tripos papers from 1824 to 1882. In 1914 the *Calendar* was taken over by the Syndics of the Press. For the years 1853–5 to 1897 much of this material was duplicated by a commercial rival: the *Cambridge University General Almanack (and Register).* In an attempt to reduce the size of what was, by now, a bulky and expensive production, full lists of college members, and forenames in surviving lists, were dropped from the *Calendar*; and after 1969/70 the almanac was also abandoned and the title was accordingly changed to the *Annual Register of the University of Cambridge.* The issue for 1972/3 lists holders of university posts, membership of university bodies, lists of prize-winners and tripos lists. Under the individual colleges only the current membership and living ex-fellows are given, with no futher duplication of the cumulative list. In 1973/4 the contents of the *Register* were split, with the first part embodied in what was again called the *Calendar* and a separate *List of Members*. The intention that two such volumes should appear annually was not realised, and the list of members now appears at intervals, interspersed with supplementary lists, while the remaining material, or some of it, finds its way into the *Supplements* of the *Historical Register*.

The Historical Register of the University of Cambridge, ed. J. R. Tanner (Cambridge, 1917, reprinted 1984) contains, as is generally known, a list of (nearly) all university officers, administrative and academic, and the holders of established preacherships and other special posts (like the Rede Lecturers), each list being preceded by a brief history of the foundation and endowment of the post. These lists are indexed at the end of the volume. There are also lists of all those awarded university (not college) scholarships and prizes, and transcripts, sometimes partial, of the *Ordo senioritatis* of BAs from 1499 to 1747, and all tripos lists from 1748 to 1910. The names listed in the *Ordo* are indexed. In addition to this material there is an abundance of further information: an account of the constitution of the university up to the time of writing (effectively 1882) and of the university courts, ceremonies, costume, discipline, public buildings and institutions. Some of the lists are in need of correction, but the volume as a whole is a mine of useful and reliable information. It was followed in 1923 by the *Index to tripos lists, 1847–1910*, compiled by C. W. Previté-Orton (with women listed separately at the end), and by a series of supplements.

The Historical Register of the University of Cambridge: Supplement, 1911–20 (Cambridge, 1922) includes, in addition to updates of holders of posts, tripos lists, prizes, etc., an alphabetical list of 'advanced students' (i.e. research students) 1897–1913; an alphabetical list of honorary degrees, both complete, for 1882–1920, and titular, for 1859–1920; and an alphabetical list of those awarded diplomas in Agriculture, Anthropology, Forestry, Geography, Medical Radiology and Electrology, Psychological Medicine, Public Health and Tropical Medicine, 1875–1920. At the end of the volume may be found an account of the university's arrangements during the First World War.

The *Supplement, 1921–30* (1932), in addition to the usual lists, offers an account of 'Changes in the university: state aid and the Commission' and of the new statutes. There is also a list of research students, i.e.

those awarded certificates of research 1920/1–23/4. On the abolition of these certificates in favour of the Ph.D., M.Litt. and M.Sc., the listing of the award of post-graduate degrees, most regrettably, ceases.

The *Supplement, 1931–40* (1942) has a new feature in that most lecturers and demonstrators are now listed alphabetically rather than under subjects as in pre-1926 posts. The *Supplements* for 1941–50 (1952), 1951–5 (1956), 1956–60 (1962), 1961–5 (1967) and 1966–70 (1972) vary from it little in the nature of their contents. That for 1971–5 (1977) incorporates sections on individual colleges as previously included in the *Annual Registers* (known up to 1949/50 as the *Cambridge University Calendar*) which terminate in 1969/70, but gives only a brief history of each accompanied by lists of entrance scholarships and prizes, of past masters and present master and fellows (including honorary, emeritus and former fellows). There are no tripos lists, just a nasty computerised index and no lists of diplomas. In the 1976–80 *Supplement* (1984) the college entries are curtailed dramatically, being limited to an account of recent developments (e.g. admission of women), and, in some cases, brief lists of awards. There is, however, a better computerised index to tripos lists. The latest *Supplement*, for 1981–5 (1991) follows the same pattern.

From 1870 the *Cambridge University Reporter* records all, or nearly all, the official transactions of the university: lecture lists, examination timetables and results, degrees conferred, reports, both of the central administrative offices and of faculties, departments and syndicates, accounts of the discussion of reports and of votes cast, and a host of other matters. The level of indexing has, over the years, improved considerably, with but a few deviations, but the use of the indexes sometimes requires much patience and diligence. The earlier issues, when faculties and departments were fewer, and the demands for statistical information less, could afford space for detailed information in, for example, reports of university institutions, on a scale which would be unthinkable in the 1990s. From the 1970s, indeed, many departments and institutions were obliged either to cease printing their reports in the *Reporter* or to offer a brutally curtailed version with a note indicating the availability of the full report from the appropriate source. The consequent loss, or at least concealment, of so much information can only be deplored, but as scientific departments in particular were driven more and more to seek external funding the necessity of printing their reports independently was mother to the invention of much more detailed, and more glossily presented, reports than had previously been seen.

Not to be despised as a source of evidence for residence is the *Residents List*, started as a supplement to the *Cambridge Review* in 1896. This unofficial publication not only frequently reveals the whereabouts of the lodgings of undergraduate and post-graduate members and the private addresses of senior members, but it is the most accessible, and often the only, source for the names of those attending short courses in Cambridge during the wars and, indeed, those coming to Cambridge in those years with their own migrant institutions.

Extracts from the statutes were first printed (along with tables of fees and the proctorial cycle for 1660 to 1716) by John Hayes in 1684. The full corpus was not printed until 1785 in an edition of 35 copies; this is invaluable not only as a source for the statutes of the university up to 1570, but also for interpretations of statutes, decrees of the vice-chancellor and Heads, forms of oaths, and tables of fees. The next printings were the product of reform and were issued between 1849 and 1858 by and for the revising syndicates, culminating in comprehensive texts in 1859 and 1861. It is in these years that Latin gives way to English as the language of legislation. Of subsequent editions, those of 1882, of 1883 (including college statutes), of 1904 (including the ordinances), and of 1926 record significant revisions, as indeed do those of recent years. After 1785, the ordinances were first published in 1858, for the Council of the Senate, and they have, since 1946, been incorporated in editions of the statutes.

BIOGRAPHICAL REGISTERS

A. B. Emden, *A biographical register of the University of Cambridge to 1500*, Cambridge, 1963

C. H. and T. Cooper, *Athenae Cantabrigienses*, 3 vols., Cambridge, 1858, 1861, 1913 (the first two covering the years 1500 to 1585 and 1586 to 1609 respectively, with the third as a supplement). The dates dictating inclusion in this or that volume and the order in which individuals are treated are the last dates in that individual's recorded career, be it his death or, say, the date of his MA. Use of the indices, which also draw attention to additions and corrections at the end of each volume, is therefore essential.

Lists of graduati were published by registraries Borlase (1787, 1800), Hustler (1823), Romilly (1846, 1856) and Luard (1873, 1884). The first of these covers the years 1659 to 1787, the last 1800 to 1884. *Matriculations and Degrees* for the years 1851 to 1900 and for 1901 to 1912 were issued in 1902 and 1915 respectively. J. and J. A. Venn, as a preliminary to their great work, below, finally published *Matriculations and Degrees 1544–1659* in 1913.

J. and J. A. Venn, *Alumni Cantabrigienses*, Part I, to 1751, 4 vols., Cambridge, 1922–7

J. A. Venn, *Alumni Cantabrigienses*, Part II, 1752–1900, 6 vols., Cambridge, 1940–54

Most, but not all, colleges have at one time or another compiled lists of past and of present members and/or of admissions. For comprehensive coverage of the last century or so the lists published by Newnham, Girton and Gonville and Caius are conspicuous for their reliability and for the amount of detailed information which they contain.

GENERAL REFERENCE

C. H. Cooper, *Annals of Cambridge*, 5 vols. (vol. 5 ed. J. W. Cooper), Cambridge, 1842–1908

C. N. L. Brooke, R. Highfield and W. Swaan, *Oxford and Cambridge*, Cambridge, 1988

J. P. C. Roach, ed., *The Victoria history of the counties of England: Cambridge*, vol. 3, Oxford, 1959

Documents relating to the university and colleges of Cambridge, 3 vols., London, 1852 (consisting mostly of university and college statutes compiled for the benefit of the commissioners)

J. Griffiths, ed., *Enactments in Parliament specially concerning the universities of Oxford and Cambridge*, Oxford, 1869

Robert Willis and J. W. Clark, *The architectural history of the University of Cambridge and of the colleges of Cambridge and Eton*, 4 vols., Cambridge, 1886, vols. 1–3 reprinted 1988

Royal Commission on Historical Monuments, *An inventory of the historical monuments in the city of Cambridge*, 2 vols., and separately boxed plans, London, 1959

Rowland Parker, *Town and gown: the 700 years war in Cambridge*, Cambridge, 1984

J. W. Clark, *Endowments of the University of Cambridge*, Cambridge, 1904

F. (H.) Stubbings, *Bedders, bulldogs and bedells: a Cambridge glossary*, 2nd edn, Cambridge, 1995

K. Taylor, *Central Cambridge: a guide to the University and colleges, 1994*

In the highly selective lists of suggested further reading below, each chronological section starts with works covering all, or at least a large part, of the period in question, and continues with studies with a narrower focus, all of them, however, selected as shedding light on the condition of the university at large and its place in society. Periodical articles, and indeed many monographs, have been brutally excluded, including, with very few exceptions, those biographical and autobiographical studies which are so essential a tool for the historian. These have been included only where they are either a uniquely valuable source for periods otherwise severely under-recorded, as with Bentley, or, as with Bentley again, and Whewell, when their subjects dominated the academic landscape of their day. Studies spanning more than one of the broad periods below have been entered in the earlier of them.

c. 1209–1500

A. B. Cobban, *The medieval universities: Oxford and Cambridge to* c. *1500*, Aldershot, 1988

J. B. Mullinger, *The University of Cambridge from the earliest times to the royal injunctions of 1535*, Cambridge, 1873

D. R. Leader, *A history of the University of Cambridge. vol. 1: The university to 1546*, Cambridge, 1988

H. Rashdall, *The universities of Europe in the middle ages* (1895), ed. F. M. Powicke and A. B. Emden, 3 vols., Oxford, 1936

M. B. Hackett, *The original statutes of Cambridge University: the text and its history*, Cambridge, 1970

S. M. Leathes, ed., *Grace Book A*, containing the proctors' accounts and other records of the University of Cambridge for the years 1454–1488 (Luard Memorial Series I), Cambridge, 1897

M. Bateson, ed., *Grace Book B, Part I, containing the proctor's accounts and other records of the University of Cambridge for the years 1488–1511* (Luard Memorial Series II), Cambridge, 1903

P. N. R. Zutshi, ed., *Medieval Cambridge: essays on the pre-reformation university*, Woodbridge, 1993

A. B. Cobban, *The King's Hall within the University of Cambridge in the later middle ages* (Cambridge Studies in Medieval Life and Thought, 3rd series, vol. 1), Cambridge, 1969

M. K. Jones and M. G. Underwood, *The king's mother: Lady Margaret Beaufort, countess of Richmond and Derby*, Cambridge, 1992

M. Rubin, *Charity and community in medieval Cambridge*, Cambridge, 1986

J. A. W. Bennett, *Chaucer at Oxford and Cambridge*, Oxford, 1974

1500–1603

J. B. Mullinger, *The University of Cambridge from the royal injunctions of 1535 to the accession of Charles the First*, Cambridge, 1884

M. Bateson, ed., *Grace Book B, Part II, containing the accounts of the proctors of the University of Cambridge, 1511–1544* (Luard Memorial Series III), Cambridge, 1905

W. G. Searle, *Grace Book Γ . . . 1501–42*, Cambridge, 1908

J. Venn, ed., *Grace Book Δ. . . 1542–89*, Cambridge, 1910 (covering only the first half of the volume, to fo. 160, and omitting the miscellaneous material inserted in the second half of the original volume)

B. Bradshaw and E. Duffy (eds.), *Humanism, reform and the reformation career of Bishop John Fisher*, Cambridge, 1989

M. H. Curtis, *Oxford and Cambridge in transition, 1558–1642*, Oxford, 1959

J. Heywood and T. Wright, *Cambridge University transactions during the Puritan controversies of the 16th and 17th centuries*, 2 vols., London, 1854

H. Kearney, *Scholars and gentlemen: universities and society in pre-industrial Britain, 1500–1700*, London, 1970

J. Lamb, *A collection of letters, statutes and other documents from the MS Library of Corpus Christi College, illustrative of the history of the University of Cambridge during the period of the reformation, from AD MD to AD MDLXXII*, London, 1838

J. K. McConica, *English humanists and reformation politics under Henry VIII and Edward VI*, Oxford, 1965

J. Morgan, *Godly learning: puritan attitudes towards reason, learning and education, 1560–1640*, Cambridge, 1986

H. C. Porter, *Reformation and reaction in Tudor Cambridge*, Cambridge, 1948; reprinted, Connecticut, 1972

D. F. S. Thomson and H. C. Porter (eds.), *Erasmus and Cambridge*, Toronto, 1963

A. H. Nelson, *Records of early English drama: Cambridge*, 2 vols., Toronto, 1989

1603–1748

J. B. Mullinger, *The University of Cambridge from the election to the chancellorship in 1626 to the decline of the Platonist movement*, Cambridge, 1911

John Twigge, *The University of Cambridge and the English Revolution, 1625–1688*, Woodbridge, 1990

J. Gascoigne, *Cambridge in the age of the Enlightenment*, Cambridge, 1989

J. E. B. Mayor, ed., *Cambridge under Queen Anne*, Cambridge Antiquarian Society, 1911

W. J. Harrison, *Life in Clare Hall, Cambridge, 1658–1713*, Cambridge, 1958

J. H. Monk, *The life of Richard Bentley, D.D.*, 2nd edn, 2 vols., London and Cambridge, 1833

J. R. Wardale, ed., *Clare College letters and documents*, Cambridge, 1903

Christopher Wordsworth, ed., *The correspondence of Dr Richard Bentley*, 2 vols., London, 1842

1748–1840

H. Gunning, *Reminiscences of the university, town and county of Cambridge from the year 1780* [to 1830], 2 vols., London, 1854

P. Allen, *The Cambridge Apostles: the early years*, Cambridge, 1978

J. P. T. Bury, ed., *Romilly's Cambridge diary, 1832–42*, Cambridge, 1967

M. M. Garland, *Cambridge before Darwin: the ideal of a liberal education*, Cambridge, 1980

D. A. Winstanley, *The University of Cambridge in the eighteenth century*, Cambridge, 1958

Unreformed Cambridge: a study of certain aspects of the University of Cambridge in the eighteenth century, Cambridge, 1935

C. Wordsworth, *Scholae academicae: some account of the studies at the English universities in the eighteenth century*, London, 1877; reprinted New York 1968

Social life at the English universities in the eighteenth century, Cambridge, 1874

The Cambridge Chronicle and University Journal, Isle of Ely Herald and Huntingdonshire Gazette (subject to alterations in title, but usually known as *The Cambridge Chronicle*), from its inception in 1762 and especially after 1849 carried much of the material which was, from 1870, to find a home in the *Reporter*.

1840–1914

Cambridge University Reporter

Report of Her Majesty's Commissioners appointed to inquire into the state, discipline, studies and revenues of the University and colleges of Cambridge, with the evidence and correspondence, London, 1852

Report of the Commissioners appointed to inquire into the property and income of the universities of Oxford and Cambridge, London, 1874

M. E. Bury and J. D. Pickles, *Romilly's Cambridge diary, 1842–1847*, Cambridge, 1994

D. A. Winstanley, *Early Victorian Cambridge*, Cambridge, 1955

Later Victorian Cambridge, Cambridge, 1947

C. N. L. Brooke, *A history of the University of Cambridge, vol. 4: 1870–1990*, Cambridge, 1993

M. Fisch and S. Schaffer, eds., *William Whewell, a composite portrait*, Oxford, 1991

G. Johnson, *University politics: F. M. Cornford's Cambridge and his advice to the young academic politician, containing the complete text of Cornford's 'Microcosmographia academica'*, Cambridge, 1994

R. McWilliams-Tullberg, *Women at Cambridge: a men's university – though of a mixed type*, London, 1975

R. Mason, ed., *Cambridge minds*, Cambridge, 1994 (essays on both individuals and specific topics)

E. Shils and C. Blacker, eds., *Cambridge women: twelve portraits*, Cambridge 1996

Sheldon Rothblatt, *The revolution of the dons: Cambridge and society in Victorian England*, London, 1968

Edwin Welch, *The peripatetic university: Cambridge Local Lectures, 1873–1973*, Cambridge, 1973

1914 TO THE PRESENT

Cambridge University Reporter

Devlin Report and evidence, 1972

A. S. F. Gow, *Letters from Cambridge*, London, 1945

A. H. Halsey, *Decline of donnish dominion: the British academic professions in the twentieth century*, Oxford, 1992

T. E. B. Howarth, *Cambridge between two wars*, London, 1978

Royal Commission on Oxford and Cambridge universities: Report, London, 1922

T. Tapper and B. Salter, *Oxford, Cambridge and the changing idea of the university: the challenge to donnish domination*, Buckingham, 1992

E. Homberger, W. Janeway and S. Schama, eds., *The Cambridge mind*, London, 1970

COLLEGES

Histories of most of the colleges were included in a series on Oxford and Cambridge colleges published at about the turn of the century, of these only those of unusual merit are listed below.

J. Peile, *Christ's College*, London, 1900

Clare College 1326–1926, 2 vols., Cambridge, 1926

R. Masters, *The history of the College of Corpus Christi and the B. Virgin Mary (commonly called Bene't) in the University of Cambridge. . .*, Cambridge, 1753

(J.) P. (T.) Bury, *The College of Corpus Christi and of the Blessed Virgin Mary: a history from 1822 to 1952*, Cambridge, 1952

W. A. Grave, *Fitzwilliam College, Cambridge, 1869–1969*, Cambridge, 1973

M. C. Bradbrook, *'That Infidel Place': a short history of Girton College, 1869–1939*, London, 1969

C. N. L. Brooke, *A history of Gonville and Caius College*, Woodbridge and Dover, N.H., 1985

T. H. Simms, *Homerton College 1695–1978: from Dissenting Academy to Approved Society in the University of Cambridge*, Cambridge, 1979

M. Bottrall, *Hughes Hall 1885–1985*, Cambridge, 1985

A. Gray and F. Brittain, *A history of Jesus College, Cambridge*, London, 1979

C. Morris, *King's College: a short history*, Cambridge, 1989

P. Cunich, D. Hoyle, E. Duffy and R. Hyam, *A history of Magdalene College, Cambridge, 1428–1988*, Cambridge, 1994

R. Murray, *New Hall 1954–1972: the making of a college*, Cambridge, 1980

M. A. Hamilton, *Newnham: an informal biography*, London, 1936

A. Phillips, *A Newnham anthology*, Cambridge, 1979

J. Twigg, *A history of Queens' College, Cambridge*, Woodbridge and Wolfeboro, N.H., 1987

F. W. B. Bullock, *The history of Ridley Hall, Cambridge*, 2 vols., Cambridge, 1941–53

W. H. S. Jones, *A history of St Catharine's College, Cambridge*, Cambridge, 1936

E. E. Rich, ed., *St Catharine's College, Cambridge, 1473–1973*, London, 1973

G. Sweeney, *St Edmund's House, Cambridge: the first eighty years: a history*, Cambridge, 1982

Thomas Baker (ed. J. E. B. Mayor), *The history of the College of St John the Evangelist, Cambridge*, 2 vols. Cambridge, 1869

J. S. Boys Smith, *Memories of St John's College, Cambridge, 1919–1969*, Cambridge, 1983

E. Miller, *Portrait of a college: a history of the College of St John the Evangelist, Cambridge*, Cambridge, 1961

C. W. Scott-Giles, *Sidney Sussex College: a short history*, Cambridge, 1975

C. W. Crawley, *Trinity Hall: the history of a Cambridge college*, Cambridge, 1976

INSTITUTIONS

M. H. Black, *Cambridge University Press, 1584–1984*, Cambridge 1984

D. J. McKitterick, *A history of Cambridge University Press*, vol. 1, Cambridge, 1992

Cambridge University Library, a history, vol. 2: The eighteenth and nineteenth centuries, Cambridge, 1986

J. C. T. Oates, *Cambridge University Library, a history, vol. 1: From the beginnings to the Copyright Act of Queen Anne*, Cambridge, 1986

S. M. Walters, *The shaping of Cambridge botany*, Cambridge, 1981 [chiefly about the Botanic Garden]

J. G. Crowther, *The Cavendish Laboratory, 1874–1974*, London, 1974

SUBJECTS

W. W. R. Ball, *A history of the study of mathematics at Cambridge*, Cambridge, 1889

W. T. Costello, *The scholastic curriculum at early seventeenth-century Cambridge*, Harvard, 1958

M. F. Geisen, *Michael Foster and the Cambridge School of Physiology*, Princeton, 1978

R. T. Gunther, *Early science at Cambridge*, London, facsimile edition, 1969

P. M. Harman, ed., *Wranglers and physicists: studies in Cambridge physics in the nineteenth century*, Manchester, 1985

J. Hendry, ed., *Cambridge physics in the thirties*, Bristol, 1984

T. J. N. Hilken, *Engineering at Cambridge University, 1783–1965*, Cambridge, 1967

J. Needham and E. Baldwin, eds., *Hopkins and biochemistry 1865–1947*, Cambridge, 1949

H. D. Rolleston, *The Cambridge Medical School: a biographical history*, Cambridge, 1932

A. Rook, ed., *Cambridge and its contribution to medicine: proceedings of the 7th British Conference on the History of Medicine*, London, 1971

P. Searby, *The training of teachers in Cambridge University: the first sixty years, 1879–1939*, Cambridge, 1982

P. R. H. Slee, *Learning and a liberal education: the study of modern history in the universities of Oxford, Cambridge and Manchester, 1800–1914*, Manchester, 1986

R. N. Soffer, *Discipline and power: the university, history, and the making of an English élite, 1870–1930*, Stanford and Cambridge, 1995

D. R. Stoddart, *On geography and its history*, Oxford, 1986

DIVERSIONS

L. and H. Fowler, *Cambridge commemorated: an anthology of university life*, Cambridge, 1984

A. Steel, *The custom of the room, or early wine-books of Christ's College, Cambridge*, Cambridge, 1949

'Hederatus', *Cambridge night climbing*, London, 1970

Robert Hewison, *Footlights! a hundred years of Cambridge comedy*, London, 1983

Roger Wilmut, *From fringe to flying circus*, London, 1980

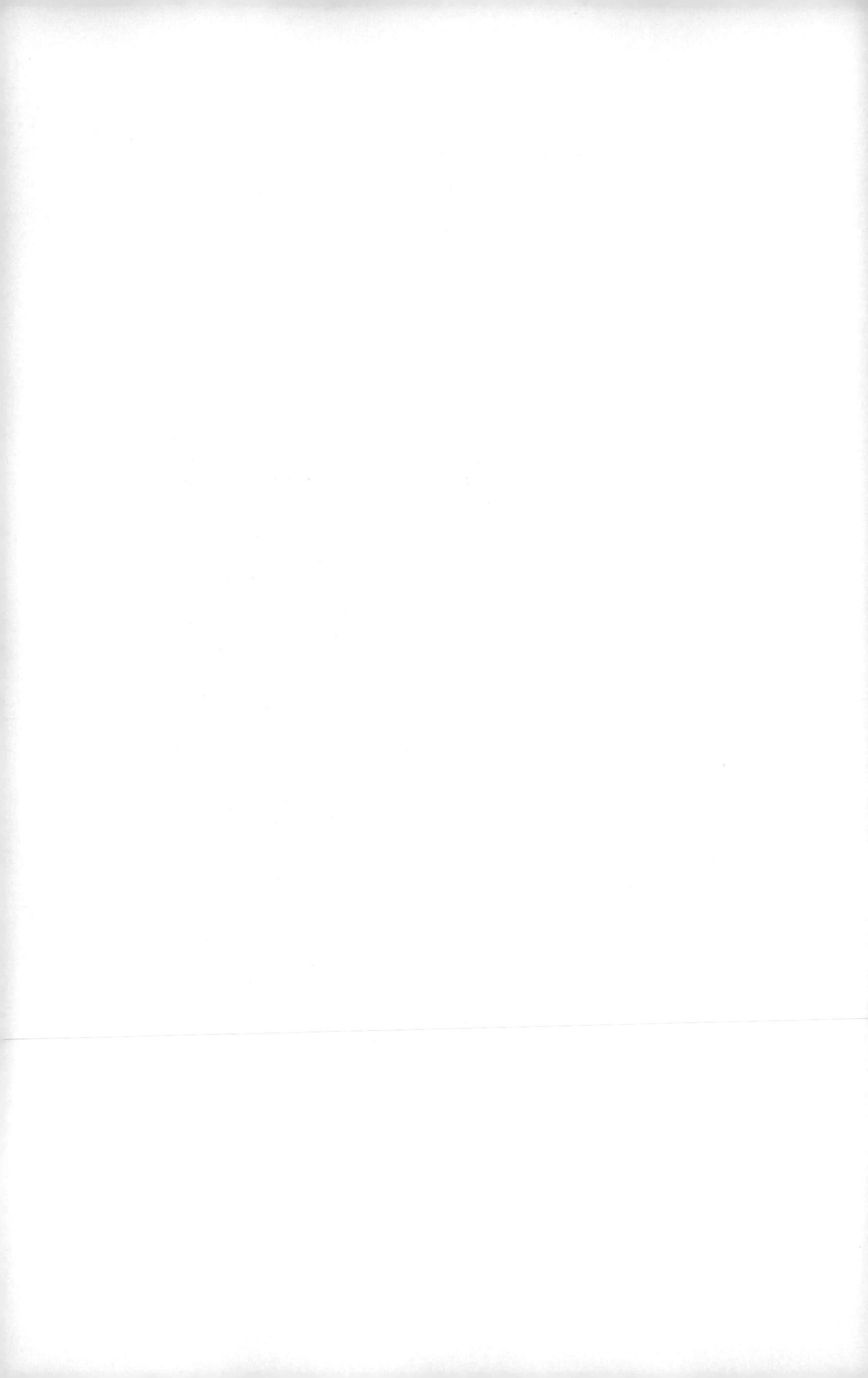

Index

Note, that certain terms, e.g. 'registrary', 'tripos', feature in this index only when reference is made either to their definition, or to their first occurrence; others, like the colleges, are indexed only where the text refers to an event which materially affected them, not, for instance, on every mention of a Fellow of that college.

English, School of, 199
Estate Management, Department of, 202